Multimodality

'Gunther Kress's *Multimodality* is the definitive statement of a social semiotic approach to communication in all its modes and their admixtures from the man who virtually invented the modern form of this field.'

James Paul Gee, *Arizona State University, USA*

'This book represents a paradigm shift beyond linguistics and literacy studies as we have known them. Yet, for all its path-breaking intellectual innovation and conceptual profundity, it contains a disarmingly clear view of meaning-making, one in which human agency is at the centre.'

Mary Kalantzis, *University of Illinois at Urbana-Champaign, USA*

The twenty-first century is awash with evermore mixed and remixed images, writing, layout, sound, gesture, speech and 3D objects. *Multimodality* looks beyond language and examines these multiple modes of communication and meaning-making.

Multimodality: A Social Semiotic Approach to Contemporary Communication represents a long-awaited and much anticipated addition to the study of multimodality from the scholar who pioneered and continues to play a decisive role in shaping the field. Written in an accessible manner and illustrated with a wealth of photos and illustrations to clearly demonstrate the points made, *Multimodality* deliberately sets out to locate communication in the everyday, covering topics and issues not usually discussed in books of this kind, from traffic signs to mobile phones.

In this book, Gunther Kress presents a contemporary, distinctive and widely applicable approach to communication. He provides the framework necessary for understanding the attempt to bring all modes of meaning-making together under one unified theoretical roof.

This exploration of an increasingly vital area of language and communication studies will be of interest to advanced undergraduate and postgraduate students in the fields of English language and applied linguistics, media and communication studies and education.

Gunther Kress is Professor of Semiotics and Education at the Institute of Education, University of London. His numerous titles include *Reading Images* (co-author with Theo van Leeuwen, 2nd edn, 2006), *Literacy in the New Media Age* (2003), *Early Spelling* (1999), *Before Writing* (1997) and *Learning to Write* (1993); all published by Routledge.

Multimodality

A social semiotic approach to
contemporary communication

Gunther Kress

 Routledge
Taylor & Francis Group

LONDON AND NEW YORK

First published 2010
by Routledge
2 Park Square, Milton Park, Abingdon, Oxon OX14 4RN

Simultaneously published in the USA and Canada
by Routledge
711 Third Avenue, New York, NY 10017 (8th Floor)

Routledge is an imprint of the Taylor & Francis Group, an informa business

© 2010 Gunther Kress

Typeset in Bell Gothic
by Keystroke, Tettenhall, Wolverhampton
Printed and bound in Great Britain
by TJ International Ltd, Padstow, Cornwall

British Library Cataloguing in Publication Data
A catalogue record for this book is available from the British Library

Library of Congress Cataloging-in-Publication Data
Kress, Gunther R.
Multimodality : a social semiotic approach to contemporary
communication/ Gunther Kress.
p. cm.
Includes bibliographical references and index.
1. Semiotics. 2. Communication. I. Title.
P99.K684 2009
302.2–dc22

ISBN10: 0–415–32060–7 (hbk)
ISBN10: 0–415–32061–5 (pbk)
ISBN10: 0–203–97003–9 (ebk)

ISBN 13: 978–0–415–32060–3 (hbk)
ISBN 13: 978–0–415–32061–0 (pbk)
ISBN 13: 978–0–203–97003–4 (ebk)

Meinen Eltern

Elly Johanna Charlotte Kress, 1912–1988
Johann Michael Kress, 1911–1987

Zwei Leben, gegen eine grausame Zeit

Contents

Illustrations

Colour plates (between pages 78 and 79)

Figures

Preface

This book has been a long time in the writing. I tell myself that maybe it will be the better for that. All this time a lot of work has been going on under the label of 'multimodality'. While I have not documented any of that here, the traces of it are evident everywhere in the book. Work in multimodality comes from quite different (disciplinary) perspectives to that taken here and one part of the task at present is to see how to make use of the connections. Carey Jewitt's *Handbook of Multimodal Analysis* (2009) gives a very good sense of the range and diversity of that work; and of the interconnections.

My aim here is to acknowledge the many people who, over a considerable time, have helped me in all sorts of ways in shaping the ideas: the smallest recognition of a great gift of conversation, of challenge and argument, of a need to explain and defend and to add; in many places, over many years. And, most important of all maybe, to have a sense of interest, support, engagement from and with like minds. I have been lucky in colleagues and friends whose ideas I admire and whose judgements I trust; who took ideas about which I felt not a bit confident as ideas just like others, with a simple 'Yes, so?'; or, more often, getting straight into a discussion, just carrying on with the conversation.

For many years I have wanted to mention Bob Hodge in that respect. We became colleagues at the University of East Anglia in the early 1970s. We taught courses jointly; with him it felt safe being ignorant. Ideas that I had never had the courage to say out aloud even to myself became the ordinary stuff of our talk, of disagreement and agreement, of discussion. That gave me the confidence to say things; to try to publish them even. In that long conversation, with David Aers and with Tony Trew too, we developed what has remained for me most important about meaning. I co-taught and co-wrote with the three of them (Aers, Hodge, Kress, 1982; Fowler, Hodge, Kress, Trew, 1979; Hodge and Kress, 1979). Roger Fowler, by then already an established author, was generously supportive in our efforts to get this work published. Out of teaching a joint course on Philosophy and Linguistics over several years, Tony Trew and I wrote a book which we called *The Chomskian Counter-revolution in Linguistics*; a book about Chomsky wresting Linguistics back from the socially oriented path set out by his teacher Zellig Harris; turning transformations from the socially/textually/discursively motivated operations they were in Harris's writing and theory, into psychological operations. It was not a notion to catch the mood of the mid-1970s; and so the book was never published.

Ten years on, in Sydney, I met Mary Kalantzis and Bill Cope: enormously generous personally; as profoundly serious in their intellectual positions as in their political views; utterly remarkable as activists. There too, Jim Martin and I joined forces to support each other's thinking around *genre*, shelving theoretical differences in favour of comradeship, support and the shared political-pedagogical aims of equitable access in schools. And in Sydney Theo van Leeuwen and I started on a project trying to figure out something akin to a 'grammar' of the visual. That project lasted a good ten years; with great enjoyment and benefit for me.

Moving to London in 1991 meant moving to the – for me – new 'site' of Education. Three research projects conducted jointly with Jon Ogborn, then Professor of Science Education, over the next nine years, here at the Institute, supplied a wonderful proving ground for developing social semiotics; as well as an intensive part-time education in matters scientific with a wonderful teacher. In the last of these, 'The rhetorics of the science classroom', Jon decisively 'scaffolded' one of my more stumbling semiotic attempts by throwing the word 'affordance' into the conversation. Carey Jewitt had come as the Research Officer on that project; she stayed on for the next one, 'English in urban classrooms'; and we have worked together since: enjoyable, illuminating, challenging, now as much as on that first project. She has been a source of inspiration and inestimable support. In London I met Brian Street. We decided early on that complementarity might be more productive than contestation; and maybe more enjoyable; and so it has proved for me and I hope for him.

At a conference in Toulouse, in 1990, I had met Ben Bachmair. Since then we have talked and worked on different projects around media and media education, talked and wrote about culture and communication. For me, his friendship has been truly delightful and an insightful means of reconnecting with things German; while his (predominantly German) sociological/historical 'take' on education has been eye-opening in thinking about issues of pedagogy. Christoph Wulf's more anthropological interest in ritual, in performance and his work on mimesis in particular, pushed me to try to become clearer about my own interests in meaning and learning, especially in relation to 'the body'. Ingrid Gogolin's coinage of the term 'mono-lingual habitus' – in her work with immigrants in Germany – made me see Bourdieu's concept concretely. In *New* London, as it turned out, I met Jim Gee. With his usual nonchalance, he made clear for me the connections of pedagogy, curriculum and 'fast capitalism', while shooting some baskets with Phillip, the youngest member of our group, in the parking lot at the back of the hotel; for me, with the same 'white light' effect of Jon Ogborn's mention of 'affordance'.

Staffan Selander had invited me to be a Visiting Professor in his DidaktikDesign group at the Laerarhoegskolan in Stockholm, between 2004 and 2006. His distinct sociological approach – broad, generously encompassing, precise and with a strangely real sense of the *geographical* proximity of Russian psychology – has been a constant stimulation and a challenge to staying alert. The time in Stockholm gave me a chance to be still; to think and talk in an atmosphere of a taken-for-granted intellectual and personal generosity. Among the scholars in that group, I benefited greatly from conversations with Eva Insulander and Fredrik Lindstrand and their work. I also came to know Roger Saljö, whose ways of thinking – with so much affinity to a social-semiotic perspective and yet so productively distinct – have proved greatly enriching for me.

In London I met Denise Newfield and Pippa Stein. Both had been working at the University of the Witwatersrand during the years of apartheid and at the same time they had worked with teachers and children in schools in Soweto. Through their experiences and in their reflection on that experience they had much more to teach me in their doctoral research than I could offer them in return. Their hopes for those students and teachers and their unbounded optimism for them in a future South Africa showed me how entirely linked inspired academic work and political action are. Pippa Stein's death since, is for me, as for so many people in many places, a vast loss.

Some two years ago Roger Kneebone approached me with a view to doing some joint research on the operating theatre seen as a pedagogic site. That has opened a whole new world of challenge, as well as truly enjoyable conversation.

My colleagues at the Institute of Education continue to inspire and support me, with coffee and conversation. I want to thank Di Mavers for her enthusiasm, energy and sharp insights into meaning-making. Jeff Bezemer brought his ethnographic take and ways of working, a great addition to the social-semiotic stew. Anton Franks has been an always insightful companion. Caroline Pelletier, Hara Sidiropoulou and Sophia Diamantopoulou have given me much material for thought from their research and their own reflections; they have – I hope wittingly – been willing to listen and respond to my ideas. Jan Blommaert brought his galvanizing energy and ideas, so close yet with an importantly different take, during his much too brief period at the Institute of Education. Norbert Pachler has been an enormously patient guide to some of the pedagogical and wider social affordances of contemporary technologies; and in that, has helped me get some real sense of its profound implications.

I have learned with all the doctoral researchers with whom I have worked. It is invidious to single out individuals; yet some need to be mentioned. Paul Mercer's exploration of forms of representation and social meanings in TV programmes remains for me an exemplary detailed study in semiosis, as well as an important re-assessment of the category of realism. Lesley Lancaster's meticulously detailed study of semiosis of a two-year-old; Shirley Palframan's study of semiosis in the work of early teenage students in classrooms, all have far-reaching implications theoretic-ally and practically for learning and assessment and pedagogic practices generally. In the work that she calls 're-genreing', Fiona English has opened new horizons on teaching and learning and representation. Elisabetta Adami came for a year and with her I was able to think again about issues long debated in Linguistics and seemingly settled – Grice's conversational maxims for instance, which get pretty well stood on their head in the triple context of multimodal representation, 'digital media' and a social-semiotic theory of communication. Sean McGovern's work on the semiotics of Japanese culture has far-reaching implications; and it has been very insightful for me. I wish to thank him for allowing me to use some of his data; I have borrowed from him the notion of 'modular composition' and want to make acknowledgement of that right here.

Marie-Agnes Beetschen and more latterly, Rebecca Elliott, have given me an opportunity, over a considerable time, to learn, in a very full sense, about the issues of representation in the practical world – in a commercial context with its pressures and demands. That has been an invaluable source of insight and of confirmation too, for me. I wish to thank them for their wisdom, insight and support. Margit Boeck gave me comments that were incisive and proved crucial at just the right moment; what coherence and order the book may exhibit is due to her clear advice.

I want to thank Lilly Ramp, who kindly took some photos of a sign by the side of a busy road in Salzburg. Rachel Kress gave me permission to use some of her images and drawings (colour plates 9, 10, 14 and 15), as have Michael Kress and Emily Kress, and for that I wish to thank them. Eve Bearne kindly allowed me to use some of her data, which has been very insightful for me; it appears as Figure 4.3.

The book draws on three research projects, funded by the UK's Economic and Social Research Council: 'Gains and Losses: Changes in Representation, Knowledge and Pedagogy in Learning Resources' (2007–2009); 'English in Urban Classrooms' (2001–2004); and 'The Rhetorics of the Science Classrooms' (1998–2000). It also draws on a project funded by the Swedish National Science Foundation, conducted in Stockholm and London 'The Museum, the Exhibition and the Visitors', directed by Professor Staffan Selander of Stockholm University and co-directed in London by myself. The deep benefits of such support will, I hope, be evident in the pages of the book.

Anyone who engages in this sort of work knows about the people who are essential yet too often remain unsung. No academic can work well without the help of those who smooth the paths of administration and who create a climate conducive to feeling 'supported'. In that respect I would like to mention Sarah Gelcich and Manjit Benning for their help; differently, and each essential.

It remains to thank the more than patient editors: Louisa Semlyen, over many years, and latterly Sam Vale Noya, whose job was not made one whit easier by my slowness; and without whose patience and increasingly firm pushing this book might still not be done.

GRK
London, October 2009

Acknowledgements

The publishers would like to acknowledge the copyright holders for permission to reprint the following material:

1935 Science: digestion from *General Science, Part III*, Fairbrother, F., Nightingale, E. and Wyeth, F.J. (G. Bell & Sons, 1935).

2002 Science: digestion from *Salters GCSE Science: Year 11 Student Book* (Heinemann Educational Publishers, 2002).

Austrian Airlines for the reproduction of their salt and pepper packaging.

The Poetry Archive for screenshots from their website at www.poetryarchive.org.

British Broadcasting Corporation for the screenshot from their 2005 website at www.bbc.co.uk/cbbc.

Every effort has been made to contact copyright holders. If any have been inadvertently overlooked the publishers will be pleased to make the necessary arrangements at the first opportunity.

1   Where meaning is *the* issue

Multimodality: simple, really

On my way to work the bus gets held up before a large intersection, even quite early in the morning. Sitting on the top deck, my eye is drawn to a sign, high up on the wall opposite; it shows how to get into the car park of a supermarket. It is not a complicated sign by any means, nothing unusual about it really. But I have puzzled about it: how does it work? Above all, how does it work *here*? It is about 150 metres before this complicated intersection. Drivers have to keep their eye on the traffic; there's no time for leisurely perusal. Of course, my academic interest in the sign lies in its joint use of image and writing. And so, one morning, when the bus is held up in just the right spot, I take a photo on my mobile phone, as one does (Figure 1.1).

If writing alone had been used, would this sign work? I don't think it could: there is too little time to take it in. A little later in the day, if shoppers tried to *read* the sign, the intersection would clog up. With writing alone, the message would, quite simply, be too complex. Using three modes in the one sign – *writing* and *image* and *colour* as well – has real benefits. Each mode does a specific thing: image *shows* what takes too long to *read*, and writing *names* what would be difficult to *show*. Colour is used to *highlight* specific aspects of the overall message. Without that division of semiotic labour, the sign, quite simply, would not work. Writing *names* and image *shows*, while colour *frames* and *highlights*; each to maximum effect and benefit.

If writing by itself would not work, could the sign work with image alone? Well, just possibly, maybe. *Writing* and *image* and *colour* lend themselves to doing different kinds of semiotic work; each has its distinct potentials for meaning – and, in this case, image may just have the edge over writing. And that, in a nutshell – and, in a way, as simple as that – is the argument for taking 'multimodality' as the normal state of human communication.

Except that, just across the road, on the other side, there is another supermarket. It too has a sign, on its side, just as high up; it shows *its* customers how to get into *its* car park. Figure 1.2 is a photo of this other sign. The sign is different: not different in the modes used but in *how* the modes are used. Colour is different, lines are differently drawn; the sign has a distinctly different *aesthetic*. Multimodality can tell us what modes are used; it cannot tell us about this difference in *style*; it has no means to tell us what that difference might *mean*. What is the difference in colour about or

Figure 1.1 Morrisons supermarket

the difference in the drawing style? What *identity* is each of the two signs projecting? What are the supermarkets 'saying' about themselves? What are they telling their customers about themselves? Are these differences accidental, arbitrary? Would the *style* of one sign serve equally well for the other supermarket?

To answer questions of that kind we need a theory that deals with *meaning* in all its appearances, in all social occasions and in all cultural sites. That theory is *Social Semiotics*.

Of course, there are many theories of what communication ought to be and how it might work. And then there is *power*. So just because something might not really work – writing by itself, in this case – it does not mean that it won't be used. There are many reasons, often more important than 'will it work?'. There is tradition, for instance. Writing has traditionally been used to do certain communicational things – *regulations* and *instructions* being just two. Then there is officialdom. Bureaucracy assumes that as long as something has been announced in writing it has been communicated and the rest will look after itself; or else it can be left to the law, where the excuse 'but nobody could have read it in that time' doesn't count. Here (Figure 1.3) is an example of that latter approach. It comes from one of the cities which played host to games in the European Soccer Championships of 2008. The sign announces temporary changes

Figure 1.2 Waitrose supermarket

to parking regulations for the duration of the championships. A rough translation might be:

> *Dear drivers!*
>
> *During UEFA 2008 the official times for bus lanes will be changed as follows. From 7 June to 29 June 2008, the normally applicable times for the bus lanes in the Griessgasse, Rudolfskai, Imbergerstrasse, Giselakai and Schwarzstrasse will be extended until 2 a.m. of the following day.*
>
> *On days when games are being played, that is, 10.06, 14.06 and 18.06 2008, the no-stopping rule in the bus lane in Griessgasse will come into force earlier, from 10 a.m.*

The instructions are not unfriendly in tone; though they are complex, official and, above all, impossible to read in the brief time before the lights ahead turn again. But then, there are times – perhaps many times – when communication isn't really the issue, and power is. That is a crucial point to bear in mind in thinking, theorizing and writing about meaning, communication and social matters.

Figure 1.3 Temporary parking arrangements, Salzburg, UEFA 2008

Simple points often have profound consequences; and so it is here: consequences for learning, for knowing and shaping information and knowledge, for attending to and communicating about the world and our place in it. Developing ways of thinking about this at once simple and complex phenomenon – that is, setting out *a social-semiotic theory of multimodality* – is what this book is about.

From semiotic *system* to semiotic *resource*

If that is the issue, then one ought to ask 'What has produced the explosive interest in the issue of multimodality over the last decade or so?' and, most obviously, 'Why now?'. *Image* has been a part of human cultures longer than *script* – though the difference between the two is not at all clear-cut. *Image* has been the subject of much interest, academic or otherwise, over millennia. *Gesture* is a presence in all cultures, even if in quite different ways. As 'sign language' it has been elaborated and articulated into a fully functioning representational resource. Whether as *gesture* or as *signing* it has been much studied (British Deaf Association, 1992). Academic disciplines have their interest in particular modes: Psychology in *gesture*; Art History in *image*, as has Mathematics, if differently so; *music* is studied in conservatories the world over. One difference is that whereas before these were the subject of interest in distinct areas of academic work, now there is an attempt to bring all means of making meaning together under one theoretical roof, as part of a single field in a unified account, a unifying theory.

A further reason, quite simply and yet most powerful of all, is this: the world of communication has changed and is changing still; and the reasons for that lie in a vast web of intertwined social, economic, cultural and technological changes.

Any attempt at a satisfactory answer to the questions 'Why?' and 'Why now?' has to go in the direction of the factors, everywhere connected, which have been and still are sweeping the world. One shorthand term which points to a collection of these is 'globalization' – which, for me, refers not only to financial globalization but to conditions which make it possible for characteristics of one place to be present and active in another – whether economic or cultural or technological. The forces of neoconservative ideology have sponsored and amplified these conditions, though they have been only partially causal. The factors at issue – let us say, forms of management, or ideologies around schooling – always impact in one locality and there they encounter locally present factors. There is a struggle of local forms and traditions with the features from outside, in which both are transformed, transformed in ways dependent on arrangements and dispositions of power in a locality.

The effects of this vastly diverse and complex phenomenon have led in very many places to the corrosion, fraying, dissolution, destruction and abandonment of older social relations, forms, structures, 'givens'. Globalization is not one 'thing'; it is differently constituted in different places, as are its effects and impacts, interacting with the vastly varied cultural, social, economic and political conditions of any one specific locality. Yet the deep effects are constant and recognizable everywhere. They have brought a move from a *relative* stability of the social world over maybe the last two centuries (as in Western Europe) to an often radical instability over the last three decades or so. Stemming from that – and generated by it – are far-reaching changes in the domain of meaning: in representation and in 'semiotic production'; in dissemination and distribution of messages and meanings; in mediation and communication. All have changed profoundly.

The semiotic effects are recognizable in many domains and at various levels: at the level of *media* and the *dissemination* of messages – most markedly in the shift from the book and the page to the screen; at the level of *semiotic production* in the shift from the older technologies of print to digital, electronic means; and, in *representation*, in the shift from the dominance of the mode of *writing* to the mode of *image*, as well as others. The effects are felt everywhere, in theory no less than in the practicalities of day-to-day living. Academic interest in the characteristics of this new communicational world, the world of the screen and of multimodality, has been relatively belated, stumbling after the horse which had left the stable some while ago. Belated or not, there is a need to catch up and get back in the saddle.

The effects of globalization are clear. From (relative) permanence and stability there has been a marked shift to provisionality and instability. Currently fashionable metaphors are always revealing in that respect. For instance, while I am writing this book, the metaphor of *mobility* has great currency, as in 'mobile technologies' or 'mobile learning'. Like others, I use such metaphors; they are attempts to name and capture something of the essence of the alterations, transformations, remakings of social arrangements and practices. *Design*, is a term I have been using since the early 1990s; for me it indicates a shift away both from the earlier social and semiotic goal of *competence* as from the somewhat later *critique*.

Design accords recognition to the *work* of individuals in their social lives and builds that into the theory. In my use of the term, *design* is about a theory of communication and meaning, based – at least potentially – on equitable participation in the shaping of the social and semiotic world. *Design*, by contrast with *competence*, foregrounds a move away from anchoring communication in *convention* as social regulation. *Design* focuses on an individual's *realization* of their *interest* in their world. The move away from *critique* has, for me, a different focus and motivation: away from engaging with the past actions of others and their effects. *Competence* leaves arrangements unchallenged. *Critique* is oriented backward and towards superior power, concerned with the *present effects* of the *past actions* of others. *Design* is prospective, looking forward. *Design* focuses on my interests *now* in relation to the likely future effects of my actions. The understanding which inheres in *competence* was essential to carry out *critique*, just as the understanding developed through *critique* is essential in the practices of *design*. *Design* draws on both these, carries their insights forward and deepens them, focused in *a social-semiotic theory of multimodality*.

As another example, take the shift from the term *grammar* to the use of the term *semiotic resources*. It indicates a shift from meanings traditionally attached to 'grammar', as fixed and highly constrained regularity. Occasionally I use the term 'grammar' to contest its meaning with my sense of '*relative* regularity of a semiotic resource'. Throughout the book I attempt to draw attention to the implications and the perspectives of the metaphors I use – *grammar, design, resource* – reflecting on their possible effects on what I want to achieve. While it may seem pedantic to do so, I spend time here and there drawing out such differences in perspectives and effects in the use of metaphors.

We do not yet have a theory which allows us to understand and account for the world of communication as it is now. Nor therefore do we have an adequate set of categories to describe what we need to describe. In their absence we tend to use the terms that we have inherited from the former era of relative stability, in particular from theories and descriptions of language, where, over a long time, a complex set of tools has been developed. But using tools that had served well to fix horse-drawn carriages becomes a problem in mending contemporary cars. Many of the older terms do point to aspects which we need to consider and shape for present purposes; at the same time we cannot afford to be reluctant in introducing necessary new terms. Many frequently used terms need careful re-examination; *representation* is one of these. The point is: adequate theoretical tools are needed to deal both with the present social, economic, political and cultural situation and the resultant conditions for semiosis.

To conclude the issue, here, of necessary theoretical resources, I will briefly return to *grammar*. Here we have a term known to nearly everyone in Western societies even though there is not much agreement as to what it might mean. There is a certain feeling – held with different degrees of conviction in different domains – that grammar is about rules, conventions, certainty: phenomena that are fixed, settled. When business leaders, politicians, media pundits, bemoan that the young leave school and are unemployable because they cannot 'write a (proper) sentence', they look back some thirty or forty years and seem to discern, through a sepia-tinged haze, that in their day the teaching of grammar had produced just such ideal conditions. They note that the young do not use the rules which they are certain that they had followed way back then; and which they think they use still, in their present practice. Adherence to linguistic convention is equated with adherence to social convention and consequently with social 'stability'. Alas, the present is deeply unstable; no amount of nostalgia can change that. The need is for a labour force that can meet the semiotic demands of conditions now. But in this, 'grammar' in its older sense of 'a stable system of rules' is an obstacle to necessary action.

Representational and communicational practices are constantly altered, modified, as is all of culture, in line with and as an effect of social changes. That inevitably makes the grammar of grammar books a record of the past social practices of particular groups, in speech as in writing: useful maybe *then*, but neither used nor useful *now*, not even for those who wish it were otherwise. If I use the term 'grammar' it leaves me with the need to contest its implied meanings of 'fixed rules', 'stable convention', and so on, or to use a term which is free of such histories of meaning. At the moment I generally choose the latter route, using the term 'resource', as in 'resources for representation'. *Resources* are constantly remade; never wilfully, arbitrarily, anarchically but precisely, in line with what I need, in response to some demand, some 'prompt' now – whether in conversation, in writing, in silent engagement with some framed aspect of the world, or in inner debate.

Semiotic resources are socially made and therefore carry the discernible regularities of social occasions, events and hence a certain stability; they are never fixed, let alone rigidly fixed. No degree of power can act against the socially transformative force of interaction. This is not the point (nor the purpose of this book) to talk about the benefits or disbenefits of *stability*, or the need for stable 'rules' in order to attempt – even if never to guarantee – relative security of communication.

Cultural difference and communication: the 'reach' of the theory and the 'reach' of modes

Most readers will take it as given that a society, its cultures and the representation of their meanings, form a tightly integrated whole, at a certain level of generality at least. If that is so, then differences between societies and cultures means differences in representation and meaning. That is close to a commonplace. We know that languages differ and that those differences are entirely linked with differences of histories and cultures. What is the case for 'language' is so for all representation – for *modes* as for *discourses* as for *genres* – and in all communication: patently so with music, with image, with clothing, food, and so on. Chinese opera is not the opera of Mozart or Puccini. For me, as someone from 'the West', it takes much focused semiotic *work* to understand its meanings, its aesthetics; roughly the same amount of work, I imagine, that it takes for someone who has grown up with Chinese classical music to make sense of 'Western' music.

The more pronounced the cultural differences, the greater are the differences in the resources of representation and in the practices of their use. This means that in theorizing and writing about communication, I can talk with some confidence about the few cultures that I know reasonably well. Where my knowledge becomes vague or more general, I can only talk vaguely and generally. I have a degree of confidence, an 'inwardness', with several anglophone cultures, and different degrees of 'inwardness' with some of the cultures of mainland Europe. I have a glancing acquaintance with some cultures in Asia and Latin America, where I have been a casual visitor. I make no strong claims about those cultures and none about those of Africa: it would be foolish for me to do so.

So what is the 'reach' – the applicability – of the theory I put forward here? How general is it, how far and where and in what ways does or can it apply? Is it confined to Western Europe alone? What claims to understanding or insight can I make for this theory outside 'the West', broadly? I have, in any case, a problem with the notion of 'universals' – such as 'universals of language', or 'universals of communication', so I am not tempted much in that direction. The universe of cultures and of cultural difference on our small planet is too vast for such generalization.

There tend to be contradictory views on how to deal with this. As far as 'language' is concerned, we know, on the one hand, that 'languages differ' in the way they name the world – in 'words' as in syntactic and grammatical forms; we know that lexical fields are close mappings of social practices. To give a banal example, English does not have the word 'Weltschmerz' and German does not have the word 'literacy'. Each may struggle to find ways of bringing the other's meanings into their culture; in the case of these two examples, with little success so far. Culture is too complex to tolerate difficult transplants readily. On the other hand, we sort of assume that 'language equals language': that is, if there is a novel in Russian it ought to be possible to translate it into English. We expect significant overlap, even if not a one-to-one correspondence. In many cases the incommensurability matters. In a debate, Germans can talk about 'Wissen' ('knowing that') and 'Koennen' ('knowing how'): when the discussion moves to translating 'knowledge' from English to German (or Swedish) it is not straightforward to know which of these to choose. Or, another example: in English there are the two words 'teaching' and 'learning', verbs with an implied directionality of authority, in which 'teachers' have 'knowledge' and 'learners' have (or used to be assumed to have) the duty to acquire this knowledge. Vast theoretical and practical edifices and industries can and have been erected on such distinctions. Yet in many languages the same lexical root is used for this social domain: in German (as in Swedish) for instance, 'lehren' and 'lernen' are morphological inflections – 'alternations' – of the one lexemic stem – 'learn' in English. That makes it likely that German and Swedish societies might develop quite different theories around 'Education' to English society; and articulate them in their languages and their institutions. In each case it is the 'accident of lexis' – not of course an accident but the expression of a history of non-accidental social differences – which leads to such ontological wild goose chases.

Two theoretical approaches have characterized this debate. One is focused on culture; the other is focused on the human brain. Noam Chomsky's *universalism* is the best known recent exemplar of the latter, through his posited link between the organization of the brain ('mind' in his terminology) and that of language – his assumptions about the 'innateness' of linguistic competence (Chomsky, 1965). This asserts that the organization (the 'nature') of the human brain is shared by all humans; the 'deep' organization of language derives from 'deep', 'innate' mental organization, so that irrespective of superficial differences, at a basic level all human languages share the same organization. From this, Chomsky derives a noble political project (to which I subscribe), namely that this profound and essential equality of humans ought to have its reflection in a politics of real equality. From this I infer that the reach of a Chomskian theory in respect to my issue here is general; it has applicability to all humans; and the social and cultural really does not enter.

My view on that is that there are some highly general *semiotic* principles, which are common to all human (as well as to most mammalian and some other animal) communication. Consequently, these are present and evident in all human societies and their cultures. The most significant of these is that humans *make* signs in which form and meaning stand in a 'motivated' relation. These signs are made with very many different means, in very many different modes. They are the expression of the *interest* of socially formed individuals who, with these signs, *realize* – give outward expression to – their meanings, using culturally available semiotic resources, which have been shaped by the practices of members of social groups and their cultures. Instead of a shared innate *linguistic competence* I assume shared *social, semiotic, communicational principles* and *dispositions* – which includes the *linguistic* as one instance. These principles and dispositions are articulated in communities in the ceaseless processes of social (inter)action. Hence the principles and dispositions take particular form, as the result of the specific social concerns of a community.

Given this stance, I assume that 'translations' across modes *within* a culture are both possible and hugely difficult; from *image* to *speech* – the 'evocation' rather than a description – of a painting in a conversation about an exhibition; or from *image* to *writing*; or from oral poetry to poetry in written form. I assume that translations across cultures, whether in the same mode (from *writing* to *writing* – from Russian *novel* to that *novel* in English; from *gesture* to *gesture* – from the 'French' shoulder shrug of indifference to an English version) or across different modes are also possible, though always achieved with enormously difficult selection; at a considerable level of generality; and inevitably with significant changes in meaning.

Stated like this, it implies that in its *most general* features, in its outline and general direction, the theory applies to all cultures. In the *specificities* of cultures there are often vast differences in the articulation of these principles, which lead to difficulty in the transfer of the theory from culture to culture. Readers need to make their assessment whether, where, in what ways or to what extent my comments, based on observations in some cultures and speculations based on these, are possible to 'translate' from one to another of the cultures with which they themselves have 'inwardness'. This features as a topic in both Chapters 5 and 6.

To give an example of principles shared by all cultures: I have mentioned the three most important: (1) that *signs are motivated conjunctions of form and meaning*; that conjunction is based on (2) *the interest of the sign-maker*; using (3) *culturally available resources*. These are principles of sign-making. There are then, at a different level, resources for making signs. Here too there are commonalities of a general kind. As one instance, for meaning-making to be possible, human cultures need and do provide means for *framing* aspects of the world to which an individual needs or wishes to attend. A culture will therefore provide its distinct semiotic resources for *framing* (complexes of) signs: what sorts of things are framed, how they are framed, what kinds of frames there are, and so on, and these will vary from culture to culture. Expressing this starkly: there is *no meaning without framing*.

These are instances of *general principles*; and of means and processes of *meaning-*making in any culture and in any mode. They provide a starting point in the analysis of meaning in any one culture. I do not call these 'universals', though I regard them as shared by all human cultures, as well as by many other species. These shared principles are based on experiences common to humans in social groups in their engagement with a world both vastly different at one level and yet presenting common challenges. If we take this line of argument we can acknowledge commonalities at a very general level and yet be able to focus on the specificities of cultural difference. The theory can then provide a shared frame at its most general level and respond to specific needs at the level of any one culture and its modes.

That represents one theoretical take on the issue of 'reach'. There is then the social and cultural aspect of that notion, namely that of the 'reach' of modes. Here the question is: 'What areas are "covered" by a mode in a specific culture?' or, differently, 'Do all modes cover the same terrain?'. In a multimodal approach it is *modes* – rather than say, 'languages' – which are compared. *Modes* are the result of a social and historical shaping of materials chosen by a society for representation: there is no reason to assume that the mode of *gesture* in Culture 1 covers the same 'area' or the same concerns, or is used for the same purposes and meanings as the mode of *gesture* in Culture 2 – quite apart from the (lexical and syntactic) differences mentioned just above.

For instance, *gesture* may be used to deal with meanings around 'attitude' in two cultures; yet what is 'addressed', made into an area of common interest within the area of 'attitude', may be quite different. The English 'eyes raised heavenward' means something different to the French shoulder shrug; though both carry meanings of a personal stance to some event or utterance. English culture does not have an equivalent to the French quick, limp-wristed shaking of the drooping hand – used by women more than men – to convey 'disapproving astonishment'. Quite to the contrary, it is likely that aspects of the cultural domain covered by a mode in one society is not covered by that mode in another culture. An area such as 'politeness' may be dealt with extensively in *speech* in one culture and by *proxemics*, by *gesture* or by *facial expression* in another. In other words, if all modes are called on to make meaning, there is no reason to assume that the 'modal division of labour' will be the same across societies. That is a radically different position to one which held when the assumption was that 'language' did all significant cultural semiotic work.

These differences have been addressed in the study of intercultural communication. Yet here too an approach focusing on modes might be highly useful. An area in which this is a real issue is that of translation. Until recently that has focused on language alone. In the subtitling of films for instance this becomes significant. But what about a translation of a movement, an action, a gesture that is entirely understood in one society and either entirely misunderstood or not understood in any way in another? We simply can no longer assume that the reach of modes is the same across different societies and their cultures. Modes occupy different 'terrains' from one society to another. We have to begin looking at the field of meaning as a whole and see how meaning is handled modally across the range of modes in different societies.

The politics of naming

Somewhat related to this is the difficulty of 'naming'. It has two distinct, maybe unrelated, aspects: one is political, the other theoretical. The political aspect is how to name the political/social/cultural world about which I am writing. It is the normal, unremarkable, ordinary world, for me. As an insider, its characteristics are difficult for me to see; however much I attempt not to do so, I use my 'insiderness' as a yard-stick in judging other parts of the world around me. Should I use names such as 'the First World', 'the developed world', 'the post-industrialized world', 'the West' in talking about the world in which I have lived and worked; and about 'the East', 'the Third' or 'Fourth' world in talking about parts of the world unfamiliar to me, different socially, economically, with profound differences in history and culture? Such ques-tions are usefully discussed in the writings of Immanuel Wallerstein (2001). Apart from the difficulty of drawing meaningful boundaries for any of these constantly multiplying and overlapping terms, each brings with it specific meanings, more often than not potentially harmful in their application, meanings which I would prefer not to import into my text.

From a semiotic perspective, all cultures, all semiotic 'worlds', are rich, if differ-ently so. Each of these domains – the 'First World' say, or 'Western Europe', the anglophone world – is highly diverse within itself, culturally and semiotically. Some parts of 'the First World' (whatever that might be) are deeply different to 'the West'; and from each other. As one small semiotic example, some societies in 'the First World' make use of character-based scripts while others use alphabetic ones. This one difference alone brings deep differences of ontology, of cultural disposition, of dispositions towards representation, to media systems; it has effects on knowledge and identity.

Absolutely related too is the issue of 'globalization'. I take it that this term names something real – for instance, the fact that in very many places around the world, economic, political, social and cultural values and practices are subject to forces which come from 'outside' the domain regarded as the immediately framed 'local' and have telling effects within it. Within that frame these 'external' factors interact with the meanings, values and practices of the 'local site'– differently therefore in different places. Semiotically speaking, this leads to constant change, transformation, 'blending'. Constant blending is by no means a new phenomenon, even though the (now fading) fashionability of the term 'hybridity' had seemed to suggest otherwise. Blending is as old as humankind itself, as archaeologists demonstrate even in parts of the globe still remote now to the 'first world'. Or as we can see everywhere around us, even now, at any time. On a recent train journey in Germany – from the northern Rhineland to Munich – three couples in their late forties or early fifties boarded the train in Frankfurt, about 9.30 in the morning. I had caught the train in Essen, about two hours to the north. Listening to the group's German dialect, I could not tell if they were from a Hessian dialect area, or from a Franconian or a Swabian one (my own dialect is middle Franconian). They were in high spirits, very friendly indeed – inviting me to join in a morning coffee-cum-picnic which they had unpacked and spread on two of the tables, with garlands across the windows; and so I asked where they were from. The answer was Germsheim: a town just north of Heidelberg, a region which just about straddles all three dialect areas. Clearly, people in this area – as in very many places (Rampton, 1995; Sebba, 1993) – are engaged in constantly assimilating, transforming features of the dialects around them and integrating them into a constantly changing yet constantly coherent resource.

What *is* new is the intensity of this phenomenon and the effect in its present manifestation, its 'pace', aided by current means of transport of economic, social and cultural commodities. Electronic forms of communication can now make aspects of any specific 'where' into features encountered everywhere, with an unspoken and urgent requirement for it to be made sense of 'there'.

What is not new however, is the set of names, the lexicon, which we have to name this differently paced social world. That is a problem, which makes the issue of theory and of naming within theory urgent. There is a need for new names. Ferdinand de Saussure suggested, at the very beginning of the twentieth century, that Linguistics – in its theory and terminology – as the then most advanced study of any semiotic system, might suffice to 'furnish forth the wedding tables' for the semiotic feasts to come in the new century. This seemed a reasonable hope, given that that expectation was expressed in the high era of abstraction in the Social Sciences: Linguistics and Semiotics included. In certain areas of the study of language in particular, concepts such as 'language', 'langue', 'parole', 'stood in' for the tendency towards achieving a grasp of the particular via very high degrees of abstraction. By entire contrast, the study of *modes* in multimodal social semiotics focuses on the *material*, the *specific*, the *making* of signs *now*, in this environment for this occasion. In its focus on the material it also focuses on the bodilyness of those who make and remake signs in constant semiotic (inter)action. It represents a move away from high abstraction to the specific, the material; from the mentalistic to the bodily.

For that, it is essential to develop apt labels for a theory of representation and communication for the whole domain of multimodal meaning as well as for the level of specific modes. The theory and the labels will need to attend to the materiality, the specificity and the histories of (social) work of any one mode. The specific aspects of mode will need to be assimilated to superordinate terms which capture what is semiotically general to all modes in that society and to modes even across cultures; even though what is general is always articulated distinctively in a specific mode.

I devote a chapter to this issue of categories of the theory and of naming. Two terms figure prominently in what I have written so far and do throughout the book: *society* and *culture*. The distinction between them is not easy to make; there is not a clear line to draw. Nor is there a generally accepted sense in which the two terms are used (Williams, 1985); for many writers the two are near synonymous. The distinction that I make has two features: *society* emphasizes human action in social groups (that is, groups organized in a recognizable fashion around goals, purposes, organizations, shared practices, values and meanings). Social groups and actions are always characterized by (differences in) power. *Culture* emphasizes the effects, the products of social actions and social work, whether physical and material or abstract and, for want of a better term, conceptual. Where the social is marked by power (difference), the cultural is marked by *values, evaluation* – itself the effect of social power. *Culture*, in my use, is the domain of socially made values; tools; meanings; knowledge; resources of all kinds; *society* is the field of human (inter)*action* in groups, always; of 'work'; of practices; of the use and effects of power.

I use the term *work*, wishing to stress social orientation and aims. *Work* involves a worker, tools and that which is worked on. *Work* produces change, in the worker, in the tools and in that which is worked on. Being social and purposive, change produces and embodies meanings. In working, the worker has experienced and learned something; the worker has changed. The tools have (been) changed by their use; and what has been worked on has changed. Each of these changes has produced meaning, new meaning. The effect of these changes is to produce cultural resources. For me, therefore, *culture* is the name for the resources which have been made, produced, remade, 'transformed', as the result of social work. Everything that is socially made and remade becomes part of cultural resources, imbued with the meanings of the work of those who have made and remade the resources. Cultural resources, being meaningful, are semiotic resources. It is 'the social' which generates 'the cultural' and, in that, 'the semiotic'.

Constant engagement in (social) *work* as defined above, with socially made cultural-semiotic resources and their constant remaking in daily actions, shapes my own inner resources in line with the meaning-potentials of these resources as encountered and remade, transformed by me. This describes the effects of communication and of *learning*: *attention* to an aspect of the social world; engagement with it in transformative action; which constantly remakes my inner resources; and in that, changes my potential for future action in and on the world. Differently seen, it describes my construction of knowledge for myself – always in social environments; with culturally available resources imbued with the meanings of those who have shaped and reshaped them in *their* social environments; responding to the needs of their times. In both of these processes – a differently focused perspective on very much the same phenomenon – I am constantly remaking myself and refashioning myself in terms of my *subjectivity* (seen from a social and political perspective) and fashioning and constantly refashioning my *identity* – the process viewed from the perspective of my biography (Endress *et al.*, 2005); a biography which shares much and yet is never identical with the biography of any other member of my or any other social group.

Throughout the book, two other terms turn up frequently: 'sign' and 'concept'. While the book does not deal with 'concept', the term names much the same territory as does 'sign' – which, together with *mode*, is at the centre of attention. The term *sign* belongs to Semiotics – the conjunction, invisible and indivisible, of form and meaning – while *concept* belongs to Psychology, and, deriving from there, to Pedagogy, where it names something called 'knowledge' in an entity called 'mind'.

A satellite view of language

Stepping outside the long tradition of seeing 'language' as a full means of making meaning, seeing it instead as one means among others, one can gain a 'satellite view' of language (Kress *et al.,* 1996). That metaphor recalls 'our' first views of the Earth through photographs from a satellite – that is, from outside the Earth, beyond its atmosphere. That view gave 'us' on Earth a startlingly different perspective; for instance showing with frightening clarity the boundedness, the limits of our planet: this is what we have, there is no more. From that time on, for many of us, it became troubling to pour old oil down the kitchen sink, because we could see, actually, that it wasn't simply going to disappear, that it would emerge somewhere else on this bounded Earth, with unknowable consequences. The satellite view showed us what we had known and had been able to ignore, in a way: that our planet, our Earth, was one small part of a much bigger whole.

A multimodal social-semiotic theory has a somewhat similar effect. It shows the boundedness of language – which we knew without knowing it – as indeed we had known about the destiny of the oil poured down the sink. 'Language' isn't a big enough receptacle for all the semiotic stuff we felt sure we could pour into it. But when I watch football or snooker, tennis or golf, I can see that the conceptual world of the football, snooker or tennis player as of the golfer is a field where semiotic work is most decidedly *not* done via *speech* – let alone *writing* – the occasional shouted 'here', 'oi' or 'Tessa' on an English football pitch notwithstanding. With snooker, the incredible precision of planning of geometrical strategies for specific shots and for the planned shape of the arrangement of the balls four moves ahead, is a domain outside (I am tempted to say 'beyond') 'language'. That is before we get to the practices of mathematicians (to which snooker or football players of course belong). The reach of *speech* or *writing* simply does not extend there. The semiotic/conceptual work done in these fields, as in countless other human social tasks, pleasures and professions, relies on modes remote from *speech* and *writing*. There are domains beyond the reach of language, where it is insufficient, where semiotic-conceptual work has to be and is done by means of other modes.

In this as in other ways, a social-semiotic approach to multimodal work makes a difference. The task is to establish, with as much precision as we might, what these differences are, in specific cases and circumstances. What new kinds of questions emerge and are made possible; how do persistent, older questions get recast, in ways possibly that lead to more plausible answers; and who might benefit in what ways from the different answers. In my area of work, the insights and benefits will accrue in all the areas of (theories of) learning, meaning, evaluation, assessment, subjectivity and identity.

In this it is important to be aware of the twin focus of the *social-semiotic theory* and of *multimodality*. The issue of 'access', for instance, can benefit from the insight that humans may have different orientations to modes and ensembles of modes – maybe with specific preferences for the temporal or the spatial, for image or speech, for the gestural or the domain of bodily movement as in dance, and so on. This could bring enormous benefits. The *theory* of social semiotics opens the route to a clearer view of evaluation/assessment in different modes. This is explored in some detail in Chapters 4, 5 and 10. Multimodality and social semiotics together may bring real benefits in understanding apt forms of communication through better understandings of design: whether in the private or in the public domain – in pleasure and entertainment as much as in work.

To give a very simple example: in a science classroom the issue of plant cells has been discussed. The teacher might ask: 'OK, who can tell me something about a plant cell?' or she might say: 'OK, who can draw a plant cell with its nucleus?'. The response to the first request might be: 'Miss, the cell has a nucleus.' The response to the second has to be a drawing – very likely of a circle with the nucleus placed – as a dot or smaller circle – somewhere in the larger circle.

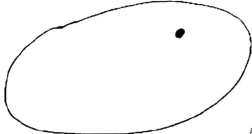

Figure 1.4 Cell with nucleus

In drawing, the student would have to make several decisions which she or he does not have to make in their spoken response. How big is the nucleus? Is it more like a dot or more like a small circle? And, most important of all, where does it have to be placed? At times I try this as a small exercise; some members of the audience are led by the seemingly implicit notion of 'centrality' in the word 'nucleus'; consequently they place the dot or small circle in the centre; others place it somewhere else. In either case, a decision has to be made about that issue: it is not avoidable. *Image* representation demands what I shall call (borrowing from Jon Ogborn) an 'episte-mological commitment': the nucleus is like *this* and it is placed *there*. Any student looking at the drawing made by the teacher is entitled to think that that is where the nucleus belongs. That 'commitment' cannot be avoided; in an image, the dot or the small circle representing the nucleus has to be placed *somewhere*. In the spoken or written response, no commitment about placement (or size or shape) has to be made. However, 'epistemological commitment' as such cannot be avoided; though in this case the commitment is of a different kind: about entities as names and their relation. A separation of 'cell' and 'nucleus' is made in the spoken or written version and a relation of possession – 'having' – is established. Now the 'cell' 'has' something, a 'nucleus'. In *speech* or in *writing* this epistemological commitment is unavoidable; in drawing no such commitment was asked, made or necessary.

This is one example. There are endless others. Theoretically, how do we now need to think about or define 'text'? How do we now think about *imagination*, when much of our thinking has been shaped and dominated by the possibilities offered in linguistic modes? What of creativity? And do we now have better means for paying attention to 'inner' representation and the 'inner' trade between different forms of representation, that is, to the entirely usual and hugely neglected process of synaesthesia? (Kress, 1997a). Is it not in that 'space' and those processes that much of what we regard as 'creativity' takes place?

2 The social environment of contemporary communication

An ethical approach to communication

Theories of communication — including the theory put forward here — set out how communication does, can or should function. Yet with the rapid shrinking, the disappearance even, of a public domain where a consensus about forms of social interaction might exist, it seems essential to consider a basic frame for ethical conduct in communication. In an era dominated by neo-liberal economics and neo-conservative 'philosophy' — 'there is no such thing as society' — older, too often implicit, values underlying communication have been challenged, negated, destroyed, forgotten out of embarrassment maybe, or have simply disappeared. In that context it seems important to set out some minimal imagined values. Here this can be no more than a personal statement; yet if it draws attention to the need for such a framework, that might be enough for now.

I assume that *full participation* by all members of a group, socially, culturally, economically and affectively in that community's affairs is a *sine qua non* for that group to flourish. That includes a commitment to values regarded as central for maintaining social cohesion. That in turn requires full access to semiotic, cultural, social and economic resources. Central among these is the potential for full participation in the *design* and *production* of representations as messages and access to the means of their *dissemination*.

In this respect, the aims of a social-semiotic theory of communication might be:

- that members of communities have access to the semiotic and other cultural resources essential to act in their social world on their own behalf and for their benefit
- that as members of a cohesive community they are able to contribute to common purposes by dealing productively with constantly new cultural, semiotic and social problems and by designing, representing and communicating their suggested solutions to them
- that in their social-semiotic actions, members of social groups have a clear sense of the effects of their (semiotic) actions on others and act so as not to impair the potentials for actions of others.

Assumptions

The means for *making* meanings and the means for *communicating* these meanings are shaped, first and foremost, by social and economic factors. In a social-semiotic theory the assumption is that the cultural technologies of representation, production and dissemination and the affordances and facilities that they offer are used within the frame of what is socially possible at any one time. Communication always has been and will remain subject to social, cultural, economic and political givens. The environments, conditions, choices are mediated by the interests of members of social groups so that practices, resources and technologies of communication respond, at different rates at different times, to social, economic and technological developments.

In anglophone societies currently, the roles and relations of 'state' and 'market' are primary among the factors shaping communication. European (nation) states have, for the last three or four decades been in a phase of rapid and deep transition. After a period of about 150 years in which the aims of the (nineteenth-century) nation-state, with a nationally conceived and to some extent nationally controlled economy, shaped conceptions and practices of communication, the trend now is towards a situation where the demands of globally organized markets are reshaping the ground of communicational conditions. The still ruling conceptions and metaphors around communication – as for other social practices and structures – come from that earlier period, shaped by its requirements and structures. One instance is the still active even though by now barely residually present nineteenth-century notion of the 'mass' – as in 'mass-society', 'mass-communication'. New social, economic, political and technological givens require new names/metaphors capable of functioning as essential guides to thought and action.

Environments for communication: social frames and communicational possibilities

The nineteenth-century nation state assumed that it exercised control of 'the market'; the situation now is one where it seems clear that markets control the major institutions of the state. In some instances the state now acts as the servant of the market – an instance might be the UK since the mid-1980s. This process has happened at a different pace in different parts of the world. The English language has acted as a vector for the spread of the relevant ideologies: neo-liberal/neo-conservative conceptions of market, state, family and the individual.

This has had effects on expectations of communication. The (nation) state's concern had been the development of citizens – social subjects whose identity was shaped by the goals of the state – and the preparation of a labour force serving the needs of a national economy and administration. That state was interested in cohesion, integration and homogeneity – however imperfectly realized. The globally framed interests of current versions of the market are neither about citizenship – shared social values, aspirations, dispositions – nor about the preparation of a labour force, whether for a national or a global economy. In advanced capitalist conditions, the market actively fosters social *fragmentation* as a means of maximizing the potentials of niche markets. Hence the market has an interest in the development and support of distinct *lifestyles*, with former (at least partly) ethical concerns swept aside. Considerations around professional practices, work, moral/ethical issues are increasingly left to individual effort, action and, significantly for communication, to forms of regulation not sponsored (let alone imposed) by the state: that is, in situations where choices around regulation are possible, given limitations or not of economic, cultural and social capital.

The subjectivity preferred by the market is that of 'consumer', a subjectivity with deeply different social, conceptual and ethical considerations and requirements to those of 'worker' or 'citizen'. The subjectivity of 'consumer', embedded in market-led conceptions of *choice*, has fundamental effects on possibilities and practices of communication when contrasted with those of 'citizen'. A citizen might adhere to notions of social responsibility and convention; a consumer is oriented to choice. The former sustains communicational framings – for instance, genres, canonical conceptions of choices of mode, as well as authoritatively given knowledge; the latter does not and assumes instead that the fluidity of social forms finds its counterpart in the fluidity of communicational practices. Theories of communication need to be clear about this and about their stance in relation to that: whether in support, in rejection, in accommodation or in developing alternative positions. Where censorship had ruled before, in all forms, ranging from direct prohibition to careful selection of materials, and often covert limitations of availability, to suggestions around 'good taste', now there is far less of such restriction. The internet is a (still) clear example in that respect in most 'Western' societies. Given the continuing existence of power and its interests, that situation is likely to become an area of contestation.

Over the last two decades, much of this debate had been framed in terms of *class* versus *lifestyle*; that debate is now more or less settled. For theories of representation and communication, the apt and more comprehensive term may be that of 'life-world' (Schütz and Luckmann, 1984). Life-worlds point to clusterings of social and cultural factors and resources, such as education, gender, age as generation, 'ethnicity', occupation/profession, regionality (where the frequently highly telling differences in availability and access to resources between city and rural-marginal areas is a basic factor). The impact, potentials and possible accelerating or ameliorating effects of technologies for production and communication of messages need to be seen in this context. Conceptions of social cohesion or of its absence are a major factor appearing as the semiotic notion of 'coherence' in the practices of shaping of texts-as-messages.

In general it might be said that notions such as *mobility* are the semiotic and informational analogue of social conditions of fluidity.

Power, authority and authorship

The factors alluded to have brought a profound transformation in social forms, structures and processes. They will continue to have shaping effects on forms, processes and possibilities of communication, on meaning-making, on environments for learning and hence on the formation of identity and subjectivity. Distributions of *power* and *principles* and *agencies of control* are generative of and crucial for an understanding of communicational environments, compared to those that had existed. In all domains of communication these rearrangements in power can be conceptualized as a shift from 'vertical' to 'horizontal' structures of power, from *hierarchical* to (at least seemingly) more *open, participatory relations,* captured in many aspects of contemporary communication. They are expressed, among many others, in metaphors such as (*hyper*) *links, webs, networks* as well as in new forms of text-making under new conditions of *authorship*.

'Authorship' in particular is in urgent need of theorizing. The debate here is marked by a profound incomprehension and hence hostility, which is evident in terms such as *plagiarism* and *cutting and pasting*. The accusation of *plagiarism* is itself now becoming an anachronistic term, harking back to a different social, semiotic and legal environment. It arises as a response to social conditions – that is, as a particular semiotic response to notions of 'freedom of choice'. That is transferred to practices of text-making where formerly settled – quasi-moral, legal and semiotic – notions about authorship, text and property are now no longer treated as relevant; or are, more often than not, no longer recognized by those who engage in text-making now. In that context, the accusation of ('merely' or 'simply') *cutting and pasting* is a response that betrays a lack of theoretical work and hence incomprehension about new principles of text-making composition. It rests on a misconceived transfer of old conceptions of authorship to new conditions. Let me hasten to say – lest I be misunderstood – that I am not in favour of intellectual theft nor of deceit, laziness or exploitation. Yet mere moral outrage alone will not produce one iota of understanding.

The redistribution of power in communication, an effect jointly of the social conditions just mentioned and the facilities of digital devices, both leading to the remaking of power-relations, has the most profound effect on conceptions of learning, of knowledge and hence on the formation of subjectivity and identity. Young people act within these understandings of (their) power. This is manifested in countless practices, whether in resistance in various ways to traditional authority or in a straightforward assumption of their agency, acting in their own interests in the domain of their 'own' culture and in their own cultural/semiotic production. The best examples here are 'user-created content' and the new genres, forms and sites of dissemination such as *blogs, wikis, YouTube* and *MySpace*.

In other words, current social and economic conditions are paralleled by and characteristic of features of the contemporary media landscape. This landscape is marked by several factors:

- The affordances of *participation* of current media technologies
- *The global and local 'reach'* of media – in many ways obliterating the difference between *the global* and *the local*
- *User-created content*
- *Accessibility/connectivity/mobility/ubiquity* of persons and information
- *Convergence of representational, productive and communicational functions* in technologies and devices
- *Multimodality*, that is, representations in many modes, each chosen from rhetorical aspects for its communicational potentials.

Social and theoretical consequences: ruling metaphors of *participation, design, production*

With former structures of power, the relation of media production to media audience had been characterized as one of *consumption*. With new distributions of power, that is giving way increasingly to one of *production* and *participation* for those who had previously been seen as audience. In early 2008, *YouTube* (founded in 2006 and sold within eighteen months to Google for $1.6 billion) witnessed a daily uploading of 60,000 videos. That may stand as a metaphor for present relations of individuals to media: *producing* for an unknown and potentially vast group; *producing* for new media and new sites; *distributing* via existing, new or yet to be created *sites*, as full *participation*. It is not clear what the social characteristics of this form of participation actually are; nor whether it could be called democratic: democracy assumes social groupings characterized by broad assent to socially agreed and legitimated practices, with rights and duties understood by members of such groups. These current forms of 'participation' may not, predominantly, be organized in former ways; here a need for social analysis and apt naming is essential.

While *consumption* (along with similar terms such as *use* and *gratification*) had been a traditional metaphor for understanding the place of 'audience' in relation to media and its power, *critique* offered a possibility of challenging and possibly disrupting its underlying relations of power: that is, from a position of lesser power to greater, from reception and consumption of messages to a refusal either to receive or consume these, subjecting them to critique instead. Engaging in *critique* is to refuse to acquiesce in and adapt to existing distributions of roles, rights, responsibilities and power in specific occasions of communication; and to attempt instead to bring these into crisis via a 'distancing analysis' of the divergent and often conflicting purposes, aims, means and interests of the makers and the assumed recipients of the messages.

In an era when social structures were inequitable yet relatively firm, stable, and in which there was a broad adherence to a sense of the semiotic 'fullness' of language as the means of representation and communication, *critique* of linguistic texts seemed a possible route of refusal to the imposition of power. In an unstable social world with differing distributions of power, *design* offers a paradigm which keeps the insights offered by *critique* and turns them into means for action in the designer's *interest*, an *interest* focused on the future. In that context, *design* is an assertion of the individual's interest in participating appropriately in the social and communicational world; and an insistence on their capacity to shape their interests through the *design* of messages with the resources available to them in specific situations. *Design* is prospective: a means of projecting an individual's interest into their world with the intent of effect in the future. It is the position taken by those who have become accustomed to *produce* (for *YouTube* even if not in or for the school) and who disseminate their messages in and to a world which they address confidently.

Personal choices: existential insecurity or agency through participation and connection

Social factors such as *generation, education, class, region* and, maybe in a newly unstable manner, *gender,* have telling effects. Generationally, members of older generations are oriented towards traditional sources of authority – whether of profession (the medical doctor, the lawyer, the 'expert' in general) – and to hierarchical social structures. Many (still) rely on *information being brought to them* rather than taking responsibility for *seeking such information* by means that are now available (Boeck, 2004). Educational and social histories play a big role here. As a consequence, in any social group there are, at the present time, differing patterns of 'participation' and 'production'. The willingness to accommodate to the global 'reach' of new media is also likely to vary, so that *ubiquitous connection* may not be a fact of communicational life for several generations in any one social group. Similarly with the ability to make productive sense and use of cultural difference.

In other words, differentiation in possibilities of access are being newly configured by social factors which had not been so significant before: for instance, *age as generation*, or *region*, playing unexpectedly significant roles, layered on top of the still-active traditional factors such as *class*. This presents a more difficult situation for many, compared to previously settled arrangements. Here lies a real danger of groups 'coming adrift' from the social mainstream. Existential insecurity can become a much heightened problem for them.

Communication and meaning: fluidity, provisionality, instability

Three features mark what is (at the moment) salient, characteristic and indicative of the contemporary media landscape – (a) *Forms of knowledge production*; (b) *Forms and principles of text-making composition*; and (c) *Social and semiotic blurring: the dissolution, abolition, disappearance of frames and boundaries.*

Forms of knowledge production

Knowledge and *text* are entirely linked. Knowledge as such comes into being in the form of some material entity, a text. The concept of *user-produced content,* that is, the 'wiki' and 'Web 2.0' software, are emblematic of this in the contemporary landscape. The 'authors' of *Wikipedia* are neither a community nor a 'team' nor necessarily at all members of the same group. Authorship is by a 'collection' of people who may be entirely diverse socially speaking, unknown to each other, rather than an integrated, coherent group. Authority is 'assumed' rather than 'achieved' or 'bestowed'. At best, these 'authoring collections' are, at the moment of their authoring, 'inceptive communities'. That is, the activity itself may lead to new forms of sociality and community. Where previously authorship had been bestowed, regulated, buttressed and protected by legal means, in wiki-like production, older notions of authorship are not an issue; texts are open to constant modification. In terms of older models, this raises the profound issue of potentials for reliability and means of discernment.

Forms and principles of text-making composition

For the generation aged 25 and below, there seems at the moment little or no concern about what were to their elders – and still are – central questions of 'authenticity' and 'legitimacy' of authorship of certain kinds of texts. In *downloading, 'mixing', cutting and pasting, mashing, 'sampling', re-contextualization*, questions such as 'where did this come from, who is the original/originating author' seem not the issue they once had been. On this issue there is, seemingly, an entire and mutual incomprehension between generations. Yet at the same time there seems to be an absolute interest in precision on the part of younger producers about 'authorship' in relation to, for them, culturally salient, valued and identity-conferring cultural artefacts.

There is, as mentioned above, an urgent need to understand the practices, epistemologies, ethics and aesthetics of the new forms of text production. At the moment they are discussed by 'authority' in terms of nineteenth-century models; hence terms such as 'plagiarism' or 'mere copying' are too quickly to hand: that is, the invocation of models of text-making from an era where conceptions of authorship were clear and legally buttressed.

Ironically, the very same processes are in use at 'high levels' in post-modern art forms and practices: in the artefacts produced in the workshops of for instance Jeff Koons or Damien Hirst; as in much contemporary architecture. Here the older attitudes to high aesthetics and to 'high theory' protects such practices.

Social and semiotic blurring: the dissolution, abolition, disappearance of frames and boundaries

The newly relevant frames and boundaries are of different kinds. Here I focus on four.

Epistemological and ontological frames: 'knowledge', fact and fiction

Examples of the blurring of the boundaries – and ensuing reactions – between *'reality'*, *'fact'* and *'fiction'* abound: whether with 'reality TV'; or in concerns about methods of documentary and 'docudrama' production – in the outrage, for instance in the UK – about photos staged for a national newspaper, of prisoners in Abu Ghraib. It was revealing that at that time it was possible for the political establishment in the UK to divert outrage away from the actual events in Iraq to the forms of representation/ documentation, that is, to the fact that a newspaper had used 'staged photographs' of these events. Equally interestingly, these events had been reported in writing several months earlier, without any particular notice being taken. In other words, outrage at the breaking of a *representational convention* was treated as more serious and overshadowed outrage at the breaking of *humanitarian conventions* on the treatment of prisoners. Entirely related are questions about 'reliability' – the truth – of non-canonical sources, such as those of the internet.

Social-interactional: issues of genre

Since the 1970s there has been an ongoing and increasingly far-reaching blurring of the boundaries of *genres* and of *generic types.* Learning and teaching materials produced for schools are no exception to this; the (former) boundary between genres of *work* and *entertainment/leisure* is being quite deliberately, knowingly and effectively erased in these materials.

Power, authority and convention: the question of 'canonicity' of semiotic forms and the reliability of knowledge

Previously 'convention' – the sedimentation of social power over time – could ensure adherence to practices in representation, for instance, the question in what mode canonical knowledge should be represented: whether as image (as *diagram*, for example) or in writing (as *report*, for example), or, what should count as official knowledge. Now these frames have virtually disappeared in many domains, including in the domain of formal education.

'Knowledge' versus information

The fraying and disappearance of social frames has begun to blur the distinction between *knowledge* and *information.* Knowledge, as a tool for the solving of problems, was unproblematic while life-worlds were stable and the problems that arose in these life-worlds were predictable. The instability of life-worlds with a simultaneous loss of authority, has led to the emergence of problems that are not predictable. With that has come the need for a constant production of *knowledge as tool* to solve these.

Information is the material from which individuals fashion the knowledge they need. That has made the line between 'knowledge' and 'information' problematic: the advent of 'user-produced/generated knowledge' is one indication. Knowledge is seen as a tool, shaped contingently in the transformation of information to knowledge by someone who has the relevant information and the capacity of transforming that information into 'knowledge as tool'.

All this demonstrates a need for a widely understood and applicable set of 'navigational aids' in relation to text-making, to reading, to the facility of discrimination of sources of knowledge/information and the means of discernment/discrimination between materials from a wide range of different sources.

A *prospective* theory of communication: rhetoric, design, production

Recognizing the dominant features of the social world fully is the essential prerequisite for a social-semiotic multimodal theory of communication. In the semiotic world, the world of meaning and the ethical world, the world of values, which is marked by instability and provisionality, every event of communication is in principle unpredictable in its form, structure and in its 'unfolding'. The absence of secure frames requires of each participant in an interaction that they assess, on each occasion, the social environment, the social relations which obtain in it and the resources available for shaping the communicational encounter.

This demands a *rhetorical* approach to communication. The hitherto sufficient requirement of *competent performance* and possibly of *critique* cannot meet the new demands. Inwardness with 'grooved convention' had, in the past, been sufficient for competent communication. By contrast, the *rhetor* as maker of a message now makes an assessment of all aspects of the communicational situation: of her or his interest; of the characteristics of the audience; the semiotic requirements of the issue at stake and the resources available for making an apt representation; together with establishing the best means for its dissemination.

In a model of communication for full and equitable participation in the new communicational world, the *rhetor's* interests need to be fully acknowledged. The *rhetor* in turn is aware of the resources needed to give material shape to these interests in the world; she/he understands the audience and its characteristics; and understands what the matter to be communicated demands. This is the basis for *designs* to shape these representations ready for their *production* and dissemination. A rhetorical approach draws on the resources both of *competence* and of *critique* and utilizes them in the process of *design*. Given the presence of modal choice in representation in a multimodal world of communication and a social world where choice is demanded and the instability of the environment of communication, a rhetorical approach is essential. *Design* meets the interests of the *rhetor* (most usually the same person) in full awareness of the communicational potentials of the resources which are available in the environment and needed for the implementation of the rhetor's interests. *Design* gives shape to the *interests* of both *rhetor* and *designer* in their world.

Production is the implementation of *design* with the resources available in the world in which the communication takes place. In *production,* meaning is made material and becomes subject to review, comment, engagement and transformation. *Production* happens both in making of messages and in their 'remaking' in a participant's engagement with and transformation of a message. *Production* has *semiotic* (form-as-content), *conceptual* (content-as-concepts) and *affective* (semiosis-as-expressive, always reflecting interest and personal 'investment') features; all three always at the same time.

A rhetorical approach is based on the agency of maker and remaker of messages. It has direct implications for *knowledge production*. *Knowledge* is made and given shape in *representation*, according to the potentials of *modal affordances*; the process of representation is identical to the shaping of knowledge. Makers of representations are shapers of knowledge.

In this conception, *knowledge production* is entirely part of social-semiotic processes and organization of *participation*. That is, knowledge is always *produced*, rather than *acquired*. *Acquisition* is a relatively non-agentive conception of the relation of individual, learning and knowledge. The new, participative *sites of appearance* and *sites of dissemination* of messages and knowledge – *YouTube, FaceBook,* but also non-legitimated sites such as those created by graffito artists – are an integral part of the new media landscape. *Sites* are associated with specific characteristics of distributions of power and agency in communication. *Sites of appearance* and *sites of dissemination* are a part of the process of knowledge production; they come with principles of evaluation as part of the logonomic rules of 'engagement'/'reading'/ evaluation in communication (Hodge and Kress, 1988). Theories of communication have to describe this world and attempt to articulate and theorize its practices both in terms of continuities and changes.

Given the changing environments for meaning and knowledge-making – multimodal representation, participative production and 'sites of appearance' – knowledge-making takes new routes in content, form and social engagement. These routes shape *what is engaged with, processes of engagement* and as a result social/individual *dispositions*. There is a need for careful considerations of *designs for meaning* and *knowledge-making*: the shaping of routes and environments of meaning-making and production of knowledge and, in this, the shaping of 'inner' semiotic resources. The *sites*, the *processes*, the *designs* all shape 'concepts' and, in that, they shape what dispositions become habituated as *subjectivities* and as *identity*.

From language and grammar to semiotic resources

In the monomodally conceived world, in other words, in a world regarded as operating with one kind of resource in a specific domain, reflection on the potentials of that resource could not arise. 'Language' was all that there was; and 'language' was regarded as a means fully capable of dealing with all human (rational) meaning. In a multimodally conceived communicational world, two questions arise: one is about the 'aptness' of the means for representation; the other is about the complexes of modes designed for achieving complex representational and communicational requirements and tasks. Instances of commonly used *modes* are *speech*; *still image*; *moving image*; *writing*; *gesture*; *music*; *3D models*; *action*; *colour*. Each offers specific potentials and is therefore in principle particularly suited for specific representational/ communicational tasks.

However, in communication several *modes* are always used together, in *modal ensembles*, designed so that each mode has a specific task and function. Such ensembles are based on *designs*, that is, on selections and arrangements of resources for making a specific *message* about a particular issue for a particular audience. *Design* is the process whereby the meanings of a designer (a teacher, a public speaker, but also, much more humbly and in a sense more significantly, participants in everyday interactions) become *messages*. *Designs* are based on (rhetorical) analyses, on aims and purposes of a rhetor, and they are then implemented through the instantiations of choices of many kinds.

Design rests on the possibility of choice – '*this* could have been chosen rather than *that*'. That permits the description of *style* as the effect of a series of choices made in the design of a message. Choice is always circumscribed by power in different ways, financial, social, cultural power, and so *style* is *the politics of choice*. *Styles* are subject to *social evaluations* and these lead to a social ranking expressed as *aesthetic* judgements. Hence socially, *aesthetics* can be seen as *the politics of style*. Questions *around ethics*, such as: 'Who benefits?' or 'Who suffers damage or hurt?', 'How are social environments likely to be changed by this?' lead to judgements of *social benefit*. In this approach, *ethics* is the *politics of value* and *(e)valuation*.

It is not fanciful to see a progression from social fragmentation and the dislodging of individuals from social bonds as forming part of a sequence of actions (where → means 'leads to'): social fragmentation and the dislodging of an individual from social bonds, forms, structures → individualism → individuation → social isolation. The social consequences and costs of that dynamic are visible now in many ways and in many places. In a period when social pathologies are increasing – aided by the dominance of the market and its values – this is a major consideration.

Mobility and portability

Currently, *mobility* is a hot topic. In my view, *mobility* is in part both an expression and an effect of larger-scale social moves towards *instability* and *provisionality*. *Mobility* tends to be discussed in terms of the affordances of currently available technologies: physically portable and hence physically *mobile* as hand-held devices of various kinds; and lending *communicational mobility* through the fast increasing range of features of the (former) mobile phone. This is the subject of discussion in Chapter 10.

The interest in *mobility* is a response to aspects of current conditions. In certain domains – institutional education, for instance – *mobility* is seen as a panacea to a range of problems. Two stand out: *effectiveness* and *motivation*. *Effectiveness* in the use of 'human resources' (i.e. teachers) promises to solve a range of financial/material problems of the school (conceived in traditional terms); as *motivation* it seems to offer a path away from the alienation from school felt by many – predominantly male – students. Portable technology offers the hope of dealing with the seemingly problematic physicality of the school, its confining time structures and its general lack of attractiveness to many students and to provide instead the physical, social and emotional mobility as freedom of the individual. Both come together in promising to match the attractions of the market through unbounded access and individual choice – as expressed in concepts such as 'the personalized curriculum'.

What is suggested for the school can serve as a metaphor for wider social domains. It is essential to subject this metaphor and the claims of *mobility* to searching scrutiny. There are profound questions about what social effects 'mobility' might have: Who or what is *mobile*?, What is *portable*? And in any case, in what ways are *portability* and *mobility* a social, cultural, pedagogic, affective, cognitive and generally human 'good'? What conditions for sociality does *mobility* propose and what kinds of sociality would these be? Is it the case that society either can or ought to 'develop', *change*, at the same pace as technological devices or in the directions indicated in the facilities of the 'new' technologies? A world of constant accessibility and availability is also a world of constant surveillance; and in that world, what opportunity is there for down time, for being 'idle', for reflection? What vision for society is entailed? The personalized curriculum is at the same time the loss of one major force for social cohesion, that of knowledge, information, values shared by all members of a group. Are total *connectivity* and *accessibility* a social good or are they markers on the road to individual and social pathologies? Are they a further instance of social fragmentation and disintegration or are they covert means for dealing with the absence of reliable social bonds?

The combined effects of these factors of communication suggest the need for *'navigational aids'* as an absolute requirement: in relation to text-making, to reading, to discernment and discrimination, to reflection on metaphors and their effects. That is, they suggest the need for communication to be founded on principles which enable affective, aesthetic and ethical judgement and evaluation as an essential response to contemporary trends towards total connectivity in the environment of market-controlled principles of 'choice'.

A word on 'pace'

Biological, individual, social, economic, political and technological developments each have their own, distinct 'pace'. The current fashion is for valuing 'speed', the assumption being that slowness is not just boring, but wasteful because inefficient. The first question in communication as in other social practices might have to be

'What is a *humane* pace' or even 'What is a *human* pace, under present social conditions?', 'Under what conditions is *slowness* of pace essential?'. The pace of technological change cannot possibly be mirrored by social institutions, even though that seems intended in calls to accommodate to every innovation as a means of furthering efficiencies: the ceaseless restructurings of organizations are one such symptom, as is the requirement of individuals constantly to adapt.

The more urgent question is to reflect what the relation between technological, institutional, social and human *pace* should be. Society cannot hope to mimic the pace inherent in every technological innovation, nor should it attempt to do so. In a healthy sociality, social, human aims and purposes must take precedence.

The need for apt metaphors

Metaphors provide (usually unnoticed) guides and framings for thinking. It is essential therefore to reflect on and make metaphors which fit the purposes and the visions inherent in the theory being constructed and used. This is at the core of my argument around 'naming', which I develop at various points in the book.

All signs are metaphors. All signs are always newly made. So metaphors-as-signs are always newly *made*, in specific environments, for specific audiences and purposes, arising from the rhetor's interest, the designer's use of available semiotic resources in an awareness of the requirements of the social environment. Signs are means of making knowledge material. Signs-as-knowledge are tools in dealing with problems in the sign-maker's life-world. As all signs are made for specific audiences and purposes, so metaphors too are made for specific audiences and purposes. That makes it essential to be aware of what and who the audiences are and what the purposes are. The fact that signs-as-metaphors and metaphors-as-knowledge are tools makes it essential to exercise the highest care in the fashioning of tools.

A sign/metaphor made for a 'lay' audience with the purpose of quick, rough-and-ready communicability cannot possibly serve for the needs of a professional audience in solving a problem or accomplishing a task; nor for the purposes of carefully establishing understanding. As one example, take the metaphor of '*multimedia*'. It seems to serve well for quick communication. But what is or are *multimedia*? What does the signifier *multimedia* refer to? What does it name? What does the metaphor project? As far as I can see the metaphor of *multimedia* has much the same relation to the present communicational landscape as the metaphor of *horseless carriage* has to the age of the car. It is a naming of new givens in terms of old frames, thoroughly lodged in a previous environment where the media of print, of sound, of photography, and so on were all discrete. Each of these dealt with specific modes: *radio* with sound as *music* and *speech* and *soundtrack*; *print* with *writing* and *image*. *Film* was, in that context, already a border category as it brought together a large variety of modes with their then still distinct traditions of production.

So, to use the term *multimedia* is to confuse past practices with present givens; to confuse the cultural technologies of *dissemination* – radio, newspaper, TV, etc. – with the cultural technologies of *representation*: writing, speech, image, etc. It is a term which effectively blocks the path to clear analysis and thinking. In the present state of social and communicational upheaval there are many such terms. I will attempt to draw attention to these and where possible suggest new namings.

3 Communication: shaping the domain of meaning

Communication as semiotic work: a sketch of a theory

Communication is semiotic work. Work changes things: the tools, the worker and that which is worked on. Semiotic work is no exception: it is work in the domain of the social; changes produced by social-semiotic work are meaningful. Meaning is made in communication, whatever its form.

Assume that we take the situation in Colour plate 1 as a normal condition of communication. Colour plate 1 shows an operating theatre; an operation is in its early stage. A 'scrub nurse' is in the foreground. Behind her, to the right, is the 'lead surgeon'; opposite him is a 'trainee-surgeon' – a qualified medical doctor training to become a surgeon. Behind them, separated by a screen, is the anaesthetist; far back on the right stands an Operating Theatre Technician. Representatives of four distinct professions are present; each with specific traditions and practices, ways of talking and doing things. Their tasks are closely interrelated and integrated. The occasion is first and foremost a *clinical* situation; an instance of (communication in) professional practice: a patient is here to be made better. It is also a *pedagogic* situation, an environment of (teaching and) learning: a trainee surgeon is here to become a fully trained surgeon.

Communication is multimodal: by speech at times, as spoken comment, as instruction or request; by gaze; by actions – passing an instrument, reaching out for an instrument; by touch. At all times communication is a response to a 'prompt': a *gaze* might produce a *spoken comment*; that leads to an *action*; *looking* at the screen by both surgeons produces a guiding *touch* by one of the other's hand; an outstretched hand is met by an instrument being passed. Communication has happened when a participant's *attention* has focused on some aspect of the communication; she or he has taken that to be a *message* and has *framed* aspects of that message as a *prompt* for her or himself. That *prompt* has been *interpreted*, becoming a new inward sign, and it in turn leading, potentially, to further communicational action. The semiotic sequence of *attention* → *framing* → *interpretation* is ceaseless; it involves all the participants here, at all times, though differently in each case.

The larger social event here can be *framed* in at least two ways – from a *clinical* and from a *pedagogic* perspective. If we *frame* the event *pedagogically*, as one of teaching and learning, the senior surgeon and the trainee move into focus. Questions then are: 'How does teaching happen?' or, with a slight shift in point of view, though within the same frame: 'How does learning take place?'. From the learner's perspective, any event may at any one moment need to be attended to: the senior surgeon might give a spoken instruction; the scrub nurse might make a slight movement – or an explicit gesture – which he ought to attend to; the anaesthetist might glance at him to draw his attention to something. At any one time, any aspect of the complex dynamic communicational ensemble might be significant for the learner/trainee, so that he has to be constantly and entirely attentive to potentially significant cues as potential *prompts*. It is his *interest* as trainee surgeon that turns any one of these – or none – into a *prompt* for him. It is his decision. Once turned into a *prompt*, his *interest* *frames* the *prompt* in a specific way and he selects features from that now specifically framed complex message as the basis for his response. Yet at the same time the trainee surgeon is there also as an assistant surgeon and needs to be at least equally attentive to *prompts* of a clinical rather than a pedagogical kind. Frequently the 'same' actions are different signs in the other frame. This kind of *multiple framing* and *multiple attention* is likely to be the norm rather than the exception in most instances of communication.

What applies to this one participant in this situation applies to the other participants; differently, depending on their position, role, perspective in the complex ensemble – and depending on their own assessment of their position. Crucially, communication in the operating theatre is multimodal: a *gaze,* a *touch,* a *spoken* comment, a *gesture,* a change in *position*, all might act as a *prompt*.

The conception of communication shown in Colour plate 1 is a very different one. For one thing, here *mode* is not an issue. It may be that *language as speech* is assumed to be the *mode* of communication; or, more likely, the focus is on a *message* as 'content' quite abstractly and generally, rather than on the material and semiotic form of the *message*.

In the Saussurean schema, two interlocutors are linked in a dyadic structure. One initiates a message; the diagram and the theory both suggest that it originates from within one interlocutor's 'head'; there it is shaped into speech, seemingly; it is uttered;

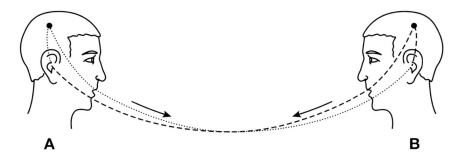

A   **B**

Figure 3.1 Saussure's diagram of communication

the other participant receives this (spoken) message; and in that interlocutor's 'head' it becomes the basis of a response.

Versions of this model had been active in twentieth-century conceptions of communication; they still haunt conceptions of communication – even if in the semi-negation of many adaptations and alterations of that model. However, the dominant conception of communication in the latter part of the century was based on the *Sender* → *Message* → *Receiver* schema of Shannon and Weaver (1948), a model derived from electrical engineering. Here the origin and active cause of communication lies with the sender, who 'encodes' a message in a *code* shared by sender and receiver, sent along a channel, to be 'decoded' by the receiver. This version received its most telling critique in Roland Barthes' (1968) article 'The death of the author', which insisted on the dominant role of the reader in communication.

In the model of communication sketched here, three concerns are in focus. One is social interaction and interchange around meaning, oriented to the processes of *making* and *remaking* meaning through the making of signs – simple or complex – in *representation*. Sign-makers and their agency as social actors are in the foreground and with them the social environments in which they make signs. The second concern is with *resources for making meaning* – on *modes* and their *affordances*. The third deals with conditions and means for *disseminating* meaning – the *media* and their facilities. A theory of communication needs to deal with the semiotic work done in relation to all three and with the meanings which result. Questions of the kind 'Who does what kind of semiotic work for whom?' are entailed by this model.

In communication, members of a community participate in the renewing, the remaking and the transformation of their social environment from the perspective of *meaning*. In that process 'the social' – as entities and forms, as processes and practices – is constantly articulated in (material) semiotic form: the social is re-*calibrated*, re-*registered* with semiotic/cultural resources. The process of (usually minute) 'recalibration' ensures that gaps between social structures and processes on the one hand and semiotic accounts of them on the other do not open too readily or too far; and that the semiotic resources remain capable of representing social phenomena. This ceaseless recalibration produces a sense of stability: the absence of noticeable gaps gives a sense to members of the community that things are as they have always been.

At the same time, social interaction via semiotic means produces more than 'documentations', 'records', more than 'ratifications', so to speak, of social change: it produces new meanings. Even the most ordinary social encounter is never entirely predictable; it is always new in some way, however slight, so that the 'accommodations' produced in any encounter are always new in some way. They project social possibilities and potentials which differ, even if slightly, from what there had been before the encounter. As a consequence, the semiotic work of interaction is always socially productive, projecting and proposing possibilities of social and semiotic forms, entities and processes which reorient, refocus, and 'go beyond', by extending and transforming what there was before the interaction.

Communication can only be understood if we see it as an always complex interaction embedded in contradictory, contested, fragmentary social environments: whether between groups or between individuals, coming together from social 'locations' which are always distinct in some respects. In the interaction, the social divergences/differences between those who interact provide the generative dynamic of communication. In the process, differences are reshaped/transformed in temporary social and semiotic accommodations. These in turn are the semiotically and socially productive force of communication: they project what is socially problematic into a public 'space' and produce temporary recordings of the social and the semiotic state of affairs; in transforming it, they shape it differently.

In other words, the hurly-burly of social life is the generative force which constantly (re-)shapes a society's semiotic resources and in doing so documents and ratifies new social givens. Communication and the resources made in that process, have the characteristics that they have because both bear the imprint of their social environments. The central point for the theory is: the social is the motor for communicational/semiotic change; for the constant remaking of cultural/semiotic resources; and for the production of the new.

To insist that 'the social has priority' is to say, above all, that the forms, the processes and the contents of communication are social in origin, they are socially shaped; that communication is embedded in social environments, arrangements and practices; that communication is itself a form of social action, of social *work*; and that communication is always a *response* by one participant to a *prompt* by other participants in social events. Some element of 'the social' *prompts* me into shaping a sign(-complex) as a message – which is my response to a prior *prompt*. Individuals act in communication, prompted by and in a social environment, with social-cultural resources.

Participants are embedded in networks of social relations with others who make meanings by making signs. *Signs* and *sign-complexes* – *messages* – have 'shape', structure and content, representing the interest of the sign-makers. Some of the signs/messages are taken up by participants in an interaction as *prompts*. As I have suggested, the two central assumptions are that *communication is the response to a prompt*; and that *communication happens only when there is 'interpretation'* (see Kress and van Leeuwen, 2001). Communication depends on the *transformative/interpretative engagement* by a participant in an interaction with a message made by another – in ways guided by their interest. *Interpretation* is the defining criterion of communication: *only if there has been interpretation, has there been communication.*

One consequence for this theory of communication and its practice is that even though an utterance has been produced as a *message* with the intention to be a *prompt*, it becomes a *prompt* only when it is taken as such by another participant. A message, intended as a *prompt*, engages the *attention* of a participant in the interaction. *Attention* derives in the first instance from the participant's *interest* – where *interest* names the momentary 'focusing' of a social history, a sense of who I am in this social situation *now*, as well as a clear sense of the social environment in which the *prompt* occurred. 'Refusal to engage' – a denial of communication – is a *social act*, the negation both of a social relation and of communication. It too is communication.

Interpretation is central in communication and so, therefore, is the *interpreter*. An *interpretation* is a response to a prior *prompt*. The characteristics, the 'shape' of that *prompt*, constitute the 'ground' on which the *interpretation* happens. An *interpretation* is therefore always a mix of features of the 'ground', as the *prompt* framed by the interpreter, with the resources brought by the interpreter. An *interpretation* is the result of a series of *transformations* in which aspects of the *prompt* and aspects of the resources brought by the *interpreter* are shaped, jointly, into a new semiotic entity.

The theory needs to be able to serve as the basis for description and analysis of all instances of communication. In suggesting that the environment of the operating theatre could be seen as 'normal', I am aware that reading the pages of a book or engaging with a website are different kinds of activities, in some sense. However, one theory should, nevertheless, be able to deal with all instances of communication.

It might be useful to say – simplifying massively – that theories of communication have veered, broadly, between dyadic, interactive models, such as Saussure's, either more sociologically or more psychologically oriented; and dyadic, unidirectional models such as the model of Shannon and Weaver (1948). Both imply social relations: unidirectional models tend be more authoritatively oriented and interactive models less so. The power relations implicitly coded in 'authoritative models' require the 'receiver' to recover – to decode – the meaning encoded by the authoritative sender; the interactive models leave the possibility of a 'negotiation' of meaning more open.

Both the models mentioned earlier were conceived of as monomodal – one depending on the mode of speech, the other on a mode(/code) based on the material affordances of electricity, modulated into 'code' by relevant technologies. Or, it might be better to say that the issue of *mode* did not arise: it wasn't 'present'. That has remained so right into the present. As mentioned, both models have been challenged in different ways – for instance by the (journalistically based) model of 'uses and gratification' (Blumler and Katz, 1974; Palmgreen *et al.*, 1985; Dervin *et al.*, 1986) in which *users* and their needs are in focus; and fundamentally by the explicitly semiotic theory of Roland Barthes in his 'The death of the author'. From that perspective, my sketch here is an attempt to give a social-semiotic articulation to the critique offered by Barthes in 1968.

To restate: in the sketch put forward here, three assumptions are fundamental: *communication happens as a response to a prompt; communication has happened when there has been an interpretation; communication is always multimodal.* Because *interpretation* is central, so therefore is the *interpreter; without interpretation there is no communication;* yet it is the *characteristics*, the shape, of the *prompt*, which constitute the ground on which the *interpretation* happens.

Seen like that, *communication* is a process with two stages. Stage one is dominated by the interest of the initial maker of the *sign-complex*, the *rhetor*, with his or her intent of disseminating the *sign-complex* as a *message* and for the *message* to be taken as a *prompt*. In stage two, the *interest* and *attention* of an *interpreter* is in focus: it leads to *selection* of what is criterial for the *interpreter* in the initial message and to the *framing of* the selected aspects of the initial *message* as a *prompt*; which is, subsequently, *interpreted*. The meaning made in that *interpretation* can become the basis of a new *sign-complex* in the making of a new *message*. From the perspective of the initial maker there is a sequence of (a prior *prompt* and its *interpretation* →) new sign-complex (based on the maker's *interest* and a sense of the audience's characteristics) → a message intended as *prompt* → the interlocutor's attention to and engagement with the message → and (possible) response. From the interpreter's perspective, it is a sequence of *message* → 'recipient's' *interest* → *attention* → *engagement* → *selection* → *framing* → *transformation* → *new* ('*inner*') *sign*. The 'inner sign' may form the basis of a new sign-complex. Both stages are instances of *semiotic work*; both result in the making of new signs.

   This does not make the semiotic work of the *rhetor* and the audience's/*interpreter's* subsequent engagement equal. They are not the same kind of work, with the same status and characteristics; nor with the same results. After all, 'setting out the ground' is very different in all kinds of ways to 'making selections' from that *ground* and interpreting aspects of it. The *rhetor* and the *interpreter* both perform *semiotic work*; but it is different work with different effects. 'Setting out the ground', whether in content, in mode, in structures, in genres, is different to making *selections, framing, transforming/transducting* and shaping these into an inner *sign-complex*.

'*Reading*' and the reader's design of meaning

This model of communication rebalances *power* and *attention*, with equal emphasis on the *interpreter* of a *message-prompt* and the *initial maker of the message,* the *rhetor*. That is the case in all forms of communication, whether in the operating theatre; in the 'reading' of a quite traditional text; in the engagement with a website; in visiting an exhibition; or in other environments. To show this, I will discuss two further examples: one, Colour plate 2, is a website – the homepage of Children's BBC; the other, Figures 3.2a and 3.2b, comes from a 'visitor study' in a museum (Selander, 2008; Insulander, 2008; Diamontopoulou and Kress, forthcoming).

   Reading is communication. In many approaches – especially in pedagogic environments – 'reading' has been thought of quite analogously to the Saussurean model, Figure 3.1, and maybe even more so to the S → M → R schema. 'Older' pages of writing embodied notions of authority and authorship quite compatible with those models: the *author* assembled and organized *knowledge* on behalf of readers and displayed that as a (well-ordered) *text* on pages of print. *Readers* engaged with that *text*-as-*knowledge* in the order set out by the *author*: an order of lines; of words on lines; of arrangements of words as syntactic elements; of genres; of texts-as-genres; of pages; of chapters. That had been the embodiment of a unidirectional, hierarchical, dyadic relationship in which power rested with the author.

Contemporary pages, whether of information books such as those produced, for instance, by Dorling & Kindersley or of websites such as the Children's BBC homepage, Colour plate 2, are designed on the basis of a quite different social relation of author, reader and meaning-making. Above all, the text/page is shaped *generically* with the assumption that engagement takes place on terms of the (child) reader's interest: an assumption based on a very different social relation to that of the 'traditional' text and its genres.

Unlike the traditional page, designed with a given order/*arrangement* for the reader's *engagement*, this *site* – a 'home*page*', which has 'visitors' rather than *readers* – is given an *ordering* by the readers' interests through their *(ordering-as-)design*. The readers' interests determine how they engage with this page. In doing so they *design* not so much a coherence for this site/'page' as an ordering which represents their interest. The sequence in which the elements are 'read' and ordered by them accords to choices which reflect their *interests*. In effect, the readers' *interests*, reflected in the manner of their engagement, provides for them the *design* for this page: readers redesign the page (see Kress, 2003). This notion of 'reading' accords with the theory of communication outlined: material is presented; and readers/viewers shape their ordering of that material. Formerly, an author, as the initial maker of the text/ message, had provided that ordering; now that is work shaped by the reader's interest.

Clearly, this (home)page is designed. In its design it embodies and assumes the necessity of the reader's semiotic work. To an older reader the page may well give an impression of incoherence; for its intended reader it provides what this reader expects: to do (at least some of) their own semiotic work of design. With this *site* the question of *modes* is unavoidable. At a first look it is not at all evident that *writing* and lexically conveyed content do provide the main path of engagement for the reader/visitor; or whether image does; or colour; nor whether *placement* of the main semiotic elements – for instance, in terms of a left–right and top–bottom order of the traditional page determines an order of engagement/reading for the reader/visitor. In the page, as it is encountered on the internet, the cartoon characters along the band at the top of the page move. *Movement* as mode provides a further point of choice; again there may be generational factors at work in shaping preferences for engagement. It is also important to observe that a formerly profound divide between the 'programme listing' and the programme itself has become blurred. Whereas differences of genre had usually been done within one mode, by a specific selection and ordering of semiotic entities – syntactic, lexical and textual – here the generic differentiation is done by means of modes: the mode of *moving image* makes the programme listing itself into performance. In some ways this is akin to a crossing of the boundaries of social-semiotic 'domains': 'work' versus 'pleasure', for instance. But the generic difference marked modally is more profound.

In considering the homepage, the question of 'reading' and generation becomes a central one. If it is the case that members of a 'younger' generation (quite likely by now to be separated by two generations from generations more 'traditionally' oriented) read according to *a design of the reader's interest* – even though on the 'ground' of someone else's *message* – it is highly unlikely that they will not carry this *habitus* into their engagement with any semiotic domain or entity in their world. These divergent practices and expectations about reading by readers of one generation (teachers) – and another (students) is, I assume, one of the major problems about 'reading' in schools. It might be objected that reading for pleasure is one thing and that reading/engagement which takes place in institutional sites – of work, of profession, of school – is another. For one thing, the issue of power is overtly and insistently present in institutional sites. Some readers will respond in alignment with power and others not; with generation playing a major role. Once developed, a *habitus* of reading is likely to be applied in all instances of communication, though the contingent factors of particular environments and the specific characteristics of readers will, as always, play their role.

My last example here – Figures 3.2a and 3.2b – comes from a research-project on visitor studies in museums (funded by the Swedish National Science Foundation). It was conducted in Stockholm and in London (at the Museum of National Antiquities in Stockholm; and at the Museum of London, in London). In Stockholm the object of the research was an exhibition on Swedish prehistory; in London two exhibitions were included – 'London before London' and 'Roman London'. The research project aimed to give insight into *how* visitors make meanings for themselves of these exhibitions; and, to a lesser extent, *what* sense they did make. Unlike schools, museums tend not to exercise power over their visitors in their engagement with an exhibition; even though they might wish to be able to so. That makes conditions of learning different in important ways.

In both Stockholm and London, visitors were invited to participate as 'couples': as grandparent and grandchild; as friends; as married couples; and so on. Those who accepted the invitation were given a camera to take photos of objects or displays which took their interest. They were videoed as they made their way through the exhibition. At the conclusion of their visit they were asked to 'draw a map' representing their sense of the exhibition; they were also interviewed briefly. Each of these four 'takes' was seen as a means of obtaining material that could serve as data to gain insight into forms of engagement and serve as evidence of 'learning'. Two maps, from the London data, each drawn by a member of each pair, Figure 3.2a and Figure 3.2b, are shown below.

An exhibition is *designed*; its designer(s) have specific aims: to *show* objects, images, reconstructions; to *tell* stories of the prehistory of a nation, and, in that, to achieve social, cultural and maybe political purposes. While these aims tend not to be overtly stated, in interviews with curators or the curatorial teams it was clear that these exhibitions were the result of much discussion, framed by policies of the museum.

Communicationally and *semiotically* speaking, an exhibition is a complex sign, designed to function as a message. It is meant as a *prompt* for the visitors' engage-ment. *Pedagogically* speaking, an exhibition presents a curriculum for the visitor/learner. In that context, the maps shown here are indications of the visitor's *interest*

Figure 3.2a
Map of a museum
exhibition 'London
before London':
'the prehistoric
camp'

Figure 3.2b
Map of a museum
exhibition 'London
before London':
'Heathrow'

which shaped their *attention*; which in turn *framed* particular aspects of the overall (design-)message. *Semiotically* and *communicationally* speaking, the maps are a *response* to this *prompt*. *Pedagogically* speaking, the maps are *signs of learning*.

The 'maps' are of interest from any perspective. They do not, of course, provide a full account either of what the exhibition offers, nor of all of the meaning made by either of the map-makers – one an 18-year-old woman, one an 11-year-old boy – in their visit. The photographs they took offered other material for data, as did the tracking video and the final interviews. Nevertheless the maps provide one lens on their engagement and transformation/transduction of aspects of the exhibition in each case. They show a clear difference in *interest*; a consequent difference in *attention* and *framing*; and distinctly different *interpretations* of the same large overall message. The one exhibition was turned into distinctly different *prompts* by the *interests* of each of the two map-makers.

Most immediately they show a starkly different sense of what a 'map' is, what it might mean, what it does or can be, based on different resources brought; in this case conceptions of what might count as a *map,* and of *what is to be mapped*. In neither case is the notion of *the map* a conventional spatial one; the exhibition had been arranged as a large 'room' with relatively indistinct sections. Some questions posed, by these map-makers, seemingly were: 'What was the central topic to engage my attention?', 'What objects did I find most interesting?'. The maps are a record of features of the exhibition, not of the layout of the exhibition; a record of the objects and tableaux that seemed most salient and interesting. In the case of Figure 3.2b, the notion of *map* is 'conceptual'/affective: one question posed, seemingly, was: ' What, for me, was (the most) significant object/entity of this exhibition, along with some others and how shall I arrange them spatially to give a sense of their relative significance?'. For the first map-maker, that which incited her attention was portrayed along with some of the entities which prompted that; for the second map-maker, the *map* was set out as a visual display, a spatially ordered arrangement, in which the most significant object has the most salient position.

From the same display/message the two visitors had each fashioned their own *prompt*, design and a distinct interpretation. A number of questions jostle for attention here. 'Whose interest has been dominant: the curator's or the visitor's?', 'Has the curator succeeded more in one case and less so in the other?', 'What interest and what resources of the visitors are evident in these maps?', 'Has one of the two visitor couples failed in their 'reading'/engagement, or have both?'. These are questions crucial and urgent for a curator; they provide one motivation for engaging in 'visitor studies'. 'Failure' or 'success' are probably not concepts the curator uses in relation to the visitors; though 'effective communication' might be. They are central and general questions within this theory of communication, irrespective of the site: whether in a museum; a school; a site for public information; a site of professional practice such as surgery; or in an ordinary conversation.

What conclusions can be drawn from these examples for this theory of communication? Taking the two maps as an instance, one response would be to say that *responses* – meanings made from the exhibition – are unpredictable, 'individualistic', 'subjective', anarchic even. Or we might say that the most significant criterion is the visitor's *interest*. Both are unsatisfactory accounts: the first amounts to an admission that there is no theory that can account for differences in engagement and reading. The second ignores the role of the maker of the initial sign-complex/message in shaping the message/prompt. That, after all, has 'set the ground' from which the seemingly 'anarchic' or 'subjective' responses are produced, a fact which is demonstrable: both maps make reference to elements of the exhibition, such as the model airplane at a neolithic camp. While the response to this complex message/prompt may not be predictable, it is not anarchic. If we stay with the perspective of the interpreter/recipient, there seems to be a sequence where the recipient's existing

> *interest* shapes
> *attention*, which produces
> *engagement* leading to
> *selection* of elements from the message, leading to a
> *framing* of these elements, which leads to their
> *transformation* and *transduction*, which produces a
> *new* ('*inner*') *sign*.

The interpreter's *interest* produces *attention*; *attention* shapes the form of the *engagement*; this leads to *selections* being made; the selections are *framed*; there is the subsequent *transformation* and *transductions* of the elements in the frame; and, in that, the ('*inwardly made*') *sign* is produced. The sequence reshapes (aspects) of the initial message, the 'ground', into a *prompt*. *Interest* is the motive force: it is the basis for *attention* to the 'ground' constituted by the exhibition, for *engagement* with that 'ground'; it shapes *selection*, *transformation* and *transduction*; and *interest* becomes evident in the new sign, the map. The maps are *subjective* in the sense of being based on the maker's *interest*; yet in exhibiting the principles of the makers' interest in a clear relation to the ground/prompt, the maps are *principled*. They are not anarchic.

This theory diminishes neither the significance of the semiotic work of the maker of the initial message, the *rhetor*, nor that of the *interpreter*: the work of *design* that fashions the 'ground' on which *interpretation* takes place is one essential element in the two-part structure of the process of communication. For the analyst as much as in everyday communication, some aspects of the *design* of the initial message must be understood in order to engage in and make sense the subsequent semiotic work of *interpretation*. The semiotic work of *transformation* and *transduction* which underlies *interpretation* is the site of the production of 'the new'. It is work which leads to semiotic entities which are always new, innovative, creative; not because of the genius of the participants in the interaction but because of the very characteristic forms of these interactions, in which one conception of the world – the 'ground' expressing the *interest* of one participant – is met by the different *interest* of the interlocutor. In the working out of that difference, with power and affect playing their part, a necessarily new conception is arrived at. Earlier, I called that 'an accommodation' to indicate both its provisionality and its emergence out of different interests, power and affect.

Practically, the curator has to ask what consequences follow from this conception of communication for her or him or for the museum in strategies of design. There are specific questions: 'What path had the curator constructed for the visitors?', 'Why and how was that path followed or not followed?'. The curator might well want to understand the principles underlying the differences in the path taken: in attention as in interpretation. The concept of *interest* provides the overarching reason. As it happened, one of the map-makers was an 18-year-old student from Germany on a self-organized 'study-trip'; her interest is expressed in the detail of attention to the objects in her map; the other map-maker was an 11-year-old boy, a highly reluctant visitor. But in different ways – each time precisely and specifically – that is the case with each one of the maps.

Provisionality in communication: rhetoric and design, newly configured

An exhibition, like any semiotic entity – a website, the operating theatre, a book, a child's drawing – is the result of *design*. *Design* is shaped by the prior analysis provided by the *rhetor* through questions such as: 'What is the environment of communication?', 'What relations of power are at issue?', 'Who are the participants in communication?', 'What are their criterial characteristics?', 'What is the phenomenon to be communicated?', 'What resources are available to make the message?'. All raise the issue of *choice*: *choices* reflecting *interest* – as policies of the museum as an institution, for instance – and of the mediation of institutional policy through the interests of the curators; as well as *choices* assumed – by the designers/curators – to reflect the *interests* of the audience. *Rhetoric* – as the politics of communication – encompasses all aspects from the initial conception of the exhibition in the environment of the museum's policies, to the overall design/'shaping' of the exhibition: in the salience given to particular themes and areas; to the selection of objects; to the modes chosen for representing specific contents; in layout; in lighting.

In all these, the *rhetor* and *designer* factor in – in different ways, with different conceptions of purpose, power and affect – the likely responses of an imagined audience. 'Are three-dimensional objects more salient, more "attractive", more noticeable than written captions or than longer written accounts/explanations?', 'Are painted scenes more engaging than three dimensional tableaux?', 'What effect does lighting have in creating *mood* and *affect*?', 'Is the distance at which visitors are able to engage with objects – for instance, whether they are permitted to touch an object, whether they are separated by a glass panel or a rail – a significant matter?'. The question of *affect* has to be addressed in all aspects of the exhibition: affect modulates the engagement of visitors.

In the map of Figure 3.2a, the two-dimensional *diorama* is represented in the mode of (two-dimensional) *image*; though elements are drawn in to the 'map' from other parts of the exhibition. The change, among other things, is from the genre of diorama to that of 'map'. The big skull at the top left of the map is located at the very beginning of the exhibition. *Selection* by the map-maker has changed a large room with many objects into an image where few objects are drawn into an entirely new coherent display. The maps, in other words, are representations shaped by *principles* of *selection*; by *transformation* – changes in ordering and configurations of elements within one mode; and by *transduction* – the change from meaning expressed in one mode to meaning expressed in another mode.

Curators might see themselves first and foremost as communicators and their response to these maps might be shaped by a wish for better, more 'effective' communication. Just like the operating theatre, the museum is more and more becoming a site which is doubly framed, as a site of *education* and as a site of *entertainment*. Governments see museums as environments for *social education*. In both framings – as a site of entertainment or of learning – curators are bound to be interested in characteristics of their audience which have an effect on both.

In the present unstable social and communicational environment, the category of *rhetoric* best serves as a basis for establishing the characteristics of communication as interaction. From a rhetorical perspective, each occasion of communication now has to be treated – potentially at least – as unknown. Each time, the *rhetor* assesses the conditions of communication: 'What are my purposes?', 'What do I wish to communicate?', 'What are the characteristics of my audience?', 'What are the best resources to do this, given the characteristics of my audience?', 'What relations of power obtain between myself and my audience?', 'What resources for communication are available?', 'How are these resources best arranged to represent what is to be communicated?' and the larger framing question: 'Am I attempting to educate, to entertain, or both?'. These are essential questions for the rhetor, in any environment, at all times. In the past, *convention* had provided 'routines' which obviated questions; now they are starkly present and need to be addressed, newly each time.

Rhetoric needs now to be seen in the two-phase structure of communication, without which it cannot deal with contemporary social givens. Communication is joint and reciprocal *work*. The sign-complex which is sketched by the *rhetor* on the basis of a preceding analysis is elaborated in detail by the *designer* and is then given material form by a *producer*. The sign-complex is presented to the audience as a (complex) *message*. Ideally, members of the audience shape the *message* as a *prompt* and each transforms that *prompt* into the new inner sign in the light of *interest* and the semiotic (and wider social, cultural, aesthetic and ethical) resources which each brings to an interaction. The *rhetor* has achieved nothing if members of the audience do not attend to and engage with and interpret the *message* meant as a *prompt* for them. Communication rests on both phases: the initial work of the rhetor and the subsequent engagement and interpretative work of the audience, seen as interpreters. To call a part of the process *engagement* is to use a relatively 'neutral' naming; it describes a state which assumes neither 'understanding' nor 'acceptance' of the message as intended by the rhetor. It does assume the *attention* to the rhetor's message. When *attention* and *engagement* lead to *selection* and the *reframing* of what has been selected as a *prompt*, there has been interpretation and communication.

The role of *rhetor* is complemented by the role of the *interpreter*. Signs are made by both the *rhetor* and by the *interpreter*. One sign-complex provides the *ground*, as *message*. The other sign-complex is the result of *attention, engagement, selection*, from that message, *framing* these according to the interpreter's *interest* as a *prompt*; and in *transduction* and *transformation* reshaped as a new, inwardly focused *sign-complex*. That suggests two possibilities of naming: to use the label *rhetor* for the role of sign-maker, whether of the initial maker of the *sign-message* or the interpreter of the *prompt*. Or we might use the label *rhetor* for the maker of the message that initiates a sequence and becomes the *ground* for the *interpretation;* and use the label *interpreter* for the sign-maker who *interprets* the *prompt*. That brings a distinction between 'setting the ground' and 'shaping and interpreting the prompt', both seen as the making of signs. I adopt that naming – *rhetor* and *interpreter* – to mark the distinction between *setting the ground* and *interpreting the prompt*. Each of the two has a distinct social function and effect. How each of them is carried out is a separate matter. It moves away, decisively, from a conception of successful communication measured in terms of the 'closeness' of the *interpreter's* sign to the sign of the *rhetor*.

The social is present twice in this framework: through the *interest* of the *rhetor*, who acts with a strong sense of the social characteristics of the audience and their relation to the *rhetor*; and through the social location and *interests* of *interpreters*. From the distinct vantage points of their social histories and present social positions, both bring their sense of the demands of the immediate social environment, of representational and communicational requirements of the phenomenon – the event or object – to be communicated and interpreted. Each brings their cultural/semiotic resources and values.

This conception of communication gives appropriate recognition to the semiotic work of curator and visitor; to teacher and student; to writer and reader; to the person who uploads a video to a social site and to those who respond to that video. It provides a shared frame of rhetorical and communicational work, modified according to the specificities of the social environment and of the technologies in use.

In conditions of political and social stability there is little need to give much or any attention to *rhetoric;* it drops out of theoretical and practical view. It is replaced by 'rules', 'conventions', 'how things are done and how things have always been done', in theory and in practice alike. Socially and communicationally, things run smoothly, in well-defined grooves; little reflection or effort is needed for what appear as unremarkable instances of interaction. Rhetorical considerations do still organize all of communication, all semiotic interaction, at all times, even in times of stability and the dominance of convention. The smooth grooves of convention obscure, obviate or lessen rhetorical effort: the semiotic work of rhetoric becomes invisible. As an issue it fades from view.

If we regard *rhetoric* as the politics of communication and regard *politics* as the attempt to shape and regulate social relations by means of power, it becomes clear why that should be so. In periods of stability the relations of power are known, predictable, naturalized – and so the frames of communication are stable, predictable, unchallenged. Usually there is little contestation of power in a social domain; the resources of representation and communication are aligned in relatively stable and predictable arrangements to ensure that this is so. Social relations appear, semiotically, in clear *generic* forms; these regulate and realize forms of interaction. Authority relations are clear; the 'appropriate' *modes* of representation as much as the 'appropriate' means of dissemination in each circumstance – the *media* – are well understood and not contested. There are canonical forms for interaction – *genres*; for dealing with 'knowledge' – *discourses*; for representing the discursively shaped world – *modes*; for distributing texts-as-messages – *media: books, radio, newspapers, television.* Unknown and unpredictable instances of social interaction are rare. The new is neither sought nor particularly valued. This is a myth of course, even in conditions of stability. It is, however, an effective myth.

In conditions of political and social *instability*, things are anything but predictable or known; the grooves of convention have been worn away or else the territory is in any case new so that there are no grooves. Relations of power are uncertain, unknown maybe: they are contingent and unpredictable, subject to constant negotiation and challenge. Things are *provisional*. For every occasion of communication and inter-action, social relations need to be newly assessed; the resources of representation have to be freshly considered in their utility for *this* instance.

An apt metaphor might be that of a 'road' across a sandy desert: a maze of wandering, diverging tracks, each forcing the anxious question: 'Is this the right track?', 'Shall we take this one or that?', 'What evidence do we have for our choice?'. Each occasion of communication requires close assessment of the social environment of communication: 'What are the rhetor's purposes in *this* specific social environ-ment?', 'What are the criterial characteristics of the audience?', 'What relations of power obtain between rhetor and audience?', 'What is to be communicated?', 'What representational resources are available?', 'What is their usefulness for representing what I need to represent?', 'What is their usefulness for fashioning the message I need to produce for this audience?'.

Environments of communication: a historical view

Communication, being social and semiotic, has a social and semiotic history. If we assume that semiotic changes 'track' social changes, we can ask about the inter-relations of social arrangements and practices and semiotic arrangements over time. We can do that in relation to any one semiotic feature or bundle of features and ask about the relation between semiotic forms and the social conditions which are mirrored in the forms and their uses. The changing uses and functions of different modes should be revealing of social changes.

In the domain of education, looking at 'teaching materials' – textbooks and, more recently, looking at screen-based materials – over the last sixty or seventy years, it is easy to see deep changes in social/pedagogic practice and in semiotic form maybe more so than, at least superficially, in content. Over the last three decades there has been a distinct move away – differently in different school subjects – from the domi-nance of *writing* as the main or at times sole carrier of meaning to an increasing reliance on *image*. This is evident in the changing functions of writing as well as in terms of quantity.

Quantifying the occurrence of modes is not straightforward; one can nevertheless attempt to count images in textbooks. Perhaps the outcome is unsurprising. In a research project ('Gains and Losses: Changes in Representation, Knowledge and Pedagogy in Learning Resources' (2007–2009)) describing semiotic changes in textbooks in English, Mathematics and Science over a period of about seventy years from the mid-1930s to 2005, the number of images in textbooks for English had increased from virtually no images at all in the1930s (average: 0.03 images per page) to two in every four pages in the 1980s (0.54 images per page), to three in every four pages in the very early 2000s (0.74 images per page). Compared to subjects like Science and Mathematics, the number for English is low, though for a subject ostensibly founded on and 'about' language, the change is surprising. It does represent by far the biggest increase proportionately among the three subjects: between 1930 and 2005, the average number of images in Science went up from 0.64 to 3.37 per page, and in Mathematics from 2.95 to 8.71 per page.

The shift in the relation of writing and image is equally marked and perhaps more significant in terms of the *uses* of modes for distinct and differing *functions*. This had happened independently of the digital technologies, which were barely emergent in the late 1970s, while the change began, noticeably, in the 1970s and carried on strongly into the 1980s: a clear indication that social forces were at work rather than that the effects were mainly produced by the digital technologies. The changes in representational practices happened within the traditional medium of the book, with its affordances and its forms of production, then still fully in the dominant position that it had traditionally held for the preceding three or so centuries, in the West.

Images are (as yet, relatively) difficult to describe and analyze since, unlike writing, they are rarely composed of clearly discrete constituent entities, as words are. Existing theories do not readily show how to describe or analyse visually represented entities. In a textbook it may not be clear at all whether a visual representation counts as one semiotic entity or as two. In Figure 3.4, for instance, are we dealing with one semiotic entity called 'the body and its digestive system' or with a series of entities: lungs, oesophagus, small intestine, etc.?

Nevertheless, there is a strong difference between the form of image of the 1935 book and that of 2002. There is an equally clear difference in the relation of written elements and image elements in the two cases. In 1935 the image was schematic and abstracted in relation to one conception of curricular need; the detail of the 1935 image has the function of providing an illustration/location for the curricular entities mentioned in the written part of the overall text. 'Curricular need' is the case also for the look of the image in the book of 2002, though now the 'curricular need' has changed. In 1935, writing was the dominant mode, carrying all the information thought to be essential or central to the curriculum; image had the function of 'illustrating'. In 2002, writing is one of two modes with seeming equal semiotic status: image no longer has the function of 'illustrating'. Image *shows* those curricular materials which are best – most aptly – represented in image. Writing deals with digestion as well, though not the physiology of digestion as before, but the bio-chemistry of digestion.

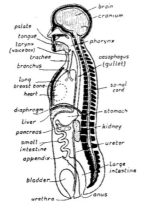

Animal Nutrition : Nutrition in Mammal 161

Digestion is the first stage of nutrition. It takes place in the *alimentary canal.* We shall now consider this process in detail.

The Alimentary Canal (fig. 148).

Food taken in at the mouth passes into and along a tube called the *alimentary canal,* the other end of which opens at

brain
cranium
palate
tongue
larynx (voice box)
pharynx
trachea
oesophagus (gullet)
bronchus
lung breast bone
heart
spinal cord
diaphragm
stomach
liver
kidney
pancreas
small intestine
ureter
appendix
Large intestine
bladder
urethra
anus

FIG. 148.—Chief internal organs of Man (simple scheme).

the hind end of the body. The opening is the *anus.* From the *mouth* onwards the parts of the alimentary canal are the " back of the mouth " (*pharynx*), the gullet (*oesophagus*), the *stomach,* and the gut (*intestine*). The whole of the canal, including the mouth cavity, is lined with a soft pink tissue

11

162   *General Science*

(*mucous membrane*), very rich in blood-vessels. The *mouth cavity* lies between the jaws. The *pharynx* and upper part of the gullet are in the neck. The remainder of the alimentary canal is within the body cavity. This extends from the root of the neck to the hind end of the body (*trunk*). A tough membrane called the *diaphragm* extends across the body cavity at the level of the lower (posterior) ribs. It divides

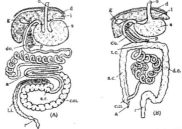

FIG. 149.—Diagram of alimentary canal of a Mammal (much simplified). (A) Rabbit; (B) Man

o - lower part of oesophagus, *d* =diaphragm, *s* =stomach, *g* =gall-bladder and bile-duct, *p* =pancreas and pancreatic duct, *l* =liver, *du* =duodenum, *li* =large intestine, *ac* =ascending colon, *tc* =transverse colon, *dc* =descending colon, *sr* =sacculus rotundus, *cm* =caecum, *a* = vermiform appendix, *r* - rectum.

the body cavity into a smaller anterior portion (*thorax*), and a larger posterior portion (*abdomen*). The greater part of the oesophagus lies in the thorax, but its lower end penetrates the diaphragm. The stomach and intestines lie in the abdomen. The general arrangement of the alimentary canal is shown—somewhat simplified—in figs. 148 and 149.

The *oesophagus* is a narrow muscular tube. The *stomach* is a large oval sac extending from left to right across the abdominal cavity immediately below the diaphragm. The

Figure 3.3 1935 Science: digestion

In 1935, writing was seen as a sufficient means for carrying the meaning that had to be carried; image was very much a supplement (Barthes, 1966). By 2002, writing and image are treated by the designers of the textbook as offering specific affordances; and these are utilized in relation to present 'curricular need' and the assumed characteristics – as likes, dislikes, preferences – of the audience.

The dominant view, that writing carried all that was crucial and significant, meant that no real attention could be paid to what image contributed. Figure 3.3 shows that image did in fact provide information not present in writing; but that was not in focus. The dominance of the mode of writing provided categories both for representation and categories for 'recognition': what was not highlighted in the lexis, the syntax or the grammar of 'language' did not emerge into visibility. So the fact that the image made specific what the diameter of the oesophagus is compared to the size of the chest cavity, was not 'visible' as a significant contribution by the image.

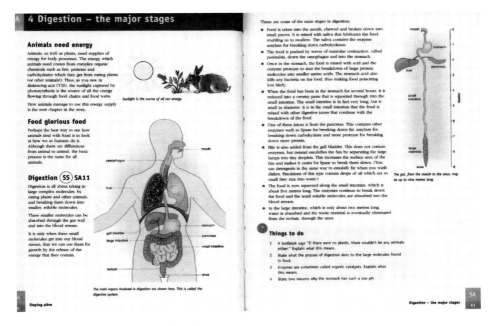

Figure 3.4 2002 Science: digestion

Refashioning social and semiotic domains: rhetoric and design

Representation and *communication* are distinct social practices. *Representation* focuses on my *interest* in my engagement with the world and on my wish to give material realization to my meanings about that world. *Communication* focuses on my wish or need to make that *representation* available to others, in my interaction with them. The dual frame of *rhetoric* and *design* permits both: *rhetoric* as the politics of communication and *design* as the translation of rhetorical intent into semiotic implementation. *Rhetoric* is oriented to the social and political dimensions of communication; *design* is oriented to the semiotic.

The *rhetor* has a political purpose: to bring about an alignment between her or his message, with its ideological position and the position of the audience with their ideological position. The *designer* has a semiotic purpose: to *shape* the message, using the available representational resources, for the best possible alignment between the purposes of the rhetor and the semiotic resources of the audience: mediating the features of what is to be communicated with the resources and characteristics of the audience.

Rhetor and *designer* share similar interests, while their tasks differ. The *rhetor* assesses the social environment for communication as a whole. She or he needs to shape their *message* such that the audience will engage with it and, ideally, *assent* to it. That is a political task. The *designer* assesses what semiotic – representational – resources are available, with a full understanding of the *rhetor's* needs and aims, in such a way that the *rhetor's* interests, needs and requirements, are met and make the best possible match with the interests of the audience, in an environment where the resources for doing so are usually inadequate. That is a semiotic task. As social environments change, so the designs of the message need to change. That is the motor which drives semiotic change *in line with* social change.

In most everyday communication, the two tasks and roles come together in one person, so that the *rhetor* is also the *designer* of whatever has to be designed in the process of communication: the social relations with the audience; the fit of modes, audience and message; the fit of the materiality of mode with the phenomenon to be represented and communicated. And designing, too, a communicational environment congenial to the audience's interest and for that which is to be communicated: for instance, designing 'everyday realism' for a younger audience in school or out; or a greater degree of abstraction for a scientific one; or with aesthetic considerations uppermost for particular audiences. Always too, designing matters of *affect*, whether lighting in a room at home, in an exhibition space, or for a film; designing the message also for the apt *medium* of dissemination and designing the spaces of display within that.

The exhibition at the Museum of London, 'London before London', shows – among many other objects, dioramas, tableaux, etc. – neolithic tools found in the Thames. They are displayed in glass vitrines, lit in a bright bluish light: much as they might be in an art gallery or in a jeweller's shop even. In the exhibition on Swedish prehistory at the Museum of National Antiquities in Stockholm, the lighting employed for the rooms dealing with the equivalent period is 'low', with greenish and reddish/brown tones. The one exhibition seems to want us to see neolithic artefacts as objects of beauty; and to think about the people who made them in that 'light'. The lighting of the other exhibition encourages us to see the period as dimly visible for us, a 'dark age' to us, even though it also displays artefacts of great delicacy and beauty in small glass cases integrated into the tableaux of the rooms.

The tasks of rhetoric and design are neither exceptional nor rare. They are part of the everyday, mundane, banal, unremarkable business of communication as much as at times part of 'heightened' occasions of interaction. *Design* is the servant of *rhetoric* – or, to put it differently: the political and social interests of the *rhetor* are the generative origin and shaping influence for the semiotic arrangements of the *designer*.

The perspective of *representation*, asks: 'What is it that *I* wish to say, write, gesture, "express", at this point?', 'What is *my* interest at this point in giving material shape and form to my meaning?'. *Representation* is focused on myself and my interest; *communication* is focused on my interest in its relation to others. With *representation* there is, first, something to which *I* want to give material realization, making some meaning tangible in the world. Second, the 'take' on what I wish to represent arises out of my *interest*: *interest* directs my *attention* to something that now *engages* me, at *this* moment. Third, my *interest* is shaped by my history, by my experiences over time in a set of communities and their cultures. And fourth, my *interest* is shaped by my sense of what is relevant to attend to in my social environment right here and now, in relation to this phenomenon or object. The question in representation is 'what are the best, the apt means for giving material form, material realization to my meanings'. That is the '*me part*' of representation.

Communication, by contrast, is to put the meanings to which I am giving material shape as a sign (as text) into an interrelation with others in my environment: to make my meanings known to my assumed audience. Now my *interest* has shifted from '*me* and the aptness of material forms to realizing *my* meanings' to the environment of communication and to those who are participants in that: *me* with *others.* The questions change: 'What is my relation to those with whom I am communicating?', 'Are they members of my more immediate social group or are they more distant?', 'What are the relations of power and how do I need to acknowledge them in my signs?', and 'How ought I to adjust and shape my representation in relation to the interests of my assumed interlocutors?'. The issue is the rhetorical one: 'How can I be most effective in disseminating my meaning so that others will engage (positively) with it?'.

Both *representation* and *communication* are social processes, but differently so. *Representation* is focused on *me*, shaped by *my* social histories, by *my* present social place, by *my* focus to give material form through socially available resources to some element in the environment. *Communication* is focused on social (inter-)action in a social relation of *me with others,* as my action with or for someone else in a specific social environment, with specific relations of power. *Interest* remains central, but its focus, its direction and attention shifts: from '*me* and my focus on aptly representing some entity or phenomenon to my satisfaction', to '*me* in inter-action with *others* in my social environment and my focus on success in engaging and persuading others'. *Representation* is oriented to self; *communication* is oriented to an other. *Representation* takes place in a social environment; *communication* constructs a social environment. Signs(-as-texts) are always shaped by both kinds of interests: by my *interest* in aptly realizing my meaning and my *interest* in aptly conveying it to an Other.

Communication is a quintessentially social activity. It may be that as humans we are defined by our need to communicate as much as by our abilities to do so. Certainly, culture is an effect, a result, of communication and not possible without it; in turn, communication is framed and shaped by culture and changes culture in the process of communication. Germanic languages have words such as: *mitteilen* in German ('mit' = with; 'teilen' = to share) – 'to have and share something in common with you, to make you and me the same in respect to some knowledge or feeling'; *Mitteilung* in German – 'sharing something about myself with you in respect to this message'; and *Medalende* in Swedish – 'letting you participate in a part of me'; as crude translations. This may be so basic and common a trait for higher-order mammals as to qualify as definitional of the species, human as well as others.

Being social, the conditions for *representation* and *communication* change with changing social conditions; at the same time, *representation* and *communication* constantly change social conditions, though each differently so. The social conditions set the ground, they lay out the arena, so to speak, for *representation* and *communication*. *Communication* constantly *(re)constructs* this social ground, the social relations and the social environment. In this, it changes the environment and in doing that it always potentially changes distributions of power. Potentially at least it makes communication politically problematic. *Representation* constantly remakes the resources for making meanings and, in the remade resources, shapes those who remake them. That is the effect of representation in the constant self-making of identity. Through their effects on power and identity, *communication* and *representation* are both *political* processes; both alter existing arrangements of power, though each differently.

Representation *happens* in a social environment. As the realization of *my socially made interest,* active in the world, it constantly changes the resources and the potentials for configuring how the world is construed. In changing the *resources for representing* the world, it changes what seems at any one moment to be settled knowledge. That makes *representation* ontologically and epistemologically problematic. *Communication reshapes, (re)constructs* the social environment; it changes the potentials for action, of agency, of those who are participants in the process of communication. That makes *communication* politically problematic. Signs and sign-complexes are shaped by both and hence they are always problematic for knowledge and power.

The effects of communication are both more overt and more likely to be subject to policing than is the case with representation. 'Policing' may range from an unnoticed adherence to conventions which have become 'naturalized', 'made mine'; to a strong enforcing of them, so that I hesitate to incur the penalties of contravention; to outright prohibition on *engaging with* or producing specific messages (censorship), with penalties for transgression.

It follows that members of a community adhere to or challenge conventions for quite different reasons. 'Normal times' might be those when conventions are known, are 'second nature', by and large regarded as essential and generally adhered to, as a matter of course. No overt policing is needed. Where they are not adhered to, penalties may take the form of disapproval; in less normal times, penalties take severe form, where power is used overtly to force adherence. A banal example might be 'littering'. At bottom, 'littering' is a matter of the boundaries of 'public' and 'private', of 'purity' and 'dirt'; while the private space is kept clean, the individual feels no responsibility about the public space (Douglas, 1984). Every act of discarding a sweet wrapper by dropping it on the ground is in that sense an act of marking and communicating boundaries of public and private. There are, even now, societies in Europe where, by and large, these boundaries work such that 'littering' is not a significant issue. It is held in check by public disapproval and even more by internalized boundaries of 'public' and 'private': 'public space' as '*our collective* space' and therefore to be kept clean. In the UK, public disapproval no longer works as a means of policing (what are now non-existent internalizations of) boundaries of 'public' and 'private': the notion of '*our* space' has broken down with the breakdown of a sense of 'a public'. The British state responds by criminalizing such actions (through the ever more frequent issuing by courts of 'ASBOs' – Anti-Social Behaviour Orders). An individual 'issued with' an ASBO is constrained not to engage in certain actions, littering for instance; or to stay away from certain spaces. In other European societies it may still be treated as a social misdemeanour and dealt with in that fashion. From this we could attempt to characterize social conditions, construct social taxonomies and calculate their likely social and political effects, and from that assess conditions of communication.

An important question is whether there is a need to distinguish between *presentation* and *representation*. Is every sign that we make a *re*-presentation in some way of (a) prior sign(s)? Is every text a remaking of prior texts? At one level the answer has to be 'yes'. The model of communication that I am proposing here assumes that communication begins as the response to a prompt. There is the possibility of seeing sign-making either as constantly transformative, as a constant remaking – the position which I adopt; or we assume that sign-making, at times, proceeds from a 'fresh start'.

In the one case we acknowledge that our utterances work on the 'ground' that has been established by the form and the content of the prompt we have received. By doing so we see ourselves as always connected to, integrated into, the (prior) actions of others. In the other case we assert that we might set the ground newly, in our own interest, in our own right; using, of course, existing cultural resources of all kinds, but using them to set our agenda newly. The concept of *representation* places us in the ceaseless chain of semiosis, which we reshape in our signs and texts, but reshape within the limitations set by that chain. The concept of *presentation* suggests that we are – at least at times – able to step out of that flow and may wish to start with our 'own' agenda.

This is a point of ideological, social and personal choice: to see ourselves immersed in the ceaseless flow of semiosis – both inner and social – and yet wish to frame an engagement with the world and its presentation in such a way that our agenda, our concerns, our interests newly set the ground for an ensuing chain. Here ideological choice shapes the theoretical frame.

4   A social-semiotic theory of multimodality

From a *linguistic* to a *multimodal social-semiotic* theory of meaning and communication

Multimodality names both a field of work and a domain to be theorized. Anyone working multimodally needs to be clear what theoretical frame they are using; and make that position explicit. Social-semiotic theory is interested in meaning, in all its forms. Meaning arises in social environments and in social interactions. That makes the social into the source, the origin and the generator of meaning. In the theory here, 'the social' is generative of meaning, of semiotic processes and forms, hence the theory is a *social*-semiotic one.

The core unit of semiotics is the *sign*, a fusion of form and meaning. Signs exist in all modes, so that all modes need to be considered for their contribution to the meaning of a *sign-complex*. The genesis of signs lies in social actions. In *semiosis* – the active making of signs in social (inter)actions – signs are *made* rather than *used*. The focus on sign-*making* rather than sign *use* is one of several feature which distinguishes *social-semiotic* theory from other forms of semiotics. In a social-semiotic account of meaning, individuals, with their social histories, socially shaped, located in social environments, using socially made, culturally available resources, are agentive and generative in sign-*making* and communication.

There are several, relatively distinct strands of Social Semiotics, which derive from the writings of Michael Halliday (1978, 1984). Viewed from a relatively abstract level, they tend to differ in relation to one issue: whether they base themselves on the *linguistic* or the *semiotic* perspective of Halliday's theory. While there is agreement both in broad outline and in much detail among proponents of either of the two possibilities, the differently placed emphases do have significant effects. The theory used here adopts the *semiotic* perspective of Halliday's theory. Rather than attempting to construct a compromise view, from here on in I use the label 'Social Semiotics' to refer to the approach set out in Hodge and Kress, 1988; Kress 1993, 1997a, 2003; Kress and van Leeuwen, 1996/2006; Kress and van Leeuwen, 2001; and, in most respects, van Leeuwen, 2005). It rests on several fundamental assumptions: signs are always newly *made* in social interaction; signs are *motivated*, not *arbitrary* relations of meaning and form; the motivated relation of a *form* and a *meaning* is based on and arises out of the *interest* of makers of signs; the forms/signifiers which are used in the making of signs are *made* in social interaction and become part of the semiotic resources of a culture. The relation of form and meaning is one of *aptness*, of a 'best fit', where the form of the *signifier* suggests itself as ready-shaped to be the expression of the meaning – the *signified* – which is to be realized. *Aptness* means that the form has the requisite features to be the carrier of the meaning.

In Figure 4.1 below, a *circle* is used – by a three-year-old boy – as the *signifier* to express the *signified* 'wheel'. The use of a *circle* to mean 'wheel' exemplifies the notion of *aptness*. In the drawing, several circles-as-wheels serve as an apt *signifier* to express the *signified* 'car'.

Figure 4. 2 is a drawing by a six-year-old boy of two footballers 'squaring up', to use the vernacular. The positioning of the two figures is an *apt signifier* to express a *signified* of 'confrontation' or 'opposition'. The drawing is a *sign-complex* made with the visual mode foregrounded and carrying major functional load. Like all *signs* and *sign-complexes* it is a *metaphor*, newly made. In a social-semiotic take on representation and communication, all *signs* are *metaphors,* always *newly made*. In its 'realist' orientation this connects with aspects of the currently popular theory of metaphor of Lakoff and Johnson (1982; also Lakoff, 1987); in its firm social basis however, Social Semiotics departs from the cognitivist approach of Lakoff and Johnson.

Figure 4.1 'This is a car'

Figure 4.2 Football: 'Arsenal vs. Chelsea'

Linguistics, pragmatics and a social-semiotic approach to representation

Before elaborating this approach, I briefly want to 'locate' it among a few disciplinary relatives, to provide some orientation. Given that thinking about meaning has in many ways been shaped by a *linguistic* understanding of language, it might help clear the decks – so to speak – of some longstanding notions around meaning and communication to sketch some differences in focus between a *linguistic*, a *pragmatic* and a *social-semiotic* 'take' on representation and communication.

The grip of the 'linguistic take' on communication rests on the long history of the study of language in European intellectual traditions. Like so much of 'European knowledge', it builds on insights from 'the East': in this case traditions going back to the grammarians of Sanskrit (e.g. the grammarian Panini, between 500 and 400 BC). These insights were transmitted by various routes – via Greece to Rome; via Arabic scholarship to medieval Europe – and much transformed along the way. In the Sanskrit grammatical tradition, concern for the 'purity' of transmission of sacred texts led to a need to 'fix' language as a necessary guarantor for that security of meaning in their transmission. In many banal but socially significant ways something like that attitude remains, adapted to contemporary givens. Now, reliance on the stability of language is seen as essential in relation to significant public texts, canonical or other. Certainty about the reliability of *linguistic* meaning is seen still as the guarantor of rationality and knowledge, of all that was and is seen as quintessentially human. Nor is the notion of purity far from current public commonsense, as witness the outrage caused by changes to 'conventions'; of which panics about the moral and social effects of 'texting' are a current instance.

If language guaranteed meaning and rationality, then theories of language could also be relied on to provide tools to explain what needed to be understood about central issues in representation; as indeed about much else of value in culture and society. In that way language and understandings about language have long since come to provide 'naturalized' access to theories of meaning and communication.

To sketch some differences of linguistic, pragmatic and semiotic approaches, I will use an example from my first years of teaching, in the early 1970s, at a 'new' university in the UK. It was not uncommon – things have become 'tighter' since – for students to ask for 'an extension' to complete some work. The approach was usually something like:

'I wanted to ask, could I have an extension for my essay?'

At that time I was teaching linguistics – undergraduate courses in (transformational) syntax, semantics, sociolinguistics, psycholinguistics, stylistics. I was trying to understand regularities of language *use* and was not comfortable with the 'correlational' approaches *à la* William Labov (1966, 1972), then dominant in sociolinguistics. To me they did not offer a sufficient explanation of what it should be possible to know and say about such utterances (e.g. 'in this environment, this linguistic or phonetic form correlates with these social features' or 'the occurrence of this form points to/indexes this social environment'). Correlations show *links* but provide no *explanation*.

The form of this oft repeated request puzzled me. It seemed that power and power-difference were the key to understanding what was going on and would lead to understanding variations in language use. My question at that time was: how can I explain the social meaning of this simple yet complex request '*I wanted to ask, could I have an extension for my essay?*' I had other, more specific questions: 'How is it that *past tense* (the morpheme (-ed), whether in 'want*ed*' or in (can + ed) ⇒ *could*) can serve as a sign of (relations of) power?'. A grammatically/syntactically founded *linguistic* approach can readily provide a *description* of clauses and their relations in this *spoken* utterance; or of the 'sequence of tenses'. It can indicate what elements and what rules of 'grammar' are being used: the use of the past-tense morphemes, for instance. The categories of a syntactic/grammatical account, e.g. *clause, subject, phrase, sentence,* or *adjective, tense-marker, noun,* can readily be used to describe formal aspects of that utterance. When this approach is used, the focus is on the *description of form* and of *formal relations*.

By contrast, a *pragmatic* (or *sociolinguistic*) approach asks: 'Under what conditions, when and where, are these forms used and what tend to be likely effects of their use?'. That provides descriptions of the environments of use and of the conditions in which such forms tend to appear. It describes the social/linguistic roles of participants; their status and relations of power; it can describe effects by using categories such as *face, repair, politeness*. To some extent the focus is on *correlation*: this linguistic form *correlates* with that social context. The orientation is to *use*, to *conditions* and *environments of use* and to some extent to *effects*. It can suggest that when the conventions of the correlation are not adhered to, there is a disturbance, which requires repair.

A *social-semiotic* approach asks: '*Whose interest* and *agency* is at work here in the making of meaning?', '*What meaning* is being made here?', '*How* is meaning being made?', 'With *what resources*, in *what social environment*?' and 'What are the *meaning potentials* of the *resources* that have been used?', 'How can *past tense* be an indicator of *power*?', 'How is it that a form that signals distance in time can signal social distance, a "distance" produced by difference in social power?'. There is an orientation to the *interests of the sign-maker* ('distancing', making her/himself 'safer'); to the *environment* in which meaning is made (the relations of power which obtain and the sanctions which exist in not acknowledging power); to *meaning* and to the *semiotic/cultural resources* which are available for the *realization/materialization of meaning* as a *motivated sign*.

That explains some of the *social-semiotic* aspects. It does not deal with the resources used, the *modes*. One response might be: 'well, the only mode here is speech, the linguistic account is sufficient, nothing else to say.' A *linguistic* account, however, is partial in two ways: first, in terms of what linguistics *recognizes* as significant about *speech*; and second, in terms of what it does or doesn't tell us about other modes involved. As far as the mode of speech is concerned, this written transcription of the spoken utterance '*I wanted to ask you, could I have an extension for my essay?'* does not tell us whether it was spoken with a rising or a falling intonation on 'for my essay?'; whether it was said with a markedly falling intonation on 'could' – to mean 'please, I am pleading with you!'; or whether either of these versions was said with a smile, a cheeky grin, a serious or embarrassed expression? Did the speaker look at the ceiling or did he or she look straight at the teacher? Did he or she come right into the room or did they stay wedged in the half-open door?

A linguistic account of speech is partial; even if it is attentive to intonation, as Hallidayan linguistics for instance is; or if it provides a careful transcription of hesitation or of rhythm – it leaves out many other essential aspects of meaning. The focus on the *semiotic* category of the *mode* of *speech* forces attention to all signs made in speech – rather than the *linguistic* construct 'spoken language' and the categories which that supplies. The *semiotic* category of *mode* attends to the potentials for making meaning of *sound-as-speech* differently to the *linguistic* category of speech. The other point here is that if a linguistic account of this *interaction* is seen as sufficient, necessarily it cannot give attention to other modes which are in play: *gaze, facial expression, gesture, spatial positioning.*

Each of the signs at issue here is *motivated*: the positioning in the half-open door as much as the shape and the extent of the intonation contours. The *ensemble of signs* as a whole makes meaning: the distancing *past tense* coheres with the *positioning* in the half-open door; as does the tentativeness of the *rising intonation*. The individual signs in the ensemble can of course be used to contrast, to contradict, to create tension: the distancing of the *past tense* can be contrasted with the person walking right *in to* the office; or with the marked fall in intonation which turns the grammatical form of *interrogative* into the semiotic category of *statement.*

As with the sign of 'circle-wheel', *motivation* here means the use of a form which, in its shape, is 'ready' – which 'mirrors' or 'parallels', so to speak – the 'meaning shape' of what is to be meant. Here, a (grammatical) indicator of *temporal distance* (the past-tense morpheme *-ed*) is used as the means for 'meaning' *social distance,* the distance of power. It is possible to call that an *iconic relation*: distance in time 'is like', 'is a likeness of', can 'stand for' distance in social positions. There is a good reason, a *motivation,* for using *this* form for *that* meaning.

A further difference between the three approaches lies in what I call the 'reach', the 'extent of applicability', of the approaches. A linguistic approach is limited to the description of linguistic forms and their relations. As *socio*linguistics, its 'reach' stops, broadly, at the description of *conditions* and *correlation*. A pragmatic approach concerns itself with correlations of *variations of use* with *variations in environments*. That is, variation in meaning is linked to variation in context.

Necessarily, the linguistic approach has nothing to say about other modes in making meaning; though the principles of pragmatics do not exclude an interest in extending its reach to other modes (Morris, 1970). In some sense both linguistics and pragmatics recognize the presence of other modes – in terms such as '*extra*-linguistic', '*para*-linguistic', '*non*-verbal' or in different kinds of acknowledgement to features of 'context'. That, however, is a recognition of the phenomenon in the same moment as its instant dismissal; a backhanded theoretical compliment: I notice you and you're not significant enough for me to bother.

Of course, as a generalization this is too sweeping. There are and have been clear exceptions (Hjelmslev, 1961; Halliday, 1978). Yet in a 'disciplinary common-sense' – if such a thing exists – it is not too far off the mark. Often this position is accompanied by an assumption that, in any case, images are organized like language, as witness terms such as 'visual literacy', 'visual language'. End of story.

Take the example in Figure 4.2. In a social-semiotic multimodal account of meaning, all signs in all modes are meaningful. Linguistic theory can tell us very little as far as the sign-complex of Figure 4.2 is concerned. It can make a comment on the written caption; and nothing beyond that. The 'core' of this sign-complex is beyond the reach of any linguistic theory. A social-semiotic theory attends to general principles of representation: to *modes, means* and *arrangements*. It can, for instance, 'say' something about meaning relations and their instantiation in image through the *spatial arrangement* of visual elements; it can elucidate a *syntax* of this visual representation – the meaning-potential of *spatial orientation* of the players standing face-to-face; the use of *colour* as an *ideational* resource, to identify the teams; of *proximity*, that is, the use of *distance* as a *meaning-resource*; about *affect* (realized by the distance at which the players stand); their *facial expression*; down, literally, to the respective size and the prominence of the studs on their boots. Should we want to use such dichotomizing terms, we could say that *affect* and *cognition* are equally and simultaneously present; though much more significantly, social-semiotic theory allows us to challenge that dichotomy, via this example for instance.

This is a multimodal text; the modes in use are *writing, image, number, colour* (and *facial expression*). Social Semiotics is able to say something about the *function* of each of the *modes* in this multimodal text; about the *relation* of these *modes* to each other; and about the main entities in this text.

To summarize: *linguistics* provides a *description of forms,* of *their occurrence* and of the *relations between them. Pragmatics* – and many forms of sociolinguistics – tells us about *social circumstances,* about *participants* and the *environments of use* and *likely effects. Social semiotics* and the *multimodal* dimension of the theory, tell us about *interest* and *agency*; about *meaning*(*-making*); about *processes of sign-making* in social environments; about the *resources* for making meaning and their respective *potentials* as *signifiers* in the making of *signs-as-metaphors*; about the *meaning potentials* of cultural/*semiotic forms*. The theory can describe and analyse all signs in all *modes* as well as their interrelation in any one text.

In relation to the example of the spoken request, Social Semiotics can say: *power* is about relative social position; it can be expressed as a *kind of distance; distance in time* can be used to signal *social distance,* the *social distance of power.* The *degree of power* felt or to be *indicated* can be regulated by a nuanced and layered use of *apt signifiers* (for instance 'I *had wanted* to *ask* . . . '; 'I *wondered, could* I *possibly ask* if you*'d mind, if . . . '*) to make ever more complex/nuanced signs of relations of power. *Distance in time* as signifier contains an ambiguity, which allows the less powerful speaker both to acknowledge the *distance in power* between him/herself and the addressee and a means – being distant in time (rather than in space) – of temporal distancing from the request; in effect saying 'I am telling you something about a past wish, about something that I had wanted to do then, whereas actually, now, I am no longer in that position.' That is, the request can be expressed and simultaneously semi-denied in this (weakened) form; it is modalized. Being modalized (Halliday, 1967, 1984; Kress, 1976; Hodge and Kress, 1979) it offers the recipient the opportunity to adopt one of the several possible readings. In linguistics this is usually treated as an instance of *ambiguity*. In the sketch of communication developed in Chapter 3, the utterance/message provides a *ground* which can readily be framed as a *prompt* in either direction, according to the interpreter's design.

In the case of Figure 4.2, Social Semiotics can say which mode is *foregrounded*; which mode carries *major informational weight* (*functional load*); which mode has *what function* in the overall textual entity (*writing* as caption, *image* as major and *number* as minor carrier of meaning). In the mode of *image* it can describe the *arrangement* of the entities of the image and their meanings – of 'opposition', of 'confrontation', of 'challenge', and so on.

Horses for courses: apt theories, useful framing

Theories, of course, are just that, *theories*: multiple, competing, often internally contradictory. Theories specify their domain, more or less explicitly and precisely; they provide categories to describe and analyse the phenomena which they construct. Language, more maybe than other social phenomena, suggests itself 'naturally' as a metaphor of the social or the political – or of their negation; and linguistic theories act as potent metaforms.

Among linguists, Noam Chomsky, a trenchant opponent of political oppression in the twentieth century, is the one who has been most insistent on separating language from social and political concerns – ever more so as his political writing has become more despairing. Yet it is not difficult to see his *politics* – affirming the equal dignity of every human – articulated in his linguistic theory through his assertion of the 'universality', the common characteristics and capacities of human brains everywhere and at all times. This (seemingly) asocial theory is a potent metaphor of his political position. A similar case can be made for the linguistic theory of Michael Halliday, though in the opposite direction. Halliday's assumptions about the generative power of 'the social' explain the close fit between social organization, human action in social environments and the meaning potential of linguistic forms and processes. That analytic edge was used in Critical Linguistics (Kress and Hodge, 1979; Fowler *et al.*, 1979; Hodge and Kress, 1993) as *the* tool for social critique: the social agent's capacity to exercise 'choice' from a complex system of *linguistic* meaning potential in the context of a specific social environment.

Shifting the frame only slightly, the choice of a theory from among the range of always ideologically founded theories is itself necessarily ideologically motivated. Positioning is unavoidable; positioning is the result of choice from among a range of possibilities; that choice is socially meaningful – it is ideological. That is the case with Social Semiotics no less than with other forms of semiotics. It is not to lapse into relativism but to acknowledge that it is impossible to escape 'positioning': socially, politically, ideologically and for me, in the end, most significantly, ethically. That inescapable choice of positioning should not, however, be confused with the very different choice of selecting a theory constructed for one domain and applying it in another. That is a quite different matter: as when a *linguistic* theory and its categories are used to describe *multimodally* constituted texts. The descriptive, analytical and ideological apparatus of the prior theory is brought along and leads, necessarily, to a mis-description of the domain to which it is now applied but for which it had not been developed.

(The choice of a) theory carries, however implicitly, potent messages about what we take to be conceptions of culture, the relations between 'representation' and culture and the fundamental characteristics of culture itself. A full theory of meaning needs a rich notion of culture and of meaning.

Multimodal Social Semiotics theorizes meaning from three 'perspectives'. The overarching perspective is that of *semiosis* – making meaning; its categories apply to all representation, to all communication and to all the *media* of communication. From the perspective of *multimodality*, the theory deals with issues common to all modes and to the relations between modes. Here there are question such as: 'What kinds of theoretical and actual entities are common to all modes and to all the types of relations between them?'. In the third perspective, of dealing with a *specific mode*, the theory has categories that describe forms and meanings which are appropriate to the specificities of a given mode – its material affordances, its histories of social shaping and the cultural origins/provenance of elements of that mode. As an instance, the mode of *speech* in English has the semiotic category of *intonation*. Even though the modes of *soundtrack* or *music* also use the material of sound – with its affordance of pitch variation – these modes do not have the category of intonation; nor of course do modes which are not time-based or which do not use sound. Another case might be looking for – or, worse still, finding – 'verbs' or 'nouns' or 'clauses' in *image*, in *music* or in *gesture*. In practical terms, the three perspectives are difficult to keep apart; yet, for certain descriptive and analytical purposes it is useful and at times necessary to do so.

Most (mainstream) linguistic theories separate meaning and form – *syntax* being the study of form; *semantics* being the study of meaning; *pragmatics* being the study of use. Multimodal Social Semiotics deals with entities in which meaning and form appear as an integrated whole, a *sign*. As signs are always newly made according to the interests of sign-makers in specific social environments, there is neither need nor place for a *theory of use*, that is, for *Pragmatics*. *Use* is, simply, a normal part of the making of every sign. A theory of use is redundant in an approach which has sign-*making* and the sign-*maker* at its centre: the sign, after all, is *made* in and for the conditions of its use. Signs are *made* in a specific environment according to the sign-maker's need at the moment of sign-making, shaped by the *interest* of the *maker* of the sign in that environment. The environments and circumstances of 'use' are, therefore, always an absolutely integral part of (the making of) the sign: they are at the centre of the concerns of the theory. The signs made are as precise as it is possible to make them to realize the sign-maker's meaning.

There are other theoretical consequences. If signs are precise, that leaves the category of *connotation* without point; it is revealed as an attempt to patch up a problem at the core of a problematic theory; a theory, that is, which had no plausible account of meaning-*making*. Similar arguments apply to enterprises such as *Semantics* and *Stylistics*. Clearly at times it is important to focus on *meaning*; and *style* is an important component of a social-semiotic multimodal theory. Yet the need or justification for (sub-)disciplines such as *stylistics*, *semantics* has gone: *style* is an outcome of successive choices of the apt relation of form and meaning in the making of signs and sign-complexes; with meaning at the core of sign-making. Similarly, the concerns of *sociolinguistics* vanish when all occasions of sign-making are embedded in and shaped by social environments.

The motivated sign

The *sign* is the central concept of semiotics. In the *sign*, meaning and form are fused in one entity. In a Social Semiotic theory, signs are *made* – not *used* – by a sign-*maker* who brings meaning into an *apt* conjunction with a form, a selection/choice shaped by the sign-maker's *interest*. In the process of *representation* sign-makers remake concepts and 'knowledge' in a constant new shaping of the cultural resources for dealing with the social world.

The two main strands of Semiotics which have dominated in 'the West' are based on the work of one or both of two major figures: Charles Sanders Peirce (1857–1913), an American philosopher; and Ferdinand de Saussure, a Swiss linguist (1839–1914), both teaching and writing in the latter part of the nineteenth century and into the very early part of the twentieth. The Peircian model offers three crucial emphases: a *classification of signs* based on the relation of signs to 'the world'; the process of *semiosis*; and the category of the *interpretant*.

In Peirce's account of signs in *use* – the process of semiosis – 'recipients'/*interpreters* of a sign make their sense of the sign they 'receive': they form an *interpretant* of that sign for themselves. The *interpretant* is the meaning of that sign for the recipient. 'Readers' are agentive and transformative in their semiotic engagement with signs. Once formed, the *interpretant* becomes (as the new *object* in Peirce's terms) the point of departure for a new sign, leading to an ongoing, constantly transformative *chain of semiosis*. In this process the 'reader'/'recipient' as *interpreter* is the maker of new signs and, in that, is the remaker of the semiotic material of the culture. It is a process of a ceaseless remaking of meaning, of *interpretants* newly formed in the transformative engagement with a prior sign.

Peirce classified signs according to the characteristics of the relation which they have to that which they represent in the world: an *iconic* sign 'resembles' what it represents – the *circle as wheel*; an *indexical* sign 'points to' (as in 'deixis') an object or event – Peirce's example was that of smoke as indexing fire; a *symbolic* sign 'stands for' a conventionally agreed relation between a form and an object or event (the Red Cross/Red Crescent as symbols for a humanitarian organization (Colapietro *et al.*, 1966). In his theory, the *function* of the sign does not – except in the case of *symbolic* signs – stand in an *arbitrary* relation to the world, but is shaped in and by those relations.

Saussure's emphasis, by contrast, was on relations of the 'outer' world to an 'inner', mental world; and on the inner relation of form and meaning *in* the sign. A relation of *reference* is established by an individual between a phenomenon in the outer world and its mental representation, the *signified*. In that inner mental world, the *signified* links with a *signifier* to produce a sign; the sign is expressed in an external, outwardly audible, visible or otherwise materially tangible form. In Saussure's sign, *signifier* and *signified* are linked in a relation which is *arbitrary* and bound by *convention*.

Both *arbitrariness* and *convention* point to social power, though in distinctly different ways: *arbitrariness* as an indication of a social power which is sufficiently strong to tie any form to any meaning; and *convention* – the effect of *social power over time* – as a social force which acts to keep signs *stable,* a stabilizing force for the community which subscribes to it. In this account, the actions of individuals cannot change signs or the relation of the sign to the system of signs (Hodge and Kress, 1988).

The Peircean approach assumes change based on the actions of individuals in the formation of the *interpretant* which becomes the object of the next sign. The Saussurian account rules out individual action as a possible means for change: the system is stable, held in place by the force of collective social power, naturalized as convention. A social account of meaning based on the significance of the agency of individuals, is entirely at odds with a conception of an arbitrary relation of form and meaning, established and held in place by convention.

The example used by Saussure to make his point was a lexical one, the French word *arbre*. There seems no reason, he suggested, why the *sound shape* [a:br] should act as the *signifier* of the *signified* – let me represent it as 'tree-ness'. In English, the *signifier/sound shape* [tri:] is linked with that same *signified*; as is [baum] in German. The relation between *sound shape* and *meaning* is an arbitrary one. That seems plausible enough.

Wittgenstein (1935) extended the scope of this reasoning, stressing the force of convention by introducing the example of a (chess) *game*. Assume, he suggested, that while we were setting up a game of chess, we discovered that a piece was missing, a pawn or a castle say, then we could use any small object, a button maybe, to replace it. This seems to confirm both the arbitrary relation between form and meaning (the *function* of the chess piece) and the strength of convention, agreed on by both players for the duration of the game.

We can push his example further. If the black pawn was missing and we had some white and some black buttons, it is likely that we would use a black button to stand in for the black piece even though the notion of arbitrariness suggests that the choice of a white button would do just as well. At this point we have made two decisions that are not arbitrary: the decision to use a button to stand for a chess piece and the choice of a *black* button. The former rests on the convenience of shape and size – a button fits more easily on a chess board than, let's say, a saucepan; the second rests on a central feature in the game, namely (likeness in) colour. Both decisions are held in place by convention: my chess partner and I have agreed on these decisions for this occasion and decided to adhere to them for the duration of this game.

Had we mislaid two black pieces of different value, say a pawn and a castle and we had black buttons of different size, we would use the larger button to stand in for the piece with the higher value: *(physical) size* of button standing in for *(size-as-)value* of the piece. If both the black and the white parties were missing a pawn, then there would hardly be choice about the colour of buttons: the game would become quite difficult to play if we replaced the missing white piece with black buttons and vice versa. It seems clear that here at any rate the principle of arbitrariness won't work.

What seems like *arbitrariness* and what is *convention* are socially motivated, by distinctly different principles. Choosing 'black' in the first example meant selecting 'colour' as the criterial aspect of the object to be represented; choosing 'size' in the second case meant taking 'value'(-as-size) as criterial. To be effective, whether in the game of chess or more so in the social *game of language* – as Wittgenstein put it – both selections need the joint agreement of the players. But the decision also needs to work effectively for playing the game: using white buttons for black pieces and smaller buttons for more valuable pieces would work against the necessary 'transparency' of signs.

That is crucial. The notion of *arbitrariness* goes directly against the notion of the sign-maker's *interest* in the making of signs and meaning. *Arbitrariness* (in Saussure's conception of it) and *motivation* each point to social principles: arbitrariness points to the strength of social power as convention and *motivation* points to *plausibility* and *transparency* of the relations of form and meaning in the sign. The *apt* relation of material form and cultural meaning is an expression of the sign-maker's interest in two ways: 'matching' form and meaning satisfies the sign-maker's wish for an apt 'realization' of their meaning and that, in turn, is needed crucially in communication as a guide for the recipient in their *interpretation*. *Convention* points to social agreement and power in sign-use. *Motivation* points to the need for *transparency* as a means towards shared recognition in the relation of form and meaning in communication.

To put this more bluntly: in Saussurian semiotics, if I want to be understood, I do so by learning the social *rules* of *use* of the semiotic resources which those around me know and use. If I don't know them, I'm in trouble. In Social Semiotics, if I want to be understood, by preference I use the resources that those around me know and use to make the signs which I need to make. If I am not familiar with those resources, I *make* signs in which the form strongly suggests the meaning I want to communicate.

Many of us have found ourselves in the latter situation and survived, using signs of gesture, of drawing, of pointing. Those signs however have to be as transparent, as 'iconic' as I can possibly make them.

Multimodal Social Semiotics does not make use of Peirce's well-known tri-partite classification of signs, as *iconic, indexical* and *symbolic.* His three terms rest on *motivation* in the relation of form and meaning, though differently in each case; and that includes the *symbolic* sign. Theoretically, to allow for 'little bits of arbitrariness' here or there, allowing maybe for the odd arbitrary sign in some environments is a profound mistake. The effect is to totally undermine the power and usefulness of a theory of the motivated sign – whether in the direction of the possibility of refutation of the theory itself or in the use of the notion as a heuristic device to hypothesize about meaning. Assuming the position that all signs are motivated conjunctions of form and meaning forces me to attempt to uncover motivation, in all cases. Once we do that, we begin to realize that the sign of the Red Cross (the Red Cross flag being a reversal of the colours of the Swiss flag) might not have been unrelated to Swiss neutrality, as a *signifier* of the *signified* of being an 'uninvolved, neutral party', 'an impartial organization of assistance' – not to mention the nationality of the founder of the organization. Nor is it implausible, given the religious meaning of 'cross', that in some societies the Red Crescent was chosen as the apt signifier for them. In that latter case it is the 'cross' as religious symbol rather than as reminder of the Swiss flag which seemed criterial.

I have not checked, but it would be revealing to find what differing versions of the Red Cross/Red Crescent there are, and what, in each case the principle of motivation is.

The inner constitution of the sign reveals the *interest* of the maker of the sign. That is of the greatest significance as a heuristic and as an analytic means, whether straightforwardly in ordinary everyday interaction or in forms of research. If the 'shape' of the signifier aptly suggests the 'shape' of the signified (e.g. the circle as wheel), it allows an analyst – whether in everyday interaction or in research – to hypothesize about the features which the maker of the sign regarded as criterial about the object which she or he represented. Positing that relation between 'sign' and 'world' is crucial; it opens the possibility of a path to understanding what in the phenomenon or object to be represented was treated as criterial by the maker of the sign at the moment of representation. That can lead to an understanding of the sign-maker's position in their world at the moment of the making of the sign. Such a hypothesis is of fundamental importance in all communication – whether framed rhetorically as critique or as design.

The everyday, the banal and the motivated sign

Saussure's mistaken assumption that the relation of *signifier* and *signified* is an *arbitrary* one was, as is all theory, a product and realization of the social conditions of his time. Here are three objections. First, *arbitrariness* takes no account either of the patent facts of the histories (of change) of semiotic resources (see in this respect Raymond Williams's (1985) *Keywords*) nor of the facts of contemporary sign-making practice in every instance. Second, it rests on a confusion on Saussure's part about the characteristics and the levels at which *signifier* and *signified* operate. Third, it denies agency to those who *make* meaning in *making* signs: in wishing to buttress one pillar of his social theory – the force of collective power; or the power of the collective – he ignored the source of that power, namely the *agency* of *individuals* in their action *collectively*. For much the same reason – the wish for a plausible social theory which does not negate the energy and significance of individual action – I stress the agency of socially formed individuals acting as sign-makers out of socially shaped interest with socially made resources in social interactions in communities.

To deal with the last of these first: observation of semiosis at any level shows constant change rather than rigid conformity as repetition or 'copying' – whatever the modes which are involved. Every example in this book provides an instance of this. The second objection rests on a confusion on Saussure's part: the *signifier* of 'tree-ness' is not *a sequence of sounds,* that is, not [a:br], but an existing *lexical-item-as-signifier*, 'tree', used in its potential for becoming a new sign. The meaning-potential of the signifier 'tree' is the sum of all the instances in which I have encountered the sign *tree* as a signifier: that enables me to make a prediction about its aptness as a signifier for the new sign that I want to make *now*. The signified TREE and the signifier 'tree' are elements *at the same level* and of the same kind: not as in Saussure's assumption where one is a *semantic* entity and the other is a *phonetic* one, one an entity of meaning and the other an entity of sound.

Assume I have bought a pot plant, a ficus. I know nothing about the plant's natural habitat or the dimensions that it reaches in its natural habitat (in Australia it is a rainforest tree which grows to huge expanse and height): my plant is about 50 cm in height. Should I call what I have bought a 'bush' or a 'shrub' or maybe something else? Or is it best described as a 'tree'? At the point of searching for a name, the signifier that I am looking for is not a string of sounds but a 'label', a name, that I have encountered before, sufficiently often to know that its meaning-potential – a woody, perennial plant, of significant size with a strong, usually single stem – best captures what this thing that I need to name is. My question is not 'will [shrub] sound best for this plant, or maybe [bush]?' Rather, my question is: 'Where does this plant "belong"? 'Does it belong with flowers, bushes, shrubs, trees?' and: 'What lexical entity will serve as an apt signifier for this plant in terms of its present characteristics or in terms of its future growth?'. Someone from Norway or from the Black Forest, used to trees as towering pines, might, on a first visit to the National Parks near Sydney, (Kuring-gai Chase to the north; the Royal National Park to the south) be unwilling to dignify the twisted, gnarled, wonderfully shaped vegetation on the sandstone plateau with the name 'tree'. The 'settlers' who encountered the Mallee trees of the South Australian inland used the word 'scrub' to name the expanses of these hauntingly beautiful, low-growing eucalypts. That gave legitimacy to uprooting thousands of square miles of that forest and sow the land to wheat – at least until the thin topsoil had blown away. The use of the signifier 'tree' is not automatic; it is socially motivated and individually enacted as *apt* for me, on that occasion.

My problem with naming the pot plant is not about the *sound* that would seem right for this plant, but about the lexical and social 'place' where it would fit. Had it been the former, then, yes, bub or sub, dub or dib, slib even, might all have served equally well as a name; though questions of euphony might have been a consideration, itself not a matter of an arbitrarily made decision. In other words, in sign-making there is a homology between *signified* and *signifier:* both are from the same *level*. In Social Semiotics *arbitrariness* is replaced by *motivation*, in all instances of sign-making, for any kind of sign (Kress, 1976, 1993, 1996; Hodge and Kress, 1988).

The banal, the everyday and unremarkable is always the best site to anchor theory. My examples here are chosen with that in mind. Colour plate 3 shows two images of sachets of salt and pepper, the kind you used to get (and still do, in some cases) on your tray, travelling in economy class on an airline. These things have a practical use: to make the meal on your tray more palatable, if you like salt or pepper. They are also *signs* and they interest me as *signs* – of salt or pepper. On a different airline the salt and pepper sachets are different (Colour plate 4); and on a third and fourth they are different yet again (Colour plates 5 and 6). This variety requires an explanation; and it demonstrates to my satisfaction that the sign-makers have chosen – differently in each case – what is to be taken as criterial about the object to be represented: how to represent 'salt' and 'pepper'. There is a vast range – infinite maybe – of possibilities of representing 'salt-ness' and 'pepper-ness'. Each of the choices provides insight into the sign-maker's *interest*. In Colour plate 3, the colours on the sachets – a kind of orange red for the iodized salt and dark brownish-grey for the pepper – point to interest and motivation: the colour of iodine and the colour of pepper.

As with the chess pieces, in each case a criterial feature of the thing to be represented is chosen. In Colour plate 3, colour is chosen to distinguish the condiments. For a passenger dealing with lunch or dinner on their tiny tray – with the light not all that good in the middle seat of the central row – the most important thing is easy recognition. Most users might agree that the greyish-brown is an apt choice as a signifier for pepper and would not work well as an apt signifier for salt. And while it might be objected that salt is rarely orangey-red, the colour does work both in distinguishing it from the pepper and in signifying that this salt is 'iodized'. With both in front of me, I am unlikely to go wrong in my selection of salt or pepper, even though I might not manage to read the word 'iodized' on the sachet. A feature of the object to be represented is selected as criterial and becomes an apt signifier in these specific circumstances.

On another airline (Colour plate 4), a different criterion is selected as a signifier for the same object – salt and pepper. There are two words, as labels; the message is 'repeated' in a way; maybe because, as in the other case, words may not be reliable enough under the circumstances. Here colour is not criterial for distinguishing salt and pepper. Instead, there is a visual reference to a culturally specific practice of serving and using salt and pepper in domestic or public environments – in salt and pepper shakers. We can ask whether colour is still important: there are bound to be colours that would *not* be apt as signifiers for either salt or pepper. If so, it would indicate that colour is significant here too, though implicitly. This too is a motivated sign, even though the signifier chosen is from an entirely different domain to that of *colour*, namely a reference to social *use*. That signifier too is apt for the signified.

The two signs show a different 'angle'. In Peirce's schema, the Delta sachets might be regarded as an indexical sign, pointing to an earlier sign, an actual shaker and its use. In Multimodal Social Semiotics this is seen as a matter of *provenance*, a reference both to a cultural practice and to the object 'salt and pepper shaker'. The question posed and answered here is 'Where does this signifier come from?' (Kress and van Leeuwen, 2001). The signs of the sachets with iodized salt belong to the Peircean category of iconic sign – of 'looking like or being like'. It is the sign-maker's decision as to what is to be taken as criterial – with any sign. The different 'angle' indicates different positioning: we are in the realm, however mildly, of ideology.

There may be other criteria. The deep navy blue colour of the salt and pepper sachets in Colour plate 4 looks to me – I am not a frequent user of the airline – like the 'corporate blue' of the airline's livery and logo. In other words, the sachet of salt and pepper may be being used to signify a 'corporate meaning', 'Delta-ness' – a feel-good factor to sprinkle on and digest with your food. *Provenance* – the question 'Where does this come from?' – puts us in the difficult waters of difference of cultural practices: in some cultures you get salt from the shaker with the one hole and in others from the one with many holes; and vice-versa with pepper. That does not change the principle of *motivation*: it points to different social histories, valuations and consequent differences in the use of these condiments in the culinary and gastronomic histories of different cultures.

In Colour plate 5, the sign refers to specific social practices: the uses of salt and pepper in the social histories of cooking – the practice of grinding the 'raw' materials in a marble mortar; a cultural reference leaning on tradition, on a specific aesthetics and evoking notions of authenticity.

The relation of signifier to signified is not an arbitrary one in any of these examples. It is doubtful whether any one of these signs will become generally accepted as signifiers for salt or pepper. The airlines' intentions, if anything, are to keep them distinctive; and maybe to allow themselves to engage in a little mild playfulness with their 'guests'. Nevertheless, the theory ought to be able to tell us under what conditions this might or might not happen. What it does show is that the relation of signifier and signified in the sign has a social and therefore 'political' and ideological component. A 'playful relation' with someone nowadays often called a 'customer' or a 'client' is to make a social and ideological point about that relation and maybe about a wider ideological frame.

In my last of these examples, Colour plate 6, 'ideology' in the sense of the suggestion or projection of a particular 'world' seems to me quite clearly present. Here the colour-scheme works together with the faint 's p i c y' printed across the bottom of one side of the two joined sachets – 'spicyness' as something that adds fun to life.

This is no longer just about salt and pepper, but about a characteristic which might define not just an individual but a community, about a whole attitude to life, about being Austrian and Viennese. Here *discourse* – in the sense of a position in and to life, the shaping of a way of being in the world, of ways of being and knowing – is most clearly evident. Equally with *genre*, as an expression of the social relation between airline and its 'guests' and the 'address' of the reader/viewer.

The crucial point is the unnoticed, near invisible social and ideological effects of the signs of the everyday, the signs of ordinary life, of the unremarkable and banal, in which *discourse* and *genre* and with them *ideology* are potently at work – nearly invisibly – as or more effective than in heightened, clearly visible and therefore resistible instances.

The concept of the *motivated sign* in no way places restrictions on sign-makers; the *sign* is as open or as restricted as the sign-maker's *interest*, which shapes the sign; an *interest* which is an effect and a realization of the histories in social environments of the sign-maker. The examples show this clearly: one speaks of health (the iodized salt); another of social practices; the third of culinary traditions, of the aesthetics of cooking and of kinds of authenticity; and one speaks of lifestyle, of pleasure and fun. All these are present, differently weighted, differently valued. The social, its histories, knowledges, its forms of social relations, its discourses and genres, are here, manifested in these unremarkable, everyday, banal objects-as-signs.

All the examples show the social embeddedness of signs and sign-making practices: histories of the value and valuation of pepper in the histories of European cooking; of social uses of salt; of their preparation in households; of the recovery of tradition; or of just being 'cool'. At an Italian restaurant near my place of work – one of a successful 'chain' – there are small, shallow, white saucer/plates on the tables, filled with coarse flaky sea-salt. They invite me to imagine myself as an Italian peasant, picking up salt with my fingers, crushing it and sprinkling it on my bread after dunking it in the saucer with olive oil. I am reminded of the one-piece heavy glass salt and pepper containers of my childhood, with two shallow 'bowls' on either side, in the middle of the table for everyone to take their pinch of salt or pepper, or 'dip' their potato or bread. These objects show that signifiers and signs carry, in their make-up, the traces of long histories of practices. The meanings of these practices are present in the signifiers as a potential for meaning and are carried 'forward' in constantly transformed fashion into new signs, remade in the light of the resources that (re)-makers of signs bring with them. In signs, sign-makers mediate their own social history, their present social position, their sense of their social environment in the process of communication; and this becomes tangible in the reshaping of the cultural resources used in representation and communication. The makers of signs 'stamp' present social conditions into the signs they make and make these signs into the bearers of social histories.

Interest and the partiality of representation

The next example shows the processes at the core of sign-making with great clarity. A three-year-old, sitting on his father's lap (mine, as it happened), draws a series of circles, seven to be exact. At the end he says: 'This is a car' (see Figure 4.1, above).

How is, or could this be 'a car'? While drawing, he had said 'Here's a wheel . . . Here's another wheel . . . That's a funny wheel . . . This is a car.' For him the *criterial* feature of *car* was its 'wheel-ness'; it had (many) wheels. Two steps are involved in the making of this sign. At the first step, 'wheels', the *signified*, are represented by circles, as apt *signifiers*. At the second step, the *signified* 'car' is represented by the apt *signifier* of '(arrangement of) seven circles'. To represent wheels by circles rests – as with the replacement of the chess pieces ('a *black* button is like a *black* piece') – on the principle of *analogy*:

> Step one:
> *analogy* → 'circles are round; wheels are round; circles *are like* wheels';
>
> Step two:
> *analogy* → 'a car has many wheels; many wheels *are like* a car'.

The outcome of the double *analogy* is two *metaphors*: 'circles *are* wheels', and 'many wheels *are* a car'. The complex sign 'car' made here, is the product of the making of two signs conjointly, a double process of analogy, resulting in two metaphors: 'circles are (like) wheels' and 'many wheels are (like) a car'; and finally as one metaphor 'this (the complex visual sign) is a car'.

To see how or why wheels could be the criterial feature for 'car', we have to adopt the point of view, literally, physiologically, psychologically, culturally, semiotically, of the three-year-old. If we imagine him looking at the family car (a 1982 VW Golf, with prominently bulky wheels, especially at the eye-level of a three-year-old) we might conclude that this sign-maker's position in the world, literally, physically, but also psychically, affectively, might well lead him to see 'car' in that way. His *interest* arises out of his (physical, affective, cultural, social) position in the world at that moment, vis-à-vis the object to be represented. His sign reflects his 'position'. Generalizing, we can say that *interest* at the moment of sign-making arises out of the sign-maker's position in the world; it shapes *attention*; that *frames* a part of the world and acts as a *principle for the selection of apt signifiers*.

Clearly, the child's *interest* is partial: there is more to a car than wheels, even for a three-year-old. Theoretically we have a choice: we can treat this as an instance of childish representation and dismiss it; or we can take it as a central feature about representation in all instances. That is the route I have taken: all representation is always partial. What the sign-maker takes as *criterial* determines what she or he will represent about that entity. An adult's choices are more shaped by a history of experiences in various social environments; and adults have greater awareness of and access to the resources for representation available in their culture. The *principle* of sign-making however remains constant. *Partiality of interest* shapes the signified at the moment of the making of the sign. At the very next moment the sign-maker's *interest* is likely to have changed; something else about 'the same' phenomenon or object has now become criterial. Nevertheless, there is nothing anarchic or arbitrary about *interest* or about *attention* or about the formation of signs as the motivated relation of a signified and an apt signifier.

At the moment of the making of the sign, representation is always partial; yet it is always 'full', 'complete'. It is *partial* in relation to the object or phenomenon represented; it is *full* in relation to the sign-maker's interest at the moment of making the sign. That is the case with this 'car' as much as with the representation of any car in any advertisement. *Interest* produces *attention*. *Attention* frames the world to be represented. *Analogy* translates *interest* and selects what is to be represented as the *signified* into *apt means* of representing it, the *signifier*. The result is a *sign*, formed on the basis of the relation of *analogy*. The outcome of that process is a *metaphor*. *All signs* are *metaphors*, always newly made, resting on, materializing and displaying the *interest* of the maker of the *sign*.

Representation – the meaning that *I* wish to realize, to make material – is not *communication*: the two are quite differently focused. *Representation* focuses on my interest; *communication* focuses on the assumed interest of the recipient of the sign. My sign needs to be shaped for the person or group for whom I have intended it to be a sign. That leads to the demand for transparency in communication.

Consider an example, well-known to most of us. We are in a plane, just before take-off. The cabin staff are going through the safety instructions, and are about to point out the emergency exits. Standing at the front of the plane, facing in the direction of the cockpit, that is, with her back to the passengers, an attendant 'performs', to the spoken announcement: 'two exits at the front, one left one right'. She raises her left arm and gestures in the direction of the left-hand exit; she raises her right arm and gestures in the direction of the right-hand exit. Her gestures are *apt* signs – the raising of arm and gesturing with her hand are *apt* signifiers – *left* arm to *left* exit, *right* arm to *right* exit. Spoken and gestural signs are in agreement. Both aptly represent what is to be represented. As the announcement continues with 'two at the rear, one left, one right', the attendant has turned around and now faces the passengers. On 'one left' she raises her *right* arm and gestures with her *right* hand to the exit which, for the passengers, is on the left-hand side; on 'one to the right' she raises her *left* arm and gestures with her *left* hand to the exit to the *right* of the passengers. She does the same to 'and four exits over the wings, two left, two right' (with an additional little wave of the hands to signify 'flapping' or 'wings'). Now there is a contradiction: her raised arms and the gestures of her hands are at odds with the spoken announcement: they are no longer *representationally* apt: 'one left' is gestured with her *right* arm and hand and 'one right' with her *left* arm and hand. In other words, in this environment the demands of communication, the overriding need, is to adopt the passengers' view-point, which makes her (complex) signs internally contradictory. The interests of the passengers have over-ridden her interests; or, better, she has factored the interests of her audience into the complex sign that she has made. The signs are *communicationally* apt. The greater demands of the communicational partner override the *representational* needs of the sign-maker for the aptness of realization of her meanings.

This may seem too obviously necessary to be useful or persuasive as an example for the theoretical point here: yet in many situations contradiction is exactly what happens; often it is the normal condition of sign-making. The sign is contradictory, from her perspective as much as from the perspective of (the luckily few) literal-minded passengers. It is also the case that most passengers would not notice the contradiction. Most passengers (like most of us at most times) assume that the world of sign-making is ordered by *our* interests, or at least on this occasion; so no contradiction is noted.

On this occasion it is the passengers who count; and so their interest prevails. Theoretically it means that all sign-making has to be founded on a careful assessment of the social environment and the relations of power in that environment. That must precede the process of communication. For the powerful, the normal situation of sign-making is that others' sign-making is ordered to fit the interests of the powerful. Power skews the semiotic world away from *transparency* into the direction of *opacity*. Much of what passes as 'politeness' (in anglophone cultures) is evidence of the skewing effects of power in communication. The more powerful the maker of the sign, the more she or he can ignore the requirements of transparency – that is, attention to the communicational requirements of others. Those others have to do the semiotic work that makes up for the neglect of the privileged.

All signs are made with these two perspectives and interests: *mine* in relation to *my* representation and interests; and *yours* in relation to *communication* and to the need for factoring in your interest and the requirements of power. While power introduces opacity into the world of signs, it does not disturb the principles of the motivated sign. A common assumption in debates around communication is that 'good communication' is 'transparent communication', that is, communication where there are no obstacles to an understanding between the person or institution who shapes the message and the individual or group who are its intended audience. The idea of 'aptness' works in that direction: the maker of the sign attempts to find the material signifier which is best fitted to 'realize' the (meaning of the) signified. However, the maker's interest cannot ever be known to the recipient. But if the recipient can safely assume that the *relation of aptness* between form and meaning will hold, then she or he can form a useful hypothesis about the signified and the interest of the maker of the sign on the basis of the 'shape' of the signifier. The recipient may not know about any limitations in the availability of signifier-resources to the maker of the sign. An example is my knowledge of French: anyone reading something written by me in French would be helped by knowing about the limitations of my resources in that language.

A usual situation is that of communication across boundaries demarcating 'cultural groups' – communities of people who by virtue of factors such as age, region, education, class, gender, profession, lifestyle, have their specific and distinct semiotic resources, differently arranged and valued. That reinforces the point I have just made: namely the need to shape my sign in relation to the person or group for whom I have intended the sign and on the effect which that is likely to have. As societies and as situations of communication become ever more diverse, that is an increasingly significant factor, an area of work which Intercultural Communication has dealt with for quite some time (Scollon and Scollon, 2000).

Social power tends to be expressed relationally, as *position* and *direction*, charac- terized roughly by the metaphors of 'up', 'down' and 'horizontal' (Brown and Gilman, 1966). Power is constantly contested, with varying potentials of success, for instance through subversive genres such as *allegory*, *joke*, aware of the degrees of superior power exerted to limit such expression (Bakhtin, 1986). Even in instances or periods of great power difference – or maybe particularly then – such challenges exist.

The current fundamental challenges to and shifts in social power in nearly all domains of 'Western' sites have had and are having *semiotic* effects. Equally, there are the potentials of *semiotic* power as means of challenge to social power. Power and its effects were the core of Critical Linguistics (Kress and Hodge, 1979; Fowler *et al.*, 1979; Hodge and Kress, 1988; Hodge and Kress, 1993), parts of which later morphed into the larger and theoretically more diffuse project of Critical Discourse Analysis (Kress, 1984/89; Kress, 1991; Fairclough, 1989). It remains one of the central interests in communication. That includes (Foucault's notion of) power from below (Foucault, 1982) or power exercised/marshalled (seemingly) horizontally. None of this affects the metaphor of *position*; in each instance, those who exert power assume the position of 'up', even if only for a moment of refusal and 'resistance' or of some other countervailing action. Refusal to acknowledge the demands of power is power; just as refusal to act is to exercise power.

We are all familiar with examples in language. In their landmark article 'The pronouns of power and solidarity', Brown and Gilman (1966) drew attention to a social and semiotic change in seventeenth-century England, when the second person plural pronoun *you* (the *vous* of French, the *Sie* of German) changed from being the pronoun of power and became the pronoun of address for everyone. Such social and semiotic change produces a far-reaching unsettling of social arrangements; it disturbs the expression of power and of power itself but it does not – and did not in that case – abolish it. New forms for expressing power needed to be and were found. In English I can address my boss as *you* and by his first name (students in higher education in the UK tend to address their teachers by their first names) but I do not address my boss with an imperative – e.g. 'Shut that window, Bill'; nor, usually, would a student their teacher.

What is the case for *speech* is the case for all modes. *Speech* provides means for the direct address of a social other in interaction, but so do *gesture*, *gaze, proximity* and *movement*. It is not difficult to test out how, with each of these modes, I can indicate *deference* to power or my *amelioration* of power in complex signs. Averting my gaze (I am talking here about 'my' social group – these signifiers and signs are highly sensitive to social difference) has a different effect to fixing someone with my gaze and holding it. Where modes are involved which do not afford the 'address' of a social other but which nevertheless inevitably represent social relations, signs both of deference and of amelioration can be produced. In a photograph the angle of power (high to low; low to high) can be varied in infinitely nuanced gradations. In watching the evening news it is possible to make reasonable inferences about the state of the 'British' economy based on the position from which the Bank of England building is shown. 'Distance' can be manipulated in a 'shot' in film or in a photo; as it can in the physical arrangements of furniture in a place of work; or in seating arrangements at a dinner table. In all these, power relations can be represented to indicate *deference* or *amelioration*. Soft focus or its opposite in photographic image; choice of words from a formal or a familiar register; the direct expression of a request or indirection; the choice of medium – not *text-message* for those to whom I defer but a more formal medium, whatever that may be at that moment; not sitting in a 'confronting position' in a meeting: all are means of expressing power or deference to power.

(Complex) signs and ensembles of signs are read conjointly so that the contradictions which inevitably exist in such ensembles provide readers with the means of making sense of any one sign and of the sign-complex overall. If many signs in the environment point to the power of a participant, then her or his use of signs of the diminution of power – in 'politeness' for instance – can be read as such and not as a sign of lesser power. This complex relation of signs (and ensembles of signs of often quite different kind) is encapsulated in the notion of the *logonomic system* (Hodge and Kress, 1988), itself a complex of signs that gives readers means of reading, 'navigating', of 'placing' the interrelations and valuations of signs in sign complexes: means for reading *contradiction*, *tension*, *opposition* and apparent or real *incoherence* as well as *irony*, *humour*, degrees and kinds of *realism*, *fictionality* and *facticity*, and so on. In that context, *contradiction* of one sign with others in a sign-complex is in no way dysfunctional but supplies essential information for an accurate reading of the social/communicative environment, which includes the maker of the sign.

Makers of signs, no matter their age, live in a world shaped by the histories of the work of their societies; the results of that work are available to them as the resources of their culture. Inevitably, what has been and what is 'around' and available, has shaped and does shape the interest and the attention of the maker of the sign. Two-year-olds can pick up pens and make marks on paper because pen and paper are there. They can (still – these materials may be passing) shape objects with playdough; make shapes with scissors and paper. Culturally provided *material* resources have their effect in shaping and directing, in the 'channelling' of interest.

A request by a primary school teacher to *write* a *story* about a visit to a museum suggests specific possibilities to the child writer, different to those of a request to *draw* an image of that same visit. The world projected in the written *recount* of the visit and the world projected in the visual account (see Figure 4.3) are likely to be profoundly different. Here is the written 'story':

When I got to the museum it looked bigger than I thought. When I went in I took off my coat and went into the men's toilet and after I ran upstairs I went into the lift. Then I went to see the mummies and all those stuff. Then we went to our cloakroom so we can get our coat and then we went to Waterloo station on a tube and a train to Clapham Junction and walked back to school and went home very happy and I told my mum, sister and my brother. The end.

The written *recount* and the *drawing* are both recollections of the visit, set down on the following day. The 'story' of the visit conforms both to the genre of *recount* and to the (semiotic) logic of *speech* – a mode familiar and congenial to a six-year-old – here present in its *transcription* into 'writing': a chronologically arranged sequence of actions and events. The depiction of the day in the *drawing* is entirely different. It too conforms to the semiotic logic of its mode: the simultaneous presence of entities, shown in spatial relations within a framed space. The *logic of speech* seems to suggest the question: 'What were the *salient events* and *actions* and *in what order* did they happen?'. The *logic of image* seems to suggest a different question: 'What were *the salient entities* in the visual recollection of the day and *in what relation to each other* do they stand?'.

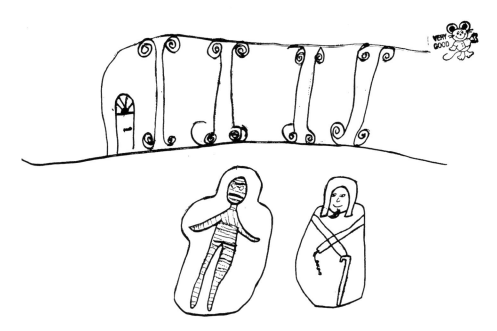

Figure 4.3 Child's drawing of the visit to the British Museum (with thanks to Eve Bearne)

The question about the image seems to be answered as 'I was really impressed by the façade of the museum, with those huge columns; and by the mummies which I saw in the museum. The two mummies were a bit different from each other, but they were equally interesting, and I drew them in front of the museum in which I saw them.'

If this is, in its brief form, a reasonable account, we might infer that the two modes of *image* and *speech* (here as written transcription) organize representation differently, that each poses specific kinds of 'questions'. Putting it more strongly, we might say that the request to make a representation of the day's experience in two *modes* leads to sign-complexes which order the recollection of the day in line with the *affordances* (and the *logics*) of the two *modes*. We might go a step further yet and ask whether a habituation to representing in one *mode* or the other could come to organize and shape our engagement with the world prior even to any request from outside or need to make a representation.

Interest is decisive because it forms the basis of the choices of what I take as criterial, the availability of modes, their materiality and their affordances. It offers potentials and imposes limitations of what can be or what is more likely to become criterial. When I *look*, different possibilities offer themselves to me (through vision) than when I *hear* (through the auditory apparatus). The modes and the kinds of uses made of mode in a society bring with them certain orientations, a certain 'take' on the world. By and large, that 'take' becomes 'invisible' (inaudible, intangible) – in the sense of explicit awareness – to those who do 'take' it. Cultural and social habituation to modes, genres and practices shapes how we represent. In time that habituation to *representation* can begin to shape our expectations about how we will encounter and engage with the world which we then represent. Within the broad range of modal choices available in a society, there is then the individual's decision to make choices to use *these* modes rather than *those* in *this* environment for *these* reasons.

Mimesis, signs and embodied experience

In the reception of a sign the *materiality* of modes interacts with the physiology of bodies. When I *see* a gesture I understand it in large part in an action of 'silent' or actual *mimesis* (Wulf, 2005): I come to understand its meaning – say the extent of the sweep of a hand-movement or its pace – mimetically both by an inner, invisible, 'parallel' performance for myself or through an outer, visible performance, in which I experience in my body what the meaning of that gesture might be. I have caught myself attempting to imitate gestures which I had noticed in order to 'feel' their meaning. There are, as well, the meanings suggested by signs in the accompanying environment. Signs made in gesture are culturally shaped as are all signs in any mode, so there is the problem of misunderstanding.

Many signs we encounter are in three-dimensional form; or they are in time; are signs we make, for instance, via the senses of *smell* or *touch*. Here too the concept of *mimesis* is crucial. We engage with the objects represented in the images in Colour plates 7 and 8 – when we encounter them in a supermarket or at home – not only through the modes of image, writing, colour, but also in actual or imagined 'inner' mimesis through touch and feel, scent and smell, in action – imagined or real. The feel of the plastic container; its texture; the shape of the 'bottle'; the action of pouring or other use suggested by the shape; its imagined and actual fit into the hand; the scent when the lid is undone; all engage more of our body in their materiality than sparser notions of 'representation' might usually suggest.

In the engagement with any sign, the materiality of modes – where *sign* and *mode* are understood broadly – interacts with the physiology of bodies. All signs, whether those that I make in my actions, or remake in my inner transformative and/or trans-ductive (re)actions, are always embodied, for maker and remaker alike. In this way the meaning potentials of the mode in which a sign is made become embodied. No sign remains, as it were, simply or merely a 'mental', 'conceptual', a 'cognitive' resource. At this point the processes named as *affect* and *cognition* coincide absolutely as one bodily effect. In this way too, *identity* is embodied and becomes more than a merely mental phenomenon, an 'attitude', maybe, that I display or perform.

At one level this is not much more than the common observation that children mimic many of the physical attributes, practices, habits – facial expressions, gestures, modes of walking, other forms of bodily hexis – of their parents or of others close to them. At another level it is a realization which forces us to reconsider, profoundly, the separation of categories such as mind and body, of cognition and affect.

From an analytic perspective of a social-semiotic theory of sign- and meaning-making, the following might be said. The sign which the sign-maker has made gives us an insight into their 'stance' in the world, with respect to a specific part of the world, that part framed by the interest of the sign-maker. As a general principle we can take all signs to be precisely that: an indication of the interest of the sign-maker in their relation to the specific bit of the world that is at issue; an indication of their experi-ence of and interest in the world. Signs are shaped by that and give us a sense of the criteria, the principles, the interest, which led to that representation. In doing that they give us an insight into the subjectivity of the sign-maker.

Taking this stance forces me to add another element to my example of the chess pieces. There I attempted to show the motivated relation between form and meaning. But in my discussion there I did not consider the *materiality* of the form of the sign. To put it simply: my characterization of playing chess was – as it were – disembodied, an abstracted mentalistic account. Chess can be (and at times is) played like that, as 'mental chess'; it is then regarded as a particularly difficult achievement. In most instances of playing, the pieces are there in fully three-dimensional extension and for a very good reason: they have a material reality; they have an aesthetic effect; they make playing chess more than an intellectual activity. At that level it comes to matter – especially if it happens on too many occasions – that the button-pawn lies flat on the board, is awkward to pick up, and takes away even if slightly from my pleasure in playing the game. My pleasure lessens. Something is different, missing. The material chess piece – carved or cast – has a tangibility and an aesthetic which has an effect on me materially, as a body in the world, with experiences, embodied, a materiality that adds to my pleasure of playing the game. I might much prefer to play with pieces with a certain dimensionality, weight, texture, aesthetic and which for reason of those qualities give me pleasure. That sensory, affective and aesthetic dimension is too often ignored and treated as ancillary. In reality, it is indissolubly part of semiosis.

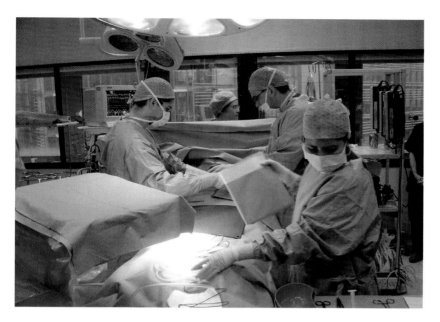

Colour plate 1 The operating theatre (Pages 32, 33)

Colour plate 2
CBBC homepage
2005 (Pages 37, 38,
175)

Colour plate 3 Salt and pepper, SAS: 'health' (Page 67)

Colour plate 4 Salt and pepper,
Delta Airlines: 'social practices'
(Pages 67, 68)

Colour plate 5 Salt
and pepper, Lufthansa:
'tradition' (Page 68)

Colour plate 6 Salt and pepper,
Austrian Airlines: 'light and
cheeky' (Page 68)

Colour plate 7 Bottle: as 'toiletry item' (Page 76)

Colour plate 8 Bottle: as 'jug' (Page 76)

But they hadn't

Colour plate 9 Lil Snail 1 (Pages 106, 109, 129)

They must have gone through here thought Lil Snail, looking out into the bright, bright light

Colour plate 10 Lil Snail 2 (Pages 106, 109, 129)

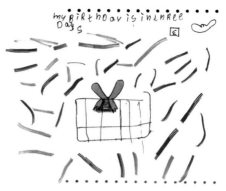

Colour plate 11 Hedgehog, Em
(Page 109)

Colour plate 12 'My Birthday': affect
(Page 109)

Colour plate 13 Lego car (Page 120)

Colour plate 14
Outside the room:
'Armenian wedding'
(Page 149)

Colour plate 15 Inside the room: 'Armenian wedding'
(Page 149)

5 Mode

Materiality and affordance: the social making of mode

Mode is a socially shaped and culturally given semiotic resource for making meaning. *Image, writing, layout, music, gesture, speech, moving image, soundtrack and 3D objects* are examples of modes used in representation and communication. Phenomena and objects which are the product of social work have meaning in their cultural environments: furniture, clothing, food, 'have' meaning, due to their social making, the purposes of their making and the regularity of their use in social life. As their primary function is not that of representation and communication, there is a question whether they should be considered as modes – even though we know that they can be used to make meaning and to communicate.

The introduction of the concepts of *mode* and *multimodality* produces a challenge to hitherto settled notions of language. After all, if all modes are used to make meaning, it poses the question whether some of these meanings are merely a kind of duplication of meanings already made in, say, speech or writing – maybe for relatively marginal reasons such as 'illustration' or for aesthetic reasons such as 'ornamentation' – or whether they are 'full' meanings, always quite distinct from other modes. If the latter is the case, then 'language' has to be seen in a new light: no longer as central and dominant, fully capable of expressing all meanings, but as one means among others for making meaning, each of them specific. That amounts to a profound reorientation. It is the route taken in social semiotic approaches to multimodal representation.

Different modes offer different potentials for making meaning. These differing potentials have a fundamental effect on the choice(s) of mode in specific instances of communication. *Writing* (in English, as in many other languages) has words, clauses, sentences, organized through *grammar* and *syntax*. It has graphic resources such as font, size, bolding, spacing, frames, colour. To *frame* its units, it has syntactic, textual and social-semiotic resources (e.g. *sentence, paragraph, textual block, genre*). In *writing*, the frames use graphic resources such as *punctuation marks*, visual means such as space between words or around paragraphs and increasingly, 'blocks' of writing, often in different colours, on surfaces such as *pages* or *screens* or others. These resources have specific forms in different cultures. Crucially, cultures may use different script systems. That makes it problematic to speak of *writing* as such; instead we need to say, *writing* in this culture or that, with an alphabetic or a character-based script. What applies in this respect to the mode of *writing* applies to all modes.

The mode of *speech* shares aspects of lexis, syntax and grammar with *writing*. The material 'stuff' of *speech* however, sound, is entirely different from the *graphic stuff* of *writing*. Sound is received via the physiology of hearing; the graphic stuff of *writing* is received via the physiology of sight. Sound offers resources such as (variation in) energy – loudness or softness – which can be used to produce alternations of *stressed* and *unstressed* elements, of *rhythm* and *accent*, which produce the rhythmic organ-ization of *speech* and the accentuation of *words*. *Pitch* and *pitch variation* (variation of the frequency of oscillation of the 'vocal' chords) produce *tone* in *tone-languages* (such as Mandarin or Igbo) and *intonation* in languages such as English. *Speech* has *vowel quality*, *length* and *silence*. *Speech* uses sound for the framing of its units. In English for instance, the contours of *intonation* are used to make and frame *intonation units*. These material entities are used to mark out *given* and *new* 'information' in semiotic entities, *information units*. (Halliday, 1967). If I say 'It was *last* Saturday he came' with high intonation on 'last' and falling away (i.e. contrasting with 'not Saturday two weeks ago'), the informational meaning is different to 'It was last *Saturday* he came' (i.e. contrasting with 'not last Sunday').

These units, held together in larger intonational frames, produce chunkings of meaning similar in some ways to the (written) paragraph and yet also quite distinct in their potentials for meaning. Sound happens in time and that allows the voice to 'sustain' a sound, to 'stretch' it as a resource for meaning – as in the lengthening of vowels and the reduplication of certain consonants: 'Aaaalbert, come here', 'yummmmy', 'pssssst!'. *Writing* uses graphic means – bolding, size, spacing – to achieve semiotic effects which are only in some respects similar to those produced by sound in *speech*. Bolding and 'loudness' differ materially; yet in some cultures they are integrated into and 'belong' to one more general semiotic category of *intensity*. Bolding in *writing* and 'loudness' in *speech* are both signifiers of *intensity* and are one means of realizing meanings (signifieds) of 'emphasis'.

In a social-semiotic approach to mode, equal emphasis is placed on the *affordances* of the material 'stuff' of the mode (sound, movement, light and tracings on surfaces, etc.) and on the work done in social life with that material over often very long periods. The distinct material of sound (in the case of *speech*) and of graphic stuff (in the case of *writing*) is constantly shaped and reshaped in everyday social lives, in the most banal as in the most extraordinary circumstances. Banality and exceptionality alike ensure that all of social life is captured in that shaping.

Social – and therefore semiotic – work with the 'same' material, *sound*, can lead to very different modes: to *speech* of course, to *soundtrack* as in film; to *music*; to *drum languages*; to so-called *whistle languages*. These rest on different use of the afford-ances of the same material features: variations in energy (loudness/softness), differences in pitch (high pitch/low pitch, rising and falling voice), changes in duration of elements (long vowels/short vowels), pauses and silence.

The social work performed ceaselessly by members of social groups with the affordances of the material, together produce semiotic resources. That is, modes are the product jointly of the potentials inherent in the material and of a culture's selection from the bundle of aspects of these potentials and the shaping over time by (members of) a society of the features selected. Hence the resources of modes, say *image* or *speech*, are both similar to and different from each other within one society: similar, in that they are shaped in the one society and by its characteristics and the needs and demands of its members, yet different in that the materiality of different modes offers different resources and potentials for social shaping. That difference in modal affordance also leads to differential use and hence to a further cause for distinctness. Modes differ in what they offer from culture to culture for exactly these reasons: the different requirements of different societies and their members and the consequent different shaping. As a semiotic resource, *image* in one culture is therefore not identical to *image* in another. Even across closely related cultures and 'languages' (such as English, French, German) differences in the cultural use of, say, *vocal intensity* (appearing as *accent* in words and as *rhythm* in extended speech) or of *pitch variation* (appearing as intonation); differences of *pace*, of *vocalic quality*, and so on, lead to characteristic variation in meanings made, in signs.

Yet there are commonalities. *Speech* happens in time. In *speech* one sound, one word, one clause follows another, so that sequence in time is one fundamental organizing principle and means for making meaning in this mode. This is shared across all cultures. By contrast with *speech*, *image* is 'displayed' on a surface in (a usually) framed space. All its elements are simultaneously present; the arrangement of elements in that space in relation to each other is one fundamentally organizing principle and means for making meanings. So while time and the sequence of elements in time supply the underlying '(semiotic) logic' of *speech*, in *image* by contrast, space and the relation of the simultaneously present elements in that (usually framed) space supply its underlying '(semiotic) logic'. The 'logics' of space and time are profoundly different and offer distinct potentials for a culture to shape meanings.

Some modes, *gesture* or *moving image* for instance, combine the logics of time and of space. In *gesture* there is sequence in time through movement of arms and hands, of the head, of facial expression, as well as their presence against the stable spatial frame (the background) of the upper part of the torso. In (older versions of) *moving image* the logic of sequence in time is provided by the succession of frames of images, each of which is itself organized by the logic of space and simultaneity.

In alphabetically written languages, *writing* is somewhat of a border category in this respect: it is spatially displayed, yet it 'leans on' *speech* in its logic of sequence in time, which is 'mimicked' in writing by (spatial) sequence of elements on the line (in script systems which use the line) on which writing is displayed. This spatial display of writing and of its elements on the line, its 'linearity', gives rise to the impression that it works like an image. However, the elements of an image can (usually) be 'read' in an order shaped by the interest of the 'viewer', while the reading of *writing* is governed by the ordering of syntax and the directionality – left to right or right to left – of the line. *Writing* is not, dominantly and finally, organized by the logic of space; as readers we are bound both by the orderings of syntax and the directionality of the line. Culturally, both *speech* and *writing* share – even though in significantly different ways – the organizing features of syntax and the resource of lexis. Superimposed on that are the distinctly different material features of sound and graphic 'stuff', also socially shaped.

Looked at in this way, there are significant differences between *speech* and *writing*, at times maybe more significant than the similarities. This makes it surprising that *speech* and *writing* have been and still are subsumed under the one label, 'language'. From a social-semiotic perspective, the use of the one label obscures their distinctness as modes with related yet importantly distinct affordances.

The resources of the mode of *image* differ from those of either *speech* or *writing*. *Image* does not 'have' words, nor sounds organized as phonology, nor the syntax and grammar of *speech* or *writing*, nor any of their entities/units. There is no point searching for syllables, morphemes, words, sentences, clauses or any other language-based category in *image*. While *speech* is based on the logic of time, (still) *image* is based on the logic of space. It uses the affordances of the surface of a (framed) space: whether page or canvas, a piece of wall or the back or front of a T-shirt. In *image*, meaning is made by the positioning of elements in that space; but also by size, colour, line and shape. Image does not 'have' words; it uses 'depictions'. Words can be 'spoken' or 'written', images are 'displayed'. *Image* uses 'depictions', icons of various kinds – circles, squares, triangles for instance. Meaning relations are established by the spatial arrangement of entities in a framed space and the kinds of relation between the depicted entities.

Given the distinct affordances of different modes they can be used to do specific semiotic work. The uses of mode constantly reshape its affordances along the lines of the social requirements of those who make meanings; that ensures that mode is constantly changed in the direction of social practices and requirements. Modal change tracks social change. Whatever is not a social need does not get articulated nor elaborated in the entities of a mode. As a consequence, the potentials inherent in *materiality* are never fully used to become affordances of a mode in a particular culture; nor are all the affordances which are available used for similar purposes across different cultures. My mention above of *pitch* may serve as the example. In tone-languages pitch is used – among other things – for lexical purposes: difference in pitch with the same syllabic (or multi-syllabic) form produces different words. In English, pitch-movement is used for grammatical purposes: for forming questions or statements. Pitch is used for lexical effect in English too, but to a much smaller extent: try saying 'Yes' to mean 'Are you really sure?' or 'Maybe' or a whole range of other meanings.

Societies and their cultures select 'materials' – sound, clay, movement (of parts) of the body, surfaces, wood, stone – which seem useful or necessary for meaning-work in that culture to be done. Selections from the potentials for making meaning which these materials offer, are constantly made in the social shaping of modes. In communities of humans who are speech-impaired, the affordances of the body – the positioning and the movement of limbs, of facial expression – are developed into fully articulated modes, so-called sign-languages. In communities where speech is available, only a narrow selection of these affordances is used, in *gesture*. Different societies have selected and continue to select differently, shaping different cultural/semiotic resources of mode.

The focus on materiality marks two decisive moves: one is the move away from abstraction: such as 'language', 'the linguistic system', 'grammar' and a move towards the specificity of a mode and its potentials as developed in social uses. The other is that it makes it possible to link the means for representation with the bodyliness of humans: not only in the physiology of sound and hearing, of sight and seeing, of touch and feeling, of taste and tasting, but also in the fact that humans make meaning through all these means and the fact that all these are linked and make meaning together. Beyond that, the focus on materiality offers the possibility of seeing meaning as embodied – as in our bodies: a means of getting beyond separations of those other abstractions, mind and body, of affect and cognition.

The 'reach' of modes

Humans engage with the world through these socially made and culturally specific resources and they do so in ways that arise out of their interests. This gives rise to the well-enough understood problems of (spoken or written) translation: certain cultural domains may be well supplied with syntactic and lexical resources in one culture but poorly supplied in another; or else a domain may be entirely missing. Any one culture only ever provides a *partial* naming or 'depiction' compared to the world that might be named or depicted. The semiotic 'reach' of modes – what is 'covered' by the modes of *image* or *speech* or *writing* or *gesture* – is always specific and partial in all cultures, though differently specific and partial. This partiality of naming or depiction, of labelling, is a feature of all modes and all cultures: there are always gaps. Areas in the centre of social attention are well supplied with semiotic resources; others less so, or not at all.

Societies have modal preferences: *this* mode is used for these purposes, *that* other mode for those other purposes. Over long periods, 'Western' societies have preferred *writing* to *image* for most areas of formal public communication. Hence there is a differential 'density' of semiotic entities, of naming and of forms of relations even within one society. If a mode is preferred for a specific social domain it will become more specialized in that respect. Not all cultural domains either can be or need to be described and elaborated equally in each mode. The material affordances of modes play into this: the 'sweep' of a gesture is infinitely variable in its expressive effect; gesture affords infinitely gradable signifiers. Gestures are impermanent – once made, no visible trace remains of them. *Gesture* may therefore be a mode with particular uses in certain social domains, as in the community of amateur fishermen.

This means that the 'reach' of modes varies from culture to culture. What may be done by *speech* in one culture may be handled by *gesture* in another; what may be well done in *image* in one culture may be better done in 3D forms in another, and so on. We cannot assume that translation from one mode to that (same) mode across cultures will work. In other words, an implicit assumption, namely that 'languages' (and now modes) deal broadly with the same cultural domains – even if less well in one culture and better in another – is likely to be unfounded. It may be that what is 'handled' by the mode of speech in this language may be handled by the mode of gesture in that; what may be handled by writing in this language may be handled by image in that other society. That difference is likely to exist in the use of modes even among cultural groups in one society. In other words, the assumption that what is represented in *speech* in Culture A will also be represented by *speech* in Culture B (of course with different lexis, syntax and genres) may be quite unfounded.

What is a mode?

The former certainties about language had acted as a barrier to posing a raft of questions, such as 'What other means for making meaning are there?' and 'What are they like; what can they be used for, what can they do?'. Turned around, that certainty could have led to unsettling questions: 'What, actually, is *language* like?'. 'Affordance' – the question of potentials and limitations of a mode – applies to all modes, and 'language' is no exception (Gibson, 1986). The idea of limitations in relation to language, however, is new. But that question is now firmly on the agenda in a multimodal approach to communication. 'Language', which had been seen as a full means of expression; as the foundation of rationality; sufficient for all that could be spoken and written, thought, felt and dreamt (Eco, 1979), is now seen as a partial means of doing these.

Considered from the perspective of multimodality, profound questions around language pose themselves where there were none before. The question of 'reach' is one of these; it has three interconnected aspects. The first is: 'What is the social and cultural domain that it covers or that it does not cover?'. The second is: 'What can this mode – *image, speech, gesture, writing* – do in the cultural domain that it "covers" and what can it not do?'. The third is: 'What semiotic features are in the mode and which are not, and why?'. These are often lumped together in the question: 'What are the potentials and what are the limitations of this mode?'. These questions apply to all modes.

Just to give a flavour of what is entailed: when a *gesture* has been made and it has been interpreted, its meaning for the interpreter is 'there' but no material trace remains. So some offensive gesture can be made, have its effect and yet be unavailable for examination. Positively, in the Science classroom a series of gestures may produce a convincing rhetorical effect yet be unavailable for interrogation after. Consider the example below, including Figure 5.1. First, a broad transcription of the teacher's talk and an equally broad indication of the teacher's actions simultaneous with the talk.

The teacher's talk (where // marks off intonation-information units):
'We can think about it // as a circle of blood like this // going round // and at various points // say // the lungs are here // the small intestines here // and the cells

are here // and the kidneys up here // okay // so it's going all the way around // and what it needs // is something to start pumping it again // to give it a bit more motion // to go around // okay //.'

The teacher's actions:
Points at head; traces finger around circle; returns hand to heart; draws on arrows; places opened hand at left of diagram; places opened hand at bottom left of diagram; places opened hand at bottom right of diagram; places opened hand at top right of diagram; draws arrows on circle; points at heart; bends elbow; arms at side, makes bellows action; makes bellows action three times; puts lid on pen.

In the final of four lessons on blood circulation, the teacher had drawn the single large circle (top, Figure 5.1) on the board before the students had come into the classroom. When the class has settled, the teacher begins his account of blood circulation. He points out that the single circle is an oversimplification, that there is in fact another circle, which he draws, to make a double circle, with the heart indicated at the juncture of the two circles. He goes on to say 'We can think about it as a circle of blood like this, going round, and at various points say, the lungs are here, the small intestine here, the cells are here, the kidneys up here, okay so it's going all the way around and what it needs is something to start pumping it again to give it a bit more motion to go around, okay?' As he says this he places his flat opened hand on the left of the diagram where the first arrow is, just to the left of the juncture, then below that, and so up to the juncture and then around the small loop. The point he is making is that the blood is pumped around to *all the organs*, that it circulates from organ to organ.

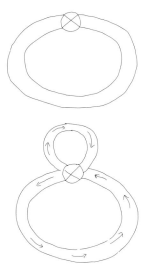

Figure 5.1
Blood circulation

The diagram, together with the overlay of the teacher's gestures, which indicate specific points on the diagram, 'show' plausibly what is going on – the movement of his hand indicating the movement of the blood from organ to organ. The position of the organs is indicated (and a little later repeated and marked with a pen), as is the movement of the blood. This mapping might serve as a topological indication of where the organs are – though as with any topology it would be best not to imagine that the kidneys are roughly at the same height in the chest cavity as the lungs, not to mention the location of the small intestine. Nevertheless, the sequence of gestures has achieved what the teacher wanted to achieve: the tangibly, mimetically witnessed movement of the blood from organ to organ. The fact that in that process the position of the organs was not accurately represented was not for him the issue *at that moment,* nor the fact that the 'cells' are not an organ in the sense of the 'lungs'; nor that they have no specific location in the body, as both *gesture* and *speech* had suggested – 'the cells are *here*'. The ephemeral character of gesture is highly useful: entirely plausible for *this* moment and for *this* purpose; physiologically felt by the onlookers, mimetically experienced in their bodies, and then gone, with no real possibility for challenge, with no commitment made beyond this 'now'. 'Sir, but you *gestured . . .*' does not have the same ontological weight as 'Sir, but you *said . . .*'.

The moment we ask the questions about 'reach', the wide diversity of phenomena assembled under the term 'language' becomes apparent. We can express that as a series of questions: 'What (kinds of) features and entities make up *gesture* or *image, writing* or *speech*?' and 'What principles of coherence might unify these features?'. With *speech* we can ask: 'What does pitch variation have in common with lexis?', 'What connects levels of energy – loudness and softness – with syntax? Or tonal variation with morphology?', 'What do rhythm and pace share with vocalic and consonantal features?'. These are entirely disparate kinds of phenomena, clamped together under the label *speech. Writing* has a no less disparate set of features and we can ask similarly: 'What does font have in common with lexis, or orthography with syntax?'. Joining all these features under one label, of *speech* or of *writing,* shows one problem. But collapsing *speech* and *writing* with their entirely different materiality into one category, thereby joining and blurring over the distinct logics of time and space, of sequence and simultaneity, exposes the implausibility of a *mode* called 'language'. It is difficult to see what principles of coherence might serve to unify all these features. So I take *speech* and *writing* to be distinct modes.

In some approaches, gesture is taken to be part of a larger complex of meaning resources, together with speech (or as part of 'language') (McNeill, 1988). Here too the issue of the entirely different materiality rules that out as a possibility in the approach here. The affordances of the material stuff of movements (largely of) hands though other parts of the body may be involved – the shrug of the shoulder, the poking out of the tongue – is entirely different.

That is one step towards answering the question: 'What *is* a mode?'. After all, treating *speech* and *writing* as modes is to accept that modes consist of bundles of (often deeply diverse) features. Questions which might follow are: 'What features are *inside* and which are *outside* a mode and why?', 'Why is facial expression not part of *speech*?'. It seems that everything that happens 'inside' the barrier of lips and nose can be part of speech; and what makes use of the physical *material of sound* is part of speech. The sarcastic curl of the lips is not. The first criterion is indecisive on the matter, the second makes it clear: a curl of the lip is not sound.

These questions are only in part of a semiotic kind; they are more about social practices and histories; about what has been essential, important, salient in a society and in its valuations. This does not, however, answer the question about potentials and limitations. To do that we would need to undertake a full inventory of each mode from that perspective, with an understanding of the potentials of all other modes in that environment. Above I attempted a small sketch of some features assembled 'in' the modes of *speech* and *writing*. There are some quite simple means of starting that task: take my example of saying 'Yes' to mean 'Are you really sure?' It shows the potential of intonation in *speech*. How could this same meaning be realized in *writing*? In *gesture* it might be the hand with the palm of the hand half turned up; in *facial expression* it might be the puzzled expression or the raised eyebrow with the corners of the mouth quizzically turned up. Such questions would begin to give an answer both about potentials of these modes – of *speech, gesture, writing, facial expression* – and of their respective limitations.

Two further means of answering the question 'What is a mode?' emphasize the *social* in Social Semiotics on the one hand and the formal requirements of a *social-semiotic* theory on the other. To put it briefly: *socially*, what counts as mode is a matter for a community and its social-representational needs. What a community decides to regard and use as mode *is* mode. If the community of designers have a need to develop the potentials of *font* or of *colour* into full means for representation, then *font* and *colour* will be mode in that community. Of course their decision to do this will not be confined to that community alone: anyone who comes into contact with their work will become affected by that decision. In semiosis, as in culture more widely, 'no man – or woman – is an island'.

Formally, what counts as mode is a matter of what a social-semiotic theory of mode requires a mode to be and to do. In this I adopt the *semiotic* approach of Michael Halliday, namely that a full theory of communication will need to represent meanings about actions, states, events in the world – the *ideational function*; to represent meanings about the social relations of those engaged in communication – the *interpersonal function*; and have the capacity to form *texts*, that is, complex semiotic entities which can project a complete (social) world, which can function as complete message-entities which cohere internally and with their environment – the *textual function*.

Unsurprisingly then, there is no straightforward answer to questions such as: 'Is *font* a mode; is *layout* a mode; is *colour* a mode?'. This flies in the face of traditional conceptions: there, what a 'language' is, was known, fixed, given.

To the question 'Is *font* a mode?' there is, on the one hand, a socially oriented answer and a formally oriented one on the other. The former seeks to establish whether there is a group of people who use the resources of *font* with relative regularity, consistency and with shared assumptions about its meaning-potentials. The second answer is concerned to establish whether *font* can and does fulfil the three theoretical/functional requirements of a theory of communication. If both are satisfied, then *font* is a mode *for that group*. Such an approach is unlike present and still active understandings around language for instance. This new approach seems improper, nearly, to those of us who had been socialized in a period when an authority decided such issues, based on power as convention and where deviations were (and still are) treated as highly problematic. For a graphic designer the meaning potentials of 'font' – its affordances – are such that it can become mode. Most of us are aware of the meaningfulness of font in our everyday representational activities. I am typing this text using 'Arial', preferring it to 'Times New Roman'. Newspapers tend to stay with specific fonts, whether for their mastheads or for particular sections of the paper, a clear indication of the meaning that adheres to font.

Take colour as another instance (Kress and van Leeuwen, 2002). Most of 'us' (where the 'us' always refers to a socially and culturally specific group) have quite a strong sense of the meanings of colour; which is not to say that we could easily articulate what such meanings are. The meaning of 'the little black dress' is both that it is little – with meanings about gender and the erotic – and that it is black – with meanings about the erotic and its links with power. Cultures where the phenomenon of 'power-dressing' exists, have their colour schemes, whether for men's suits, shirts and ties, or for women's skirts, shirts and shoes. In other words, meaning can be made through the affordances of *font* as it can through *colour*. These meanings are socially made, socially agreed and consequently socially and culturally specific.

With the socially oriented approach, shared understandings and practices are in focus. With the *theoretically* oriented question 'What is a mode?' the focus is on the communicational task we expect to be able to do with the semiotic resource: neither font nor colour can be a mode if they do not meet the theoretical requirements stated. An approach via such general functions allows us to test 'candidates' for mode status; we can ask whether and how any semiotic resource meets these criteria in instances of use. With that in mind I ask: 'Is layout a mode?'.

Is layout a mode?

Consider the figure first shown in Chapter 3, which is shown again here as Figure 5.2a. It is from a textbook for 13–14 year olds, published in 2002. My three questions are: 'Can layout form message-entities which are internally coherent and which cohere with their environment?' (the textual function); 'Can layout represent meanings about the social relations of those engaged in communication?' (the interpersonal function); and 'Can layout represent meanings about the world of states, actions and events?' (the ideational function).

The question 'Can there be versions of this "semiotic entity" (the "page", the "double-page spread") which are *incoherent* internally and externally?' deals with a central requirement of the *textual function, coherence*. This 'semiotic entity' appears in a school; for a class in the school-subject Science, in a science lesson; and in a school year for which it was designed; it has a place in a curricular sequence, and so on. Clearly, the text coheres with its environment. Conversely, we can imagine any number of environments in and with which it would be incoherent. As far as internal coherence is concerned, a simple test is to ask: 'Will changes in the "arrangement" of the elements which make up this "semiotic entity", produce a different text?', 'Will such changes produce incoherence?' or 'Will such changes make no difference at all?'. If, no matter what change we make, the text remains coherent then there is nothing to say as far as the textual function is concerned: it does not apply.

In relation to ideational and interpersonal meanings, the formal technique of *commutation*, borrowed from structuralist linguistics, can be used to test for the effect of changes in arrangement. The technique allows me to ask 'What happens if I alter the arrangement of the elements in the text I am concerned with, by substituting this element for that?'. Take the difference between *The sun rose and the mists dissolved* and *The mists dissolved and the sun rose*. The two clauses 'the sun rose' and 'the mists dissolved' remain the same; their order has been changed by commutation of one with the other. As a consequence, the meaning of the two sentences differs.

To apply this test we need to know what the elements of the larger unit are. In my example just above, the elements are the two clauses *the mists dissolved* and *the sun rose* and the conjunction *and*. In Figure 5.2a, on the left-hand page the immediately obvious elements are the two columns – of writing and of image. I call that the 'highest' level, Level 1. Within each of the columns there are further units. The column of writing consists of three 'blocks', each with a heading, at Level 2. At one level further down, Level 3, the top-most block consists of two segments and the bottom-most block of three. Turning to the image-column, at Level 2, the column consists of two images, the one at the bottom much larger than the one at the top. The top-most image, Level 3, is relatively easily analysable into three elements: the left-most, the central and the right-most, together with the arrows which connect the left-most element to the central element and which connect that in turn to the right-most. In the original, the lower image (Level 3) shows a division of a pale pink background and a greenish-blue foreground, e.g. the digestive organs.

This simple description allows both the identification and the rearrangement of entities at the various levels. At Level 1, I can switch the left–right ordering of two columns, as in Figure 5.2b. I can commutate elements from Level 3 across the two columns, as in Figure 5.2c. Now the sun no longer causes photo-synthesis but shines instead on the nether regions of the digestive system.

The effect is clear: when the two columns are inverted, the meaning is changed; though the page stays coherent. With other such changes neither the page-as-text nor the two largest elements any longer cohere (Figure 5.2c). There was coherence before; now there no longer is.

The ideational aspect – meanings about the world of states, actions and events in the world – is clearly involved in the commutation of Figure 5.2b. In a culture with

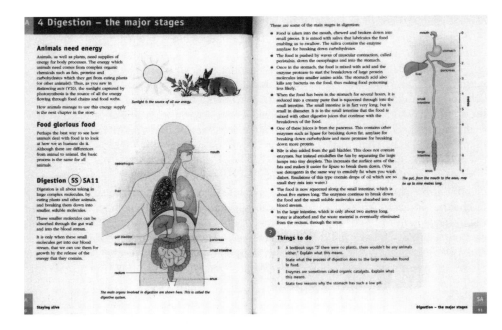

Figure 5.2a 2002 Science: digestion

a left-to-right reading direction, left-most and right-most position have different meaning-potential: 'left', as the point from which I start, and 'right' where I am moving to, give different information value to what is placed there. So in Figure 5.2b, the physiological aspects of digestion are taken as 'given', as 'established', as 'what we already known'; while in Figure 5.2a it was the bio-chemical aspects which were presented as already known.

Figure 5.2c however, is not a coherent layout. Take the example of the change in arrangement of the Level 2 element, the image of *sun–arrow–plant–arrow–rabbit*. Here the original has a broadly (causal) meaning of 'sun (unit 1) provides energy (the arrow, unit 2) to a plant (unit 3) which (in a transformed state, suggested by the arrow (unit 4)) a rabbit (unit 5) ingests'. A rearranged version, say 4–5–3–2–1, has nothing like that meaning. We can labour and give it a reading 'a rabbit, identified by an arrow, has turned its back on a plant; for some reason it seems interested in the writing to its left, while the sun sets'. The rearrangement has led to a change, and to considerable puzzlement if not incoherence for a possible reader.

However, it might be said that this reordering affects elements of the mode of *image* rather than settling the question about *layout* – the arrangement of elements on a *site of appearance* – as mode.

Before answering this second question I turn to the third: 'Does layout enable us to represent meanings about social relations between those engaged in communication?'.

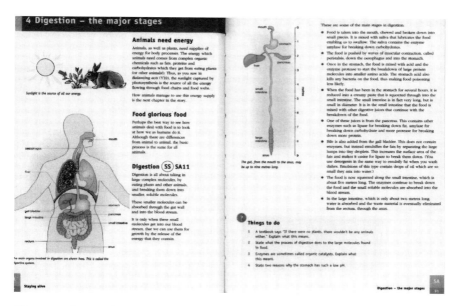

Figure 5.2b The digestive system: columns reversed

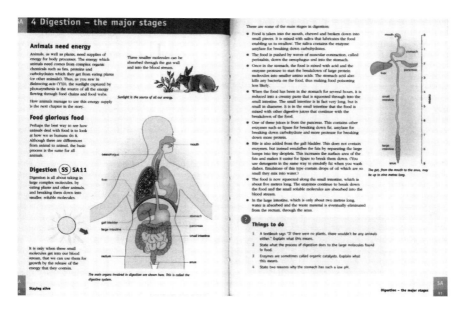

Figure 5.2c The digestive system: rearranged

In Figure 5.2b, the order of the two columns is inverted. In this 'Western' example, the taken-for-granted reading direction ('where we start from and where we go to') is from left to right. In the culture for which this page is made the left–right ordering bears a general meaning of: left = information assumed to be 'known' and as 'socially given', and right = information regarded as 'new' information, as not known to the addressee and not shared by the social group.

The classification of information as either 'already known to the audience' or as 'new to the audience' has social and ontological consequences. In each case a particular status in relation to knowledge is (implicitly) ascribed to the audience, and further communication, further social interaction proceeds on that basis. That distribution of 'given' and 'new' ascribes, whether correctly or not, specific social characteristics to the audience. That ascription organizes the communicational relation of maker and receiver of the message in a specific way and, in that, has effects on their social relation. That meets the theoretical requirement of the interpersonal function.

To return then to the question of ideational aspects of this mode, which may be the most vexed. The organization of material through layout produces and realizes specific social and ontological arrangements in the world of this interaction. In social-semiotic approaches to multimodality it is an absolute assumption that modes have different affordances; *speech* and *writing*, for instance, 'name'; *image* 'depicts'; *gesture* 'enacts' and 'indicates', emphasizes and 'sketches out' themes and topics. *Layout* does not name or depict; it does however 'dispose', organize and indicate aspects of the social/ontological 'status' of representations, as 'known' and 'given' or as 'new' and 'unknown'. In doing that, *layout* 'orients' viewers/interactants socially, as 'part of my group or not'; epistemologically, as 'knowing or not'; and ontologically, in indicating the 'social status of knowledge'.

The disposition of elements in a framed space – a page, a screen – does not 'name' as words do and it does not 'depict' as (elements in) images do. It does however dispose information in semiotic space; it positions semiotic elements and their relations; it 'orients' viewers/readers to classifications of knowledge, to categories such as 'centrality' or 'marginality', 'given' or 'new', 'prior' and 'later', 'real' and 'ideal'. These are states of affairs in the socially made world, aspects of the ideational/experiential function; different to, yet as significant in their ways as 'naming', 'relating', 'depicting'.

If we do accord to *layout* the status of mode, it has consequences for how we think about the scope of the ideational function in comparison with the affordances of all other modes. Here as elsewhere, thinking about meaning and communication had been shaped by a previously unquestioned focus on 'language' as a full means of representation. We cannot afford to let older 'language-based' thinking to constrain how we see mode, in a semiotic theory. The consequence of a multimodal approach, of taking meaning seriously, is that rethinking, new thinking and, with that, new naming becomes essential. As I have pointed out in preceding chapters, what is needed are categories at a level general and abstract enough to encompass all the meanings of contemporary social life in the multimodal communicational world.

Mode, meaning, text: 'fixing' and 'framing'

A multimodal approach to representation offers a choice of modes. Depending on the rhetorical requirements and the media involved, there are different possibilities: do you wish to realize your meaning mainly as *writing* or mainly as *image*, as *moving image* or as *speech*? The existence of such choice reveals that 'meaning' does not 'exist' other than when it has become materialized, realized as mode or as a multi-modal ensemble.

Semiosis, the making of meaning, is ongoing, ceaseless. Occasionally there is a 'prompt' to make that internal process visible, and there is then an 'utterance', an out-ward material sign-complex, always as a response to the prompt. It is a *punctuation* of semiosis: the ceaseless process of inner meaning-making is halted for a moment. It is 'fixed' and it is 'framed' (Kress, 2001). The example below, first discussed in Chapter 4, is an instance. A class of six-year-olds in a school in South London are taken by their teacher to the British Museum. On the day after their visit she asks them to write a 'story' and to draw a picture of their visit. The 'story' is reproduced again here.

> When I got to the museum it looked bigger than I thought. When I went in I took off my coat and went into the men's toilet and after I ran upstairs I went into the lift. Then I went to see the mummies and all those stuff. Then we went to our cloakroom so we can get our coat and then we went to Waterloo station on a tube and a train to Clapham Junction and walked back to school and went home very happy and I told my mum, sister and my brother. The end.

The topic of 'story' and drawing were the same: the visit to the British Museum. Yet the mode of writing, leaning, at the age of six, heavily on the organization of the mode of *speech* and the spoken *genre* of *recount*, with its semiotic logic of temporal sequence of action/events (here in chronological order) leads this young man to an entirely different representation to that in the mode of *image*. The written *recount* implicitly poses the question: 'What were the salient *events* and *actions* and in what order did they occur?' The *image* with its spatial logic implicitly asks the question: 'What were the salient objects for you in that day and what ordering do they have for me?'

The relation of meaning and mode presents itself in three ways: First as a rhetorical issue, a matter jointly of modal affordances and of rhetorical requirements. Which mode is apt and therefore to be selected, given the rhetorical task to be achieved? Second, given the different orientations of modes and their different 'takes' on the world, it presents itself as an ontological and epistemological issue; this will be explored in the next example. Third, in the case of arrangements of several modes simultaneously, in 'multimodal ensembles', it presents itself as the question of which modes are to be selected and in what 'arrangements', a matter discussed in Chapter 8.

In a social-semiotic approach to meaning-making, it is seen as both social and external and social and 'internal'. There is outward social (inter-)action in which meaning is constantly created, in a transformative process of interactions with and response to the prompts of social others and of the culturally shaped environment; and there is constant 'internal' action, an (inner) response in constant engagement with the world. Most of this semiotic action never sees the light of day, so to speak. When it does, when this flow is arrested momentarily by social and individual need and design, the question is: 'In what mode(s) should meaning be "fixed"?'. I am borrowing the metaphor of 'fixing' from older forms of photography, where a chemical substance on a film was the means of 'fixing' light and thereby 'fixing' that which was the subject of the photograph. Different kinds of chemical coating provided for different effects: most noticeably the difference between black and white and colour photography. This is the sense in which I take 'modal fixing'. *Image* and its affordance provides a distinctive 'take' on the world; a different take is provided by the affordance of *gesture*.

In the following two examples the topic of blood circulation is fixed in *writing* (in the genre of 'diary') and in *image* (in the genre of 'concept map'). The data comes from research in Science classrooms in London, with students around the age of 13. After four lessons on blood circulation, the teacher asked the students to 'write a story, imagining that you are a red blood cell travelling round the body'. This is one such 'story', in the genre of *diary*.

1 second	Dear Diary, I have just left the heart. I had to come from the top right chamber of the heart (Right atrium) and squeeze my way through to the Right ventricle where the heartbeat got stronger and I left the heart.
3 seconds	Dear Diary, I am currently in the lungs, it is terribly cramped in here as the capillaries are tiny and there are millions of us. We have just dropped off oxygen and picked up some carbon Dioxide.
5 seconds	Dear Diary, we have entered the liver where we had a thorough wash.
7 seconds	Dear Diary, we have just visited a kidney where we dropped off some water which will be turned into urine.
10 seconds	Dear Diary, I have just finished my journey round the body by stopping off at the heart.

In the written text, the affordances of *speech* are clearly in evidence, as actions/events in sequence: '*I left the heart; I had to come . . . ; (I had to) squeeze through . . . ; the heart beat got stronger; I left the heart.*' The genre of *diary* with its chronological sequencing, complements the organization of the semiotic logic of *speech* in its temporal sequencing. In the mode of writing, the topic is shaped ontologically through the affordances of the mode as (events in) temporal sequence: the actions/events as well as the scientific 'entities' presented in the text-genre, are arranged like pearls on a string, in sequential order: *the top right chamber of the heart, the right atrium, the right ventricle, the lungs, the capillaries*, and so on. The *genre* of *diary* fits with this entirely: the temporal logic of *mode* complementing the chronological sequencing of *genre*.

The *diary* was written as homework by one student; the *concept map* was produced by two students jointly in class on the following day. Many of the same scientific entities appear in both, though now organized through the affordances of *image*, using the semiotic logic of *space* and the modal affordance of spatial relations between simultaneously present entities. This is a profoundly different ontological organization: not as temporal or linear sequence, but as a hierarchy.

Whether for science or for everyday issues, it matters which mode is used to 'fix' meaning. Scientific conceptions as much as everyday 'common sense' are shaped by that decision. Once a particular means of 'fixing meaning' has become habitual – whether in *image* and formal accounts of 'proportions' as in the *genre* of *pie charts*, or in *writing* as actions and events in *genres* such as *diary* or *recount* – it is likely that the world represented through these *modes* and *genres* comes, ever more, to be seen like this 'naturally'. *Modal fixing* provides the material from which text, ontology and 'knowledge' can be shaped via framings of different kinds; the frame of *genre* being one such. That then provides a 'take' on the world which comes to organize and shape our encounters and engagements with that world.

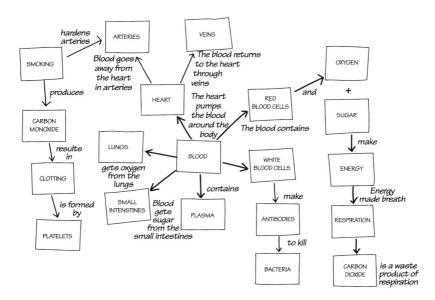

Figure 5.3 Blood-circulation: concept map

Mode as technology of transcription

The 'take' on the world – in manner, in potentials for engagement – has consequences. In many social domains it is important to be as specific as one can be in the context in which one is writing, acting, talking, researching. Each requires tools of a specific kind. Research needs specific data to answer the research questions posed. So maybe the first step is to ask: in what domain am I operating? Is it that of politics, of public information and awareness-raising? Am I addressing policy-makers or teachers, parents or journalists? Am I attempting to produce useable accounts of complex phenomena by means of academic research?

My interest is in developing precise tools for understanding the interrelation of resources of representation and forms of knowledge; of the effects of both in shaping environments; and these in relation to the facilities, affordances, potentials and limitations of contemporary technologies of representation/production/communication.

In much of this area there is a current fashion to use the term 'literacy'. Multimodality in a social-semiotic frame offers a different approach. If modes differ in their affordances, it is evident that they configure the world differently, often profoundly so: as the earlier discussion was meant to show. They can then be seen as 'technologies of transcription'. If *image* shows the world, then that is different from words in *speech* or writing *telling* the world. In that perspective, modes offer distinct ways of engaging with the world and distinctive ways of representing the world. They offer different and distinct potentials for presenting the world; distinct possibilities of *transcription*; and, with that distinct 'cultural technologies' of *transcription*.

'Literacy' might usefully be the name of one such technology, offering one specific form for the transcription of specific kinds of meanings. However, it names just one of many such *cultural technologies* of transcription. One problem then becomes describing the different technologies for transcription potentially available in any one society and finding apt names and terms for them. The other, more significant part, is to develop adequate descriptions of the *affordances* of all the modes and identifying their potentials in representation and communication. Questions such as: 'What semiotic work needs to be done?' need to find an answer; or: 'What semiotic work can be done with a particular mode?' and 'What are the best means for achieving my rhetorical aims in my semiotic designs?'.

We've been taught to think that writing has been developed to transcribe speech; we also know that, really, that isn't the case. Here comes the first problem: in talking about 'literacy' are we talking about *writing* or about *script systems* or maybe both? Alphabetic and character-based scripts both developed from image-based forms of recording. In the case of alphabetic scripts, image-script developed – among other things – into a means of transcribing (aspects only, of) speech. In the case of character-scripts that route was not taken, or not to anywhere near that extent. In so-called literate societies, alphabetic writing is only rarely used to transcribe speech: it can be, but that is a relatively marginal use. Yes, there is a constant semiotic trade between speech and writing and not only in forms such as texting, or MSN. But most of the time writing is used as a means of transcribing phenomena, events, objects, ideas that are about in the world, directly, not via the route of speech. The *minutes* of a meeting for instance – an event in which speech is the foregrounded mode – are not a transcription of the actual speech-sounds (or words or phrases) of what was spoken but represent the 'gist' of what was transacted.

With the concept of *transcription* come questions such as: what is (required to be) transcribed; what is not (to be) transcribed; what can and cannot be transcribed with any one technology of transcription? Both the potentials and the limitations of transcriptional resources come into focus. We know that the alphabet does not transcribe intonation. At the same time we know that – in speech – intonation can be as important and at times more so than words in syntactic order; and so can hesitations, loudness or softness, pace or 'tone of voice'. Every technology of transcription has potentials and limitations, *speech* and *writing* not excepted.

The digital media of representation/production/communication facilitate the use of many such technologies of transcription: modes such as *speech, moving image* or *still image, writing, colour, layout* all appear and are available to be used. Multimodal representation is possible at little 'cost'; the affordances of multimodal representation are readily available for use in designs of environments of communication or of learning. In multimodal design one needs to ask specific questions about what is to be transcribed, what can be transcribed or for whom the transcription is intended. This requires precise tools and if not (yet) settled then certainly useable understandings of the capacities, the affordances and facilities of these tools. But more: we need to know about what kinds of meanings are made in the various cultures of our societies. Which of these meanings can or should be transcribed in what environments and by what technologies of transcription, by what modes? Do we actually understand the meaning effects – ontologically, epistemologically, politically, socially, affectively – of different transcriptional technologies?

Assume that we continued with present uses of the term 'literacy'. How do we deal with the differences between an *alphabetic script* and a *character script* and their profound meaning-effects? What questions do and do not emerge; which can and cannot be posed?

Here are two bits of material 'stuff', which need some accounting in a theory of communication, meaning and learning. The 'writing' in Figure 5.4 was done by a three-year-old girl. At one level I see it as her attempt to make sense of alphabetic writing. If my perspective now is that of learning, I will want to see and understand it as a 'sign of learning': what does this semiotic object reveal about what this child has learned? Well, the 'writing' is displayed on a line; its elements are simple; some of them look as though they were repeated and some not; the elements are in sequence; many of the elements are connected; the writing has directionality.

Figure 5.5 shows a similar and different example. The effect of the different script system is evident immediately. As with the alphabetic 'writing', this is the trace of semiotic work done on a bit of the culture with which the child has engaged. In describing this we might say: the writing is displayed on a line; its elements are

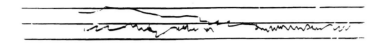

Figure 5.4 Alphabetic writing

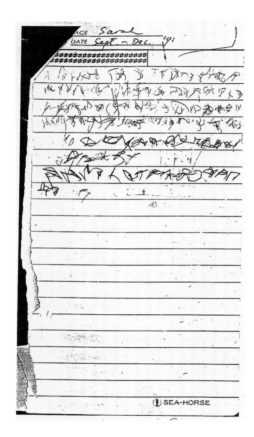

Figure 5.5
Character-based writing

complex; each differs from all others, none are repeated; they are in sequence; each is separate; elements are not connected; there seems to be directionality.

There are common features – display on a line, directionality, sequence – and there are features which are distinct. But there is another issue, at a more abstract level maybe, which relates to meaning and learning: the issue of learning, of the body, of embodiment and identity. It relates to actual material, bodily, production: the physicality of the placement of a letter on the line, movements of linking, the length of down-strokes and up-strokes, the shape of curves and lines. What is learned and embodied in these actions? Linearity, sequence, spatial disposition, limits of size and extent; but also notions of repetition, of the relative simplicity or complexity of the entities. What is learned is how the hand moves, which, in the case of the forming of a character consists of very different movements to those in the forming of a letter; the pen or pencil held differently; the hand not resting on the surface of inscription. In the case of the production of alphabetic writing there is the insistent feature of the line; in the case of the production of a character, there is the placement/balancing of the character in a square – actually present on pages designed for the early stages of learning; and later on present as an imagined square.

There is also – a different matter – the fixed sequence of strokes to be learned. Learning the fixed sequence of strokes in the making of the character entails the learning of a metaphor of social order, equally firmly fixed. The perfect balancing of the character in the actual or imagined square naturalizes a specific framing of the world, just as the placement on the line 'teaches' and naturalizes linearity, sequence and progression. Both script-systems embody and 'naturalize' ontology, epistemology and social order.

At this point we can give an answer to the question 'What has been transcribed here, in the writing of these two young people?'. Part of that answer is: 'All of the above.'

This approach raises the question whether 'literacy' – as script or as writing system – is separable from other 'cultural' organization? The meanings which inhere in the script-system are meanings produced in that society as general semiotic features. Is it an accident that cultures which use alphabetic writing have representations of time as linear, sequential, directional? I want to explore some aspects of this issue by means of a few examples. These come from the research work of Sean McGovern, to whom I am indebted for permission to use examples from his data. He shows how semiotic organization appears in different technologies of transcription/realization. In that view 'literacy' (the script system together with the grammar and syntax of writing) as well as spoken language and its organization, are one kind of manifestation of a 'deeper' cultural and semiotic organization which also emerges in specific ways in other, different 'transcriptional systems', with the different materiality of the resources in which a mode (as transcriptional resource) is realized.

Here, to frame this bit of the discussion, is an entirely usual Western timeline (Figure 5.6). The question is: is it an accident that in Sean McGovern's data, the 21-year-old students who were invited to *draw* their 'biographies', represented time in a variety of forms which, in one way or another, seem to be shaped by and to realize the notion of 'centrality'? One of these, Figure 5.7, was titled 'The tower of my memories'. The drawing is placed centrally on the page; it is composed of modular elements. It is not directional in the sense of Aristotle's arrow of time in the timeline of Figure 5.6, going from left to right. Experience is represented as *spatial* and *modular*, as a spatial *composition*; the tower is built of modules of experience. It is not *temporal* and *continuous*, as a chronological *display*. At the moment captured in the drawing, this person might be asking 'where does the next module-block of experience fit?' Experience, time and future are very differently conceived here compared to Western notions.

Figure 5.6 Western timeline

Figure 5.7
The tower of my
memories

Two more examples can illustrate the notions of centrality and modularity. Figure 5.8 comes from an exercise in which the student subjects were asked to explore the highly abstract notions of 'dependence' and 'independence'. Both *module* and *centrality* are used as compositional elements and principles.

Figure 5.9, lastly, shows the well-known lunch-box of Japanese take-out. Modularity is the dominant principle. From one perspective one can see 'the meal' as shaping and prefiguring the modular organization of the lunch-box; from another one can see the form of the lunch-box (pre)figuring, shaping and constraining the organization of the meal. Both perspectives are valid: these are mutually constructing and determining social practices and cultural forms.

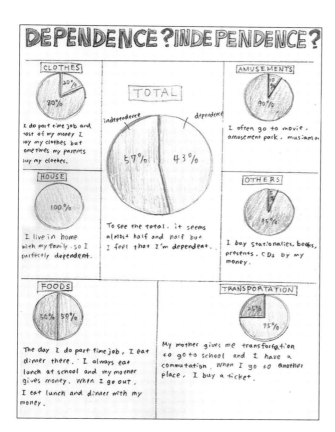

Figure 5.8
Modular layout:
'dependence'/
'independence'

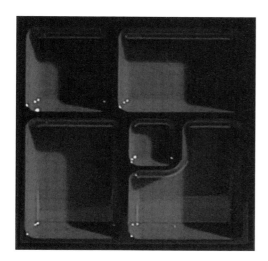

Figure 5.9 Bento box

This discussion is motivated by the need for precise theoretical/descriptive/analytical tools. The distinct affordances of modes offer the potential for better transcriptions of the world or those parts of it that we want to transcribe, along the lines of what is offered by each mode. Imprecise tools hold out the promise of answers; and they mislead. The term 'literacy', whatever the prefix (e-, media-, mobile-, computer-, visual-, emotional-) becomes ever more vague the further it is extended. In the end it obstructs the uncovering of central aspects of meanings that ought to be transcribed in any culture, whatever the means of representation and dissemination. There are specificities of meaning to which we ought to attend. Using the term 'literacy' has one advantage: it draws attention to the fact that 'there are things to attend to here'. As a message to policy-makers, teachers or parents, that is important. As a tool for research or theory-making it obliterates vast areas of significant specificities. For the everyday task of drawing our attention to that variety of meaning which we make and which surround us it is too blunt an instrument.

When referring to script and writing, the notion of literacy is problematically imprecise. It becomes an obstacle when extended to other modes and processes of representation. The distinctive affordances of modes are brushed over and become invisible, whether those of *speech* and *image*, *writing* and *sound-as-music*, *moving image* or *three-dimensional objects*. Multimodal production is now a ubiquitous fact of representation and communication. That forces us urgently to develop precise tools requisite for the description and analysis of the texts and semiotic entities of contemporary communication. Social diversity requires attention to careful design in representation. The increased availability of resources and the facility for the design of messages bring the need for careful questioning of what meanings are to be transcribed and what resources are best suited for their transcription. In this, the presence of the digital media, if anything, adds complexity and urgency.

6 Meaning as resource: 'naming' in a multimodal social-semiotic theory

Naming aptly

The Arts, the Humanities, the Social Sciences, have all paid attention to modes other than *speech* and *writing* in their distinct disciplinary fields. Each names the phenomena from the perspective of its concerns and its questions. The problem is not a shortage of 'names' but one of 'fit'; and that problem has three aspects. One is how to bring all areas of meaning and all *means of representation* within one theoretical and practical frame, without introducing problems about compatibility, coherence and a sensible integration of existing terms. The second is that the newly integrated field will exhibit gaps which point to possible new kinds of relations that were not visible or did not exist in the formerly discretely framed and bounded areas. The third aspect is that questions arise about the 'fit' of the kinds of entities, relations and processes necessary to describe that unified, larger and yet, at some level still highly diverse field.

Each of the disciplines has had and still has its distinct perspectives; each with a lens that focuses on specific aspects of the world under investigation. The names used reflected that focus and the interests of a specific discipline. So for instance, (how) do we now use terms such as *text* or *concept* in the integrated field? *Text* comes from Linguistics by and large; *concept* from Psychology. Naming the new field in a full and coherent manner is the task of *social-semiotic* theory. New entities, new relations, new processes need new names. The problem is that the names – as *words*/signifiers – which already exist are full of the meanings of the places from which they come.

When Thomas Edison discovered that an electric current, passed through a wire placed in a glass container in which a vacuum had been produced, would make the wire glow, he realized that this could revolutionize means of lighting. There was then the small problem of how to name that new object. Obviously, 'light' might be an important aspect of the name and so might the shape of the object. From among the names which seemed plausible for the shape, 'bulb' – as in an 'onion-bulb' – was chosen. And so English speakers learned to live with 'light-onions'. To German speakers, the cause of the light – the glowing wire – was significant; and the shape seemed more like that of a 'pear' and so they got their 'glowing pear' – the *Glühbirne*.

The question 'Which is the more plausible?' hardly mattered in this case. Speakers of each language have managed fine with the metaphor that they got; even if it does give rise to some mild amusement when one points out the literal translation from one language to speakers of the other. In matters of *theory* the choice – 'light' versus 'glowing' – is significant, the metaphor orienting its users towards *effect* in one case and *cause* in the other; while orientation to *vegetable* or *fruit* seems less relevant. If we were to name the field of multimodal meaning with names borrowed from theories of language or of film, we might be led to look for *shots, pans* and *edits* in writing; or for *nouns, adjectives, tense markers* or *sentences* in image and film. That choice would matter.

A multimodal social-semiotic approach assumes that all *modes of representation* are, in principle, of equal significance in representation and communication, as all *modes* have *potentials for meaning*, though differently with different *modes*. The assumption that modes have different potentials for meaning makes the point about *apt naming* interestingly significant. The meaning-potentials of modes are the effect of the work of individuals as members of their societies over very long periods. These meaning-potentials become part of the cultural resources of any one society. But being made in *one* society, even if over long periods, and embodying the meanings and values of that society, should mean that all modes express, in some way or other, these socially made and culturally shared meanings. After all, they all have their origins in and give material expression to the 'same social'.

Yet it is a fundamental assumption in this book that modes have different affordances: the material of sound has been used in nearly all human societies as *speech* to realize meaning; these meanings differ from those afforded by the materiality of marks on a surface in *writing*. For me, the solution is to assume that at a lower level of generality they do differ and at a 'higher' level they don't. Following Halliday's notion of social/communicational *functions*, I assume that each mode expresses meanings about states, relations, actions and events in the world; that it expresses meanings about the social relations of those who interact in communication; and that it has the capacity for forming semiotic entities which cohere internally and with their environment. How these functions have been developed in each society and with what materials is then a matter of that society's history, the constraints of the material and the demands of a social group. No mode, therefore, offers the same resources as any other; yet every mode does, at a general level, realize the three functions mentioned.

At the level of *mode*, each has its specific *potentials* – its *affordances*. This entails that the terms developed for the description of any mode cannot readily be used as names in the description of other *modes*: they are unlikely to aptly describe the *materiality*, the *entities*, the *relations* and the *processes* in that society. Putting it too simply in a quasi-slogan form: *images* do not have *words*; nor do they have *sentences*, *tenses, subjects*; *writing* does not have *depictions*; nor *vectors, centrality, diagrams* or *top–bottom arrangements*.

New frames, new names

Mainstream linguistic theories of the twentieth century had emphasized abstraction and generalization: the 'linguistic system' – coherent, stable; 'grammar' as a set of fixed rules; the 'phoneme' as an abstraction away from the messiness of actual speech. The theory was both a product and mirror of larger-level, modernist conceptions of stability, integration, coherence, of versions of power and of a state which fitted and exemplified these. A multimodal social-semiotic approach to *representation* by contrast puts the emphasis on the *material*, the *physical*, the *sensory*, the *bodily*, 'the stuffness of *stuff*', away from abstractions, toward the specific, the variable. In the constant *reshaping* of *entities, relations, processes* in *interaction* and *communication,* the semiotic potentials of the *material* of modes is constantly newly shaped – pushed, extended, remade. And, going just one but a significant step further, whereas Linguistics had treated language as one integrated phenomenon, attention to the *materiality* and *logics* of modes, to their distinct and specific *affordances*, suggests that *speech* and *writing* need to be treated as distinct *modes* rather than as superficially differing variants of the one mode of 'language'.

Given that, it is clear that a theory and the terms produced for any one *mode* cannot deal adequately with the different potentials of other modes used for making meaning. The *materiality*, the *potentials*, the *social shaping* in history and hence their *characteristics*, their *uses in interaction* and their *functions* in specific cultures all differ – *speech* and *writing* included. Careful theoretical work needs precise instruments. It needs labels-as-tools which are not seriously misleading, as metaphors can be: tools which can account for the whole domain of *representation*, its *entities* and *relations*; which do so aptly for the specificities of each *mode* and not just, in effect, for one or other or both of the linguistic modes of *writing* and *speech*.

A *social-semiotic theory of multimodality* is a fork with two prongs, so to speak – the *semiotic* and the *multimodal* prong. The former attends to signs, meaning, to sign- and meaning-*making*; it needs names apt for those. The latter attends to the material resources which are involved in making meaning, the *modes*; it needs names/labels adequate for those. Names are needed which aptly describe the functions and purposes of multimodality overall, which name *processes* and *features* common to all *modes*. Because *modes* are distinct in their *materiality* and in their social/cultural histories, a further set of terms is needed which *aptly* names the features and characteristics of *specific modes*.

As the briefest exemplification: how *signs* are made; how *meaning is shaped;* what *discourses* and what *genres* are available and how they are used; what *texts* are and how they work; how *representation* and *communication* function; that *modes* occur in *ensembles*: all these belong to the first prong, the *social semiotic*. What the potentials of each mode in these *ensembles* are, the fact that *modes* – *image, architecture, speech, gesture* – have specific affordances and differing *semiotic means* – differing means for *framing*, for instance – belongs to the second prong, the multimodal. Together, *Social Semiotics* and *Multimodality* provides an encompassing theory of *representation and communication.*

Does this mean that we ignore all that has been thought and done before in the field of *representation* and *communication*? Do we now throw out all that past social/cultural/theoretical work? And if not, how can past insights be integrated and made coherent with present conceptions? It would be foolish to ignore the work and the insights of those who, over many centuries, have engaged and thought profoundly about such issues, whether around 'language' or other modes. Yet simply taking over past theories and their terminologies and constructing a patchwork of categories cannot work. A theory is a response to a set of issues which have arisen in and pose significant problems in specific social environments; theories carry the characteristics of the problems and the environments with them. New environments and new problems cannot be solved by patching together elements of diverse theories made to solve other problems. To do that would produce a social, epistemological and ideological hotchpotch (Kuhn, 1968).

In each case, one has to ask what *general semiotic principles* can be drawn out about *this* category or *that*, coming from its theory. 'Do the principles implicit in the category apply in present circumstances and how can they be brought into a *coherent* account?' Much of different linguistic theories and their description is relevant to understanding the modes of *speech* and *writing*. In *Language as Ideology* (Hodge and Kress, 1979) we used the notion of *transformation*, borrowed and changed, from Chomsky's work; and we twined that together with the linguistic functions and many of the linguistic categories taken from the work of Michael Halliday; as we did in *Social Semiotics* (1988). Nevertheless, the insights from Linguistics, like those from other disciplines – Art History, Psychology, Design Studies, Dance, Drama – need translation, via such general semiotic principles.

To make this somewhat more concrete: all semiotic entities – all texts – express indications of kinds of realism. These tell us whether we are meant to read something as an actual representation of something that exists in the world or as a theoretical account or as a fiction of some other kind (Kress and van Leeuwen, 1996, 2006).

Consider Colour plates 9 and 10. If we are aware members of the culture where these images originate and belong, we are unlikely to see them as representations of everyday 'realism'. We do not see them as everyday representations, taking them along to our local garden centre, to show the experts there the look and scale of the problem and ask for an ecologically safe snail repellent. There are several features to help us: the image is not produced with the most up-to-date available technological means; nor is it the realism of scientific drawing (see Kress and van Leeuwen, 2006). Signs of *realism* are semiotic navigational devices for the viewer, reader, observer, part of the logonomic system of the society. They allow us to ask: 'Am I in the domain of *children's story* or in that of a *report* for a biologist?' or, in other instances 'Is this a joke or a report to be taken seriously?', 'Should I get outraged that this has been said?'.

The general question is: 'How is a general semiotic feature – say, "indication of reality" – conveyed in any one mode?'. The materials, the mode and the genre-specific realizations of general semiotic categories cannot simply be taken from one mode and its theoretical descriptive categories and applied to *modes* which differ materially and which have been shaped in different social histories.

That does leave the question whether the semiotic categories and features which appear in one or more modes are present in every mode, in some way, at some level; and if so, in what material shape? Take *time* as a semiotic entity. Does every mode have the potential to indicate time? If the answer is 'yes', what features are used in any one specific mode for this? Can we indicate past time or future time in the mode of *gesture* (I am not here talking about the highly elaborated semiotic resources of sign-'languages') and if so, how is this done? If *gesture* has the means for indicating time, can these means be compared to the *signifiers* of time in *speech*? If they differ, how do they differ? Or – assuming they are present – those in the mode of *image*? The sepia colour or the faded appearance of a photograph indicates the age of the object 'photograph'; it is not a representation of *time* shown in the tableaux or events in the photograph. When sepia tones are added now, as a signifier, to a photograph, a sign about *time* is being made – though still only of the object 'photograph' and not of *time* in the image itself. How does that differ from the indication of time in *gesture* or in *speech*? In the previous chapter I argued that *layout* may function as a mode in many environments: so does *layout* have means for indicating time? My answer would be 'No'. Yet layout has the capacity to express many other aspects of the ideational function; some that are not present in *speech*, say. There is no reason to assume either that all cultures or all modes in every culture will have means for the expression of time: certainly not 'time' in the 'Western' sense, and certainly not in a recognizably similar fashion from culture to culture. In that respect, the work of Benjamin Lee Whorf remains important and more than merely 'suggestive' (Whorf, 1966).

In developing a new field we need care in the use of names. For academic work, catchy metaphors turn out to be blunt instruments – a bit like using the term 'chisel' as the name for a tool in carpentry, bricklaying and brain-surgery alike. The *metaphor* of the chisel treats the world to be chiselled – whether timber, stone or the bone surrounding the brain – as, in essence, the same. But the interests of both patient and surgeon are better served by nuance and accuracy, by precision in the shaping and by subtlety in the use of tools.

The aim in this chapter is to set out *names* for some central concerns – entities, processes, units, of *a multimodal social-semiotic theory of communication*. The aim is not and cannot be comprehensiveness or exhaustiveness but to indicate principles that might be of use in naming. The chapter, from here on, focuses on the issue of resources and types of meaning. Chapter 7 focuses on the question of design and arrangements of these meanings. Meaning is the focus in both chapters.

Making signs: resources, processes and agency

Multimodal social-semiotic theory deals with *meaning* and *meaning-making*; with *sign-making* and *signs*. 'Making' implies a 'maker'; hence *agency* is central. 'Making' has effects; and the various effects need naming. In a *sign* something to be meant is brought together with a *form* which can mean it; that is, which can carry and express that meaning. Two questions are 'What kinds of meanings are there, to be made as signs?' and 'What are the means for making these meanings as signs?'. *Meaning* and *resources* are in the crowded centre of the theory. They jointly mark out the domain to be named: 'meanings to be made' and 'means for making meanings'. To keep the theory as simple as is commensurate with usefulness and need, two overarching labels capture what has to be dealt with: *meanings* and *arrangements*. Meaning forms the core of this chapter.

Meaning

The distinction between *meanings* and *forms* is not an absolute one; it is not a difference of 'substance' or 'kind', nor is it permanently fixed. It is a matter of the perspective demanded at a given moment. Something which functions as *meaning* at one moment may be used as a *form* the next; a sign at one moment functions as signifier in the next sign made, as Roland Barthes showed in his essay 'Myth today' (Barthes, 1978): a (red) rose can be a *form/signifier*. When combined with the *meaning/signified* 'love' it is a sign, which, once understood, endows the *form/signifier*, the rose, with an expanded potential for meaning. In its potential for meaning *love*, it can become a *form*/signifier for a new *meaning/signified*, 'all embracing care' let's say, or 'peace', maybe. Socially made form is meaning(ful*)*; that is, *form* carries the potential for expressing meanings of a certain range. Conversely, by that process, meanings can serve as signifiers, that is, as *form*. Where there is a choice, of sepia-tinged and 'normal' photograph, the meaning of the sepia-coloured photograph can become a *form/signifier* in a new sign of (age-as-)'nostalgia', maybe. *Meanings are accessible only through the form in which they appear as signs.* The elements that appear as *meaning* at one moment can at the next moment appear as *form*. I could therefore rephrase my two questions as two different headings. Here the heading would be: '*What kinds of meanings are there to be arranged?*'. In the next chapter it could be: '*How and with what means is that meaning arranged?*'.

So, what kinds of meaning are there to be arranged? Meanings arise in social life, in social action and interaction, even though signs-as-meanings are always individual. The social is the domain of (at least some) regularity; it is shaped by the aggregation of the experiences of its many members, over past time and now. 'The individual' draws on that regularity, though individual use is shaped by the contingencies of individual experience, always in specific environments, expressed as *interest*. To say that meanings are individual is to indicate that signs are integrated into an individual's set of experiences and emerge in a specific moment as *interest*. Semiotically speaking, meaning is made twice: 'inwardly productive', it is established when the sign of an other has been interpreted in transformation with the individual's existing meanings-as-signs; 'outwardly productive', it is established in materialization/realization of sign-making.

In Colour plate 11, the meanings made in the sign of a hedgehog rest on this four-year-old's experiences: encounters with images and stories of hedgehogs; maybe an actual encounter with a hedgehog in the garden or a park. From this she formed her meaning, inwardly: the bumpy look, the spikiness, the wild messiness of the 'fur'. The meanings we hold as most 'private' are no less shaped in social environments, with socially made cultural resources, than are those we regard as 'public'. This is not to deny that we may 'hold' meanings which are entirely 'ours', as this sign of the hedgehog is; meanings which we have shaped for ourselves in a myriad of diverse experiences, kept to ourselves, never made into signs, not outwardly at least. Even though these meanings may never have been outwardly materialized as a sign, the stuff we have used to form the meanings 'internally' was social stuff.

So when I speak of 'meanings', I refer to semiotic resources encountered in the many communities in which I have participated and in which I now lead my life. To quote myself from just above 'the domain of (at least some) regularity; . . . shaped by the aggregations of many experiences' constantly transformed in my encounter with these as signs and constantly reintegrated into my inner resource of meaning.

What kinds of meanings are there and what kinds of meanings are they? There are meanings of different *kinds* at different *levels*. All derive in some form from and deal with the social world, always from a specific perspective, transformed in the light of my own semiotic resources. In Colour plate 12 there are meanings that might be called *conceptual* or *ideational* – the box present; the careful wrapping; its bow. There is the written heading. Above all there is *affect* as meaning; maybe the major, certainly the foregrounded meaning here: materialized in the carefully drawn bow; in the exuberance – the length, the angle; the 'freedom' of the coloured 'strokes'. The image strongly suggests that it is impossible to separate the *conceptual* – not to mention the 'cognitive' – and the *affective*. But so does the image of Colour plate 11; and I would say, the image of Colour plates 9 and 10. The physical world around us is accessible directly: I can feel uncomfortably cold or hot, feel hungry or not, feel the sharp pain when I stub my shoeless toe on a bit of the furniture. In communication however, the world is mediated and made accessible through the semiotic categories that culture provides. *Affect* is inevitably part of such mediation; it must have a central place in this theory of meaning. Indeed, my inclination is to erase the boundary of *affect* and *cognition* in this frame; it is the now entirely misleading construct of theories with their specific social, historical and political/ideological origins.

Resources

The *terms* and *names* here may be quite usual ones; in their use here as terms/names/signifiers they indicate a perspective toward entities, objects, practices and events as all treated as social and seen semiotically (Brice-Heath and Street, 2008; Hodge and Kress, 1988). The distinction between 'terms' and 'names' indicates an orientation to a place in theory for a 'term'; and 'name' indicates an orientation towards 'the function or characteristics 'being named' in the latter. Using this distinction, a *vector* is a *term* in a theory of visual representation which *names* the *function* of connecting depicted entities in images in specific semiotic relations; an *adjective* is a *term* in theories of the modes of *speech* or *writing*; it *names* the *function*, broadly, of 'adding' a quality – to qualify a noun.

Discourse

Discourse deals with the production and organization of *meaning* about the world from an institutional position. Following the work of Michel Foucault (Foucault, 1982; Kress 1984/89; Kress and van Leeuwen, 2001; Fairclough, 1989, 1993), *discourses* are taken to be meaning-resources available in a society to make sense of the world, *social* and *natural*, at a larger level. The term 'discourse' *functions* in the theory as a resource for constructing epistemological coherence in texts and other semiotic objects. *Discourse* refers to 'institutions' and the knowledge they produce about the world which constitutes their domain (Kress, 1984/1989). Knowledge about the world which is the institution's domain of relevance and responsibility is continuously produced. Examples of such institutions are education, medicine, science, law, 'the church', and more often and somewhat less tangibly, institutions such as 'the family'. Knowledge is produced in and shaped by the perspectives of a particular institution. 'Discourse' *names* both the complex as well as the understandings derived in encounters with such knowledge. In these encounters 'we' produce what we then hold as our knowledge about our world. *Discourse* shapes and *names* the routes through which we (have come to) know the socially shaped world as one kind of *knowledge*.

We encounter discourses in and via *semiotic objects*: buildings, texts, rituals may serve as examples of such semiotic objects. Texts and objects are the site of emergence of several discourses: intersecting, cross-cutting, running in parallel, contesting. Figures 6.1a and 6.1b show two photographs of the Senate House building of the University of London to illustrate this point.

The monumentalist style has strong affinities both with some public buildings of Germany in the 1930s, associated with the name of Albert Speer, as it has with some of Stalinist Russia – the central tower of Moscow State University for instance – but apparent also in the architecture of the 1930s in many places, whether in Europe, in the US, in Australia (for instance, some of the early buildings of the University of Queensland, in Brisbane). Wikipedia's entry (5 March 2009) on the Senate House building is informative, especially when read in relation to a Foucauldian concept of discourse. In the building itself, a discourse of monumentalism is overwhelmingly evident. In its entrance hall that discourse is linked with classicist 'Art Deco' ornamentations, a combination which, for me, is entirely reminiscent of buildings constructed in the 1930s in Nuremberg for the annual rallies of the National Socialist Workers' Party of Germany, the NSDAP. Wikipedia's entry on Art Deco is revealing in that respect: 'Although many design movements have political or philosophical roots or intentions, Art Deco was purely decorative. At the time, this style was seen as elegant, functional, and modern' (Wikipedia, 5 March 2009).

Figure 6.1a Senate House, University of London

Figure 6.1b Entrance hall, Senate House

   The connection with 'political or philosophical roots' points directly to *discourse*; the disarmingly naïve 'Art Deco was purely decorative' points in the opposite direction; as much aesthetic discussion does. Two points are important to add: the signifier of 'monumentalism' could serve to realize a nuanced range of (political) signifieds – whether those of 'National Socialism' in Germany; those of Stalinist communism; or various splinters of the global movement of fascism, as in depression-ravaged 1930s Australia (where the official opening of Sydney Harbour Bridge was interrupted by a member of the far-right 'New Guard', Francis de Groot, opposed to the Labour State Government of Premier Jack Lang, intending to signal the start of a putsch); or early 1930s Britain. *Discourses* draw their sustenance somewhat deeper and have a life independent of the surfaces of party-politics; yet are intricately linked to them.

   One point here is about the 'institutions' which stood behind the global phenomenon of fascism; as indeed can be asked at any time about such 'global' movements. This is decisive for my interest in the 'banal': the revealing of social life; in some ways such signs lie closer to where discourses are shaped. From this it also becomes clear that *discourses* have a 'reach' which goes well beyond specific societies and cultures including their – in this respect – relatively superficial political arrangements.

   A second point is to draw attention to the 'overlapping', the 'conjunctions' and 'layering' of *discourses* in texts or other semiotic entities and the effects of these complex ensembles of discourses in the production of ideology. The 'purely decorative' Art Deco ornamentation of Senate House combined with its 'monumentalism' serves to aestheticize the brutality of the latter; as it did on the rallying grounds of the National Socialist Workers' Party in Nuremberg; as did the 'wedding cake' decorations in a somewhat differently motivated conjunction in Moscow, some twenty years later. Yet while 'Art Deco' could serve to aestheticize a species of brutalism, its conjunction with that brutalist discourse gives some hints of the potentials for meaning of Art Deco as a signifier/sign: and *its* ideological functions.

   The conjoining of discourses into complexes as *ideology* is neither accidental nor merely contingent; it serves specific, describable social purposes. *Semiotic objects*, whether as buildings, written texts, stories casually told, films, gardens and their layout, video games, the layouts and contents of museums and supermarkets are the material sites for the conjoining of discourses and their emergence in material and naturalized form.

Genre

As a term in the theory, *genre* addresses the semiotic 'emergence' of social organization, practices and interactions. It names and 'realizes' knowledge of the world as *social action* and *interaction* – that part of the social world which is about my actions in interrelation with others, in social relations. It comes through participation in *events* formed of such actions experienced as recognizable *practices*. These *events* and *practices* are experienced by the participants as having relative regularity and stability. *Terms* for the *events* in their semiotic (rather than their social) guise are *ritual, genre. Genre* and *ritual* indicate and *name* the *participants* in these (inter-) actions in terms of their social *relations*. The *meanings* of genre are a function of my experience of practices and events, in their social and in their semiotic guise.

Mode

Mode is the third *term* here; as an organizing and shaping meaning-resource, it is at the same level as *discourse* and *genre. Mode* is meaningful: it is shaped by and carries the 'deep' ontological and historical/social orientations of a society and its cultures with it into every sign. *Mode* names the material resources shaped in often long histories of social endeavour and available as meaning resources. In that guise, of meaning-resource, it belongs here. The potentials of *modes* are encountered in the *signs* made with a *mode.* At the same time, *mode* sits somewhat uncomfortably here: as a means for realizing/materializing meaning – as a response to the question 'With what means?' – *mode* belongs in the next section; and Chapter 6 deals with just that.

We might put it like this: *discourse* offers meanings to be realized; it shapes the world of knowledge as ideational 'content'; and provides a social-conceptual location. *Genre* offers the means for contextualizing/locating/situating that meaning in social spaces and at the same time provides an account of the social characteristics of those spaces. *Mode* offers meaning-laden means for making the meanings that we wish or need to make material and tangible – 'realizing', 'materializing' meanings.

The two terms, *discourse* and *genre,* make it possible to refer to '*the what*' and '*the how*' of meaning-making and of meanings in the world; they account for 'what the world is *about*' and 'what is *going on* in the world': who is involved, in what ways, in the events themselves as much as in the actions of communicating about them. *Modes,* in their varying affordances, make it possible to make meanings material with specific ontological effects, according to the intentions of rhetor and designer.

There are few *names* for discourses: the ones we do have are vague and too widely used, even though they are not securely established nor agreed on. In their naming they hover between the (usually negatively) evaluative – *sexist discourse* for instance, or *racist discourse* – or the more descriptive, such as *discourses of gender.* They do point, generally, to phenomena which are easily recognized and difficult to describe; as with *religious discourses, legal discourse.*

The term *discourse* has been subject to cavalier usage – rivalled maybe only by the term *literacy.* This rests on confusions in several different directions. On the one hand, and in a sense trivially, the term as introduced from (Socio-)linguistics is used to mean, broadly, 'any extended stretch of language'. In that use it is often treated as synonymous with *text.* On the other hand, in the use of the term introduced from Sociology it means broadly 'a socially salient domain of concern with its entities, participants, relations and processes'. In many forms of discourse analysis, the emphasis tends to be on describing socially produced complexes of knowledge rather than on the formal semiotic means of their realizations. As a consequence, this semiotic domain is under-lexicalized: it lacks terms and names. The different uses and their different implications swirl about, giving rise to vague and casual use, where the words 'discourse' and 'topic' or 'issue (of social interest)' (e.g. 'fashion discourse', 'shopping discourse', 'discourse of family', 'discourse of war', 'discourse of the economy') are readily interchangeable. Frequently, 'site' of interaction — 'classroom discourse', 'internet discourse' — becomes the referent for this *name*.

Genre labels are somewhat more secure; some have a solid standing in ordinary usage — *film noir, novel, Spaghetti Western, family picnic, photo romance, editorial, wedding photo, flowchart, Sunday Mass, piano concerto, weather forecast, lesson.* Here too there are few labels compared to the number of semiotic entities and events which clearly are generically organized; and here too agreement on the applicability of the terms is unreliable. We know what a *passport photo* looks like compared to a photo a friend has taken of me at a party. There are explicit instructions surrounding the passport photo (Figure 6.2): what the photo must show; how much neck; head positioned looking straight-on at the camera; no smiling. These signs document a specific, regulated social relation of subject to authority: for political reasons more tightly policed than ever before. The passport photo shows me as imagined by the purposes of authority. The 'posed shot' — Figure 6.3 — shows me in a different institutional frame, that of the professional practices of studio photography. We know what an *interview looks, sounds* and *feels* like for quite similar reasons; or what a *news broadcast* looks and sounds like.

Figure 6.2 Passport photo   *Figure 6.3* Posed shot

Genre mediates between the social and the semiotic: it points to *social organization* and provides semiotic *arrangements* which realize these: hence my comment that genre provides 'means for contextualizing/locating/situating'. Depending therefore on the degrees and forms of power at work in the social environment, a relatively pliable, flexible, dynamic resource for arrangements, or, as in the case of the passport photo, of a quite inflexible kind. It is necessary of course, as always, to recognize power also in its ameliorated or disguised forms, as in the *family snap*. It is useful to ask what would *not* constitute a *family snap*: what regularities would need to be contravened, in what manner? In a *genre* social roles and relations are described and prescribed, more or less rigidly. *Interactions* are social events; as *genres*, interactions become shaped by *discourse* and through *mode*. So in the mode of *speech*, an interaction can be a *conversation* or an *interview*; an *argument* or a *discussion*; a *tutorial,* a *lecture* or a *sermon*. Each specifies and projects particular social relations and organization. The shifts in genre are responses to and parallel social shifts; though it is essential to be aware that shifts in semiotic form can, equally, produce shifts in social givens. If social actions have semiotic effects, it is also the case that semiotic work has social effects. One might say, provisionally: from a social perspective there are *actions, interactions* and *processes* and one can ask what social relations are at issue. From a semiotic perspective there is a *text* and one can ask what *genre* is shaping and organizing the text. From that one can hypothesize about and get an indication of the social environment which generated the genre.

The shapes and boundaries of *genres* are by no means firm; they vary with social changes: something which, no doubt, has always been the case. Yet in my social world, the rate of change in generic forms over the recent three decades or so has proceeded at an increasing pace. This acceleration is an effect of the acceleration of change in social settings and environments. In any case, *framings* are always weaker in informal settings than in formal settings – a tautology, but maybe useful to point to the effects of power in this.

Discourse answers the questions: 'What is the world about?' and 'How is it organized as knowledge?'. *Genre* answers the question: 'Who is involved as a participants in this world; in what ways; what are the relations between participants in this world?'. *Mode* answers the question: 'How is the world best represented and how do I aptly represent the things I want to represent in this environment?'.

Most social actions and interactions are not treated as semiotic events nor seen in generic terms. A game of tennis is a game of tennis and as such a *social* event; it is entirely possible, however, to see it as a *semiotic* event. Cricket, that once quintessentially English game, is or at least had until very recently been seen in what Barthes called mythic terms, a sign of what Englishness was about. Hence discussions of the kind: 'Is something (to be seen as) a genre or not?', 'Should it have a genre label or not?' are best settled by reference to whether and how it has been interpreted. *Action* is not a genre label, nor is *interaction*; unless either is interpreted as a semiotic event, as an actual or a quasi *communication*; it is then seen as a semiotic event and it has become a semiotic *term*.

Actions and processes

Actions and *processes* happen in time and they 'take place' somewhere, in social, semiotic and physical space; they have temporal and spatial location. A semiotic theory has to provide resources to indicate the *locations* of *participants, actions* and *events*: the two terms *orientation* and *deixis* might serve. Cultures and *modes* in cultures vary widely in their development and use of these features.

Orientation serves as a *term* which *names* an effect on the person who engages with a semiotic object: the *genre* of *sermon* orients me as to what social situation I am in; the *discourse* emerging in and through the *genre* of sermon orients me as to the *knowledge domain* I am in; not, for instance, a Darwinian account of creation. The past tense form of the *genre* of *narrative* orients me to the fact that I am in the world of a fictional past. While the genre of the *lobby* of a public building orients me socially/ institutionally; the decor of the lobby – the discourse there – orients me discursively. *Orientation* describes (the establishing of) a position in the social and the (culturally mediated) natural world; a position in the affective dimensions provided by a culture; in time and in space, themselves seen as socially produced categories. *Orientation* is about *social navigation* semiotically done: much as the fixing of latitude and longitude became essential in the long history of seafaring.

Deixis can serve as the *term* which *names* locations and directions within the semiotic object, which *direct* participants. 'Signage' in a building or in public spaces generally has a deictic function: arrows in the paving of a railway station may mark the way to the taxi rank.

Other signs tell me to pass *here* and not to enter *there*. In an *image* the gaze of a depicted entity leads me to 'follow' that gaze – 'What's that cat looking at?'. In English, many words are deictically marked, as are many grammatical particles: *come* vs. *go*; *lend* vs. *borrow*; *to* vs. *from*; *leave* vs. *return*; and so on. In a waiting room, the arrangement of the furniture tells me where to go and where not to go. The handles of secateurs instruct me with which hand and how I should hold and use them; the shape of urinals in the men's room issues quite explicit directions. *Deixis* names the process whereby my *attention* and that of others is directed to specific entities, objects, aspects of the social and physical world in specific ways: '*where* I am' in relation to you or to some location; '*where* you are'; but also '*how* you are' (an attitudinal/ affective positioning); and '*who* you are' (a positioning in terms of social identity).

Orientation and *deixis* answer questions such as 'Where am I?' and 'How do I know my way?' 'How can I/do I locate myself and others?' Figure 6.4 shows the stamps used to mark the passports of non-EU citizens at the borders of countries belonging to the Schengen group; these exemplify deixis in one kind of visual form. The rectangle of each stamp is, in this environment, an apt signifier for the domain of the respective state – itself indicated by capital letters, say S for Sweden, DK for Denmark. The arrow pointing in to the little rectangle (bottom, left) suggests 'entered'; the arrow pointing out suggests 'departed'. *Location* suggests *space* more than it does *time,* so it is a term subordinate to orientation and deixis. Orientation and deixis are independent

Figure 6.4 EU passport stamps, 'entered' → and 'departed' ←

Figure 6.5 Giorgia

and connected features: knowing that I am in a *sermon* (*orientation*) still leaves me in need of features so that I can navigate (*deixis*) in that (discursively organized) social space.

In Figure 6.5, a drawing made by four-year-old Giorgia, *orientation* and *deixis* are evident in a number of ways: as orientation, in the domain, that of the *family*; in a domain of *affect* and *aesthetics*; in the social domain of the child framed by the house, by her parents, in her family, in between mum and dad; affective, spatial, social. Spatial *deixis* is present in overt markers of place and position – between the parents; in her drawing herself as being quite small; of her admiration of her mother shown in the 'colourfulness' of the drawing of that figure.

Deixis is a socially produced cultural-semiotic resource. Consequently the deictic resources of cultures differ widely and at times in ways that seem inexplicable. The Dyirbal are an Australian Aboriginal people living along the escarpment of the Great Dividing Range in far North Eastern Australia. The terrain is cut by steep ravines and deep valleys; it is covered by dense rainforest. Dyirbal, the language (Dixon, 1976), has an enormously finely articulated set of deictic particles; not just the English *that, this, there, here*, but forms which allow a pinpointing of the kind 'there, 200 yards upstream across the creek, at the base of that hillside over there', or 'up there, in the undergrowth on the side of that creek'. In the rugged terrain – the rainforested escarpment – which is the home of the Dyirbal, that degree of precision is essential for ordinary day-to-day social and spatial navigation.

Linking

Linking of entities – humans with humans, with places, objects; objects with objects; objects with processes; processes linked with processes – is a major resource for making meaning. Much of semiosis is about *linking* of various kinds: *linking* by and through actions; by adjacency and proximity, temporal or spatial. Again, cultures differ vastly in what their societies have regarded as essential, as central, as marginal or as simply not present, and not visible therefore. Modes differ in how their affordances for realizing such relations have been developed, along the demands of the society in which the mode has been used.

Human action and (inter-)action in and on the world, involves *relations between participants* – people, objects, phenomena; human, animate, inanimate – in processes of *action* and of *relation*, of *doing* and *being*, spatially, temporally, socially. *Participants* are involved in various ways – as '*doers*'/'*actors*', as '*done to*'/'*sufferers*', as those who are '*beneficiaries*', or as those who are simply '*involved*' in some *circumstantial* way. The range and kind of such relations varies from culture to culture. *Actions* and *relations* are *initiated* by one or more of the *participants*; or actions and relations may be represented as *simply happening, as simply 'being the case'*, in *image*, in *movement* and *actions in space*. Relations may affect one participant alone or many participants – as in *games* played in a school playground – or they may involve reciprocal actions between the participants.

The possibilities of *realization* of such relations vary from mode to mode. Whatever the mode and its affordances, its *forms* of linking and separating – of participants, objects, events – are always meaningful. Originating in one mode, say in *play* in the schoolyard, a meaning moves across to another mode and genre – in a *spoken recount* of the game, for instance, in forms apt for that mode. It repays close attention to see what actions, relations and processes exist in any mode, and what relations can be imagined or are implied in that mode: whether in the tableaux which young children constantly make on the floor of their bedrooms; in a comic strip; in textbooks; in an illustrated book for children; in a Lego construction (Kress, 1997a).

The three-dimensional features of Lego blocks and their constructions (Colour plate 13) afford meanings about *balance* and *symmetry*, something far less available in two-dimensional drawing and not available – or utterly differently – in writing or speech. These are the building blocks of *arrangements* of all kinds, in all modes, as *actions* and *events in time* – to *precede*, to *follow*; as *actions, events* and *relations in space* – to be *before* or to be *after* – to *invade*, to *occupy*, to *inhabit*; to be *at,* to come *from,* to be *with,* to go *to,* to lag *behind*; as relations of *action* and *interaction*; as relations of *existence* and *being* – to *be*, to *become*, to *happen*. There are actions which more directly *show*, or *demonstrate* or *name* social links – to *involve*, to *follow*, to *co-operate,* to *join*; in *actional* and *non-actional relations* such as to *be inferior*, to *be below*, to *equal*, to *be above* (Hodge and Kress, 1979).

Many events, phenomena, objects, are *linked*, that is, they have been *brought together, collected together*, as the result of social decisions and judgements. These relations are handled in distinct ways in any society and its cultures and hence handled distinctively semiotically. *Linking* may be the most useful general term. The question socially and semiotically is 'What *forms of linking* are available in a particular social and cultural world?'. Are the links made through actions or through various forms of non-actional relations? Are they links of spatial or temporal contiguity and proximity? Other terms name specific relations of linking: *conjoining, adjacency*, for instance; each of these being specific in particular ways. There is a judgement to be made between the need for general, less specific terms and those needed to name particular relations.

Processes and effects: making and remaking meaning

The *processes* described in this chapter relate to meanings as resource. The *representation of meanings* is the subject of the next chapter. In social-semiotic theory other *processes of semiosis* also need to be described. '*Semiotic work*' names all processes which are part of the *making of meaning* – in the ongoing process of semiosis, *externally* and *visible*, or *internally* and *not* (immediately) *visible*.

Processes of semiosis

The *processes of semiosis* are specific; and in this chapter several are identified and named. The making of a *text* – as an externally realized *semiotic entity* – entails that the *flow of semiosis* be *arrested* for a moment. That constitutes a momentary *punctuation* of *semiosis* in which *processes of framing* play their part. Preceding, though also concurrent with and in a lesser way following that moment there are *rhetorical processes*. In these, the *rhetor* analyses and assesses the *environment of communication* and reflects on the *resources* needed to shape the *message* and the *media* to be used for maximally persuasive effects with the *audience* of the *message*. Using the term *rhetoric* responds to the new social and technological givens and provides a necessary frame for considering *communication* at all points.

Rhetorical processes

Rhetorical processes underlie, precede and then become *design processes*. The *rhetor's* task is a political one, with *political* and *communicational* effects, namely to provoke and produce the rearrangement of social relations by semiotic means. The *designer's* task by contrast is a *semiotic* one; to transform political intent into semiotic form. In the present period it may be essential to focus on the contrasts between *design* and *critique*. While *critique* attempts to uncover 'political purposes' in the effects of past uses of power, of *past rhetorical action* as it is manifest in existing *texts*, *design* aims at implementing rhetorical intentions, which will have their effects in the future. *Critique* is necessarily backward-oriented, focused on the past actions of (usually) powerful others; *design* is *prospective*, future-oriented, focused on putting the *rhetorical conceptions* of the *rhetor/designer* – most often the same person – into the world.

Before the *processes* of (*material*) *framing* can take place, the *meanings* to be framed need to be *fixed* modally – using *fixed* in the sense of the *fixing* of light on the prepared chemical surfaces of older forms of film. The *fixing of meaning* has several aspects: in choice of *modes*, of *discourse,* of *genre* – as an answer to such usually entirely naturalized and therefore implicit questions 'In what *modes*, in what *discourse(s)*, in what *genres* shall we present the meaning?'. The *selection* of *modes* affects choice of discourse and vice versa, as each of these does with *genre*, with its questions about the social relations which shape and appear in the *text*: as *editorial* in a newspaper; as a *contribution to a professional journal*; as an *entry on a website*; as an uploaded video on *YouTube*; and so on. In other words, meaning is *fixed* three times over – *materially* and *ontologically/semiotically* as *mode*; *institutionally* and *epistemologically* as *discourse*; and *socially* in terms of *apt* social relations, as *genre*.

Framing

Framing of various kinds is essential in all decisions about *punctuation of semiosis* and the subsequent *fixing of meaning* in *modal, generic* and *discursive form*: through *mode* and its entities; through available types of *genres*, through available *discourses*; and *framing* in forms of its *display* on/in *sites of appearance* and media of *dissemination*.

The *process* of making a *text* can be imagined as a sequence: starting with *a prompt* and the *interpreter's* interpretation of that *prompt*. On that basis the rhetor *shapes* a message as a response, influenced and shaped by the assessment of the communicational environment and their interest in that environment. The rhetor's assessment and interest leads to *design processes* in which the modal implementation, as an *orchestration* of modes, apt for the *rhetor's meaning*, is settled and *shaped*, using available *cultural/semiotic resources*. This is a new punctuation of semiosis; with meaning fixed in *modes* and *frames* – modal, generic, discursive – apt to the social environment. This constitutes – at the same time – the *processes of production*, leading to *orchestrated multimodal ensembles* as *material text*.

Semiotic work has social effects. *Social* as much as *semiotic work* is preceded by yet other processes: of *attending* (*attention*) to an aspect of the *social/semiotic world*, in this case the *prompt*, of *choosing* (*choice*) of *processes* and *resources* and of the consequent *apt selection* of these in the shaping of a *response*.

Process and change

The origin of decisions to *link* and the principles for doing so – depending on the kind of *linking* involved – are judgements about similarity and difference, relatedness, complementarity, functions which link actors and objects, objects and objects, according to culturally specific criteria. As a consequence, *linking* entails and rests on *classification*, more strongly or less so. In any one society and its cultures, *classification* and the forms of *arrangements* available are strongly related.

Classification

Classification is a social and semiotic process carried out by semiotic means. Its effect is to stabilize the social world in particular ways; as such it has far-reaching consequences. *Classification* provides the legitimation of present and future actions, processes, judgements and valuations. *Classification* reaches from the most innocuous – the 'private' *holiday snap*, the *class photograph* to the more cuspish *wedding photograph*, to the anything but innocent *official photograph* of participants at some significant meeting (e.g. the once famous photos of the leadership of the former Soviet Union arranged on the dais of the Kremlin Wall on the anniversary of the October Revolution). The processes of *classification* are active in all semiotic processes and entities: whether in *architecture*, in newspaper *layout*, in domestic *design*, in *family relations*. Its seemingly innocuous character helps to make its political effects more effective. Given that the semiotic resources of a society are constantly (re)fashioned in the social-semiotic work of interaction, through the resources of its signifiers, *classifications* reflect the social organization which has produced them and which is constantly reaffirmed, remade and naturalized through them.

Meanings of *causality* (as against a-causal meanings) are entailed, more strongly or less, through 'action' as well as through the *ordering* of events, states or processes and the participants involved. *Ordering* rests on and suggests an interpretation of the 'priority' among phenomena, where 'prior' can have any one of a number of meanings: prior in 'significance'; prior 'temporally' or spatially; prior causally in relation to the subsequent phenomenon. This can be realized in spatial relations within and between images; as 'first' in a sequence or as last; in moving images and their temporal relations. *Classifications* can be established using signifiers capable of suggesting ordering of any kind.

In the two images of Colour plates 14 and 15, 'prior' and 'later' depend on a sequential ordering, suggesting 'entering' and 'leaving', for instance. This is a different means of achieving a 'similar effect' to the placement of the arrows in the passport stamps. Such meanings have distinct material and formal articulations in different modes. Some modes have a more elaborate set of terms in one semiotic area than do other modes. What is expressed by spatial or temporal adjacency, or as position in the sequence of a linear arrangement in *image*, may be expressed as a preposition in *speech* or in *writing*; what is expressed as the word 'follow' in *speech* or *writing*, can be expressed through temporal order in *speech*, *dance*, in *gesture*; or through spatial *ordering* in other modes. Some terms and the meaning-potentials named by them, may not exist at all in some modes; or, putting it in terms that I have used just now, some modes may not have the potentials to realize certain semiotic features.

In Figure 4.2 (page 55), a drawing by a six-year-old football fan, *linking* is done through spatial proximity. Additional meaning is conveyed by the degree of proximity and by the orientation of the players, facing each other. In London teenage speech the heading might be 'You look'n at me?' spoken with steeply rising intonation, aggressively challenging in tone of voice. The mode of writing adds information, though in a plain form.

Many of the meanings discussed here can be realized in different *modes*. How they are depends on history and culture. In the passport stamps (Figure 6.4) the direction of the arrow – either pointing *in* to the little rectangle or *out* – 'realizes' what in writing would become words such as 'entering' or 'departing'. Certainly, the stamp 'means' that, and yet it also 'means' differently and more: it is, literally, 'spatial', in a way the word 'enter' is not. That is a reminder that 'meaning' exists in its specific realization, when it has been fixed in a specific mode and framed modally/ontologically, generically/socially and discursively/ideologically.

It is not difficult to verify this for oneself by constructing 'glosses': 'translations' and transductions of images such as Figure 4.2 (Chelsea vs. Arsenal) – a visually/spatially realized form of a meaning that might be realized as 'confrontation' in speech or writing.

Translation

Translation is a process in which meaning is moved. It is moved 'across', 'transported' – from mode to mode; from one modal ensemble to another; from one mode in one culture to that 'same' mode in another culture – what has been regarded as translation from one 'language' to another. Meaning is moved from one genre to another; from one discursive/ideological complex to another. Meanings connect across modes, genres, objects. The processes and facts of *classification* as they appear in *architecture* are connected with *classification* as it appears in the organization of a family or of a business; they in turn are reflected in *classifications* apparent in *photographs* or in the organization of a business, reflected as in the visual *organogram* of its management structure.

Processes of 'moving meaning' and of relating meanings across modes need a name. The term *translation* most readily suggests itself. Here it is used to name a major re-articulation of meaning, of whatever kind: from one 'semiotic domain to another'; from one semiotic category to another. This might be within one culture, for instance, from a text in one genre to a text in a different genre, staying in the same mode. Or it may be a move from a mode in one culture to the 'same' mode in another culture: a *novel* can be translated from English to Russian, staying within the mode of *writing*. Or it may involve shifts in mode, from *writing* to *speech, sound track, music*, as in the translation of a *short story* to a *radio play*. It may involve shifts in discourse; either within the same mode or with a change in mode. Here, *translation* is the term used to describe significant shifts in meaning: across *genres*, across *modes*, across *cultures* and across any combination of these. If *translation* is used as the most general term to name changes in representation, it leaves the need for terms to name changes of a more specific kind.

The two terms used here are *transduction* and *transformation*. When the re-articulation of meaning involves a change of *mode* it necessarily entails a change in the *entities* of the *mode*. As mentioned before, the modes of *writing* and speech have *words*, the mode of *image* does not. The change of entity in the re-articulation is a thoroughgoing process; for instance, it involves a change in ontological orientation. The term *transduction* is used to signal this process of drawing/'dragging' meaning across from one mode to another. In *transformation* the process involves no change in mode. As a consequence, there is no change of entities; the process operates on and with the same set of entities. The process is not as thoroughgoing: for instance no change in ontology is involved. *Orderings* of entities are changed, but staying within the set of entities of the one *mode*.

To restate: there are two kinds of moving meaning and/or altering meaning: one by moving across modes and changing entities (and usually *logics*) – *transduction*; the other, staying within a mode (and staying therefore with the same logic) but reordering the entities in a syntagm – *transformation*.

Transduction

Transduction is seen as subordinate to – as one kind of – *translation*. It names the process of moving meaning-material from one mode to another – from *speech* to *image*; from *writing* to *film*. As each *mode* has its specific *materiality* – sound, movement, graphic 'stuff', stone – and has a different history of social uses, it also has different *entities*. *Speech,* for instance, has words, *image* does not. That process entails a (usually total) re-articulation of meaning from the entities of one mode into the entities of the new mode.

As a (not so) simple example, imagine the transduction of the meaning of the image in Figure 6.5: not as a *description*, as in: '*In this image I see three figures, one seemingly a child . . .',* but as a full recasting of what that image means, though now in a spoken 'story' or recount: '*I think my mum is the most beautiful mum in the world. I love it when she lets me wear my party dress. My dad is very nice. He has a bad leg and has to carry a stick.'* In the image there are no '*names'* for any of its entities or their relations; nor for the attributes of entities – if we should even describe it like that; words have to be found for these, but the selection of these words rests on our selection of specific aspects of the meaning of that image: others could have been selected by other 'transductors'. Where in the image there is colour, size, distance, height, and so on, to realize *affect* for instance, words now have to be found. There is a need to ask seriously how a meaning realized in one mode can be newly articulated as meanings in the new mode(s); that is, how the meaning of the original can be (re-)articulated in the 'translating mode'. In *gesture,* for instance, movement is used to 'mean' movement – an iconic relation of meaning and form; in *writing,* movement is conveyed by a name – 'he *walked slowly'.*

Many of the examples in this book involve *transduction.* The change from the *diary* account of blood circulation to the *concept map* involves *transduction.* It is an absolutely common, constant, ordinary and profound process in everyday interactions: our dreams are made of it. Here is one other example. Figures 6.6a and 6.6b exemplify a number of points about *transduction* and about the process of *synaesthesia,* on which *transduction* rests.

Figure 6.6a is a page made up (by me) of six small square pieces of paper from a phone notepad. One summer weekend, the then five-year-old had been drawing these images, unbeknown to his parents, who were entertaining friends in the garden. Seeing him laying them out in pairs on the floor in the hallway of their house, I asked what he was doing. Of the first pair he said: 'The boy is in life and the dog is in life, so they're in the correct order.' Of the second pair he said: 'The plane is in the air and the bomb is in the air, so they're in the correct order.' Of the third pair he said: 'The patterns are in the correct order.'

Some few weeks later, at the end of the school year, he brought home his school exercise books. On leafing through them, somewhat aimlessly, I discovered the page shown in Figure 6.6b, a page from a school exercise book. The date on the page reveals that the exercise had been done some four weeks before the images in Figure 6.6a.

Figure 6.6a Michael: classification 1 (home)

Figure 6.6b is an exercise in classification – 'linking like with like'. When that was completed, time left in class had been spent, it seems, in colouring in the shapes: an exercise in control of pens and a means of filling time enjoyable to the children. My question is about the relation between the two events, separated by several weeks, one done in school as 'work', the other out of school and done out of the child's interest, unbidden. *Classification* connects the two, though in the interval the characteristics of that notion seem to have changed significantly: 'like' is still connected with 'like', though now the notion of 'like' has become more *abstract*, much more *general*.

Semiosis, involving classification, had clearly continued, silently and invisibly, so to speak. At a particular point – the prompt is not known to me and I did not ask – 'inner' semiosis became external; it was *fixed, punctuated, framed*. The conception of 'like' was 'framed' and modally 'fixed' in the shape of the six images as well as in their

Draw a line to join the things which are the same.

Figure 6.6b Michael: classification 2 (school)

laying out as pairs on the floor. In Figure 6.6b, the process of linking 'like' with 'like' was done manually; the manner of holding the pen and of drawing the lines typical of a five-year-old is visible in the lines. The act was physical/manual and semiotic/ conceptual at the same time: as indeed it had become in the later instance, now with a much more general sense of 'like'. Again there is the material stuff, the bits drawn on paper. That material act of laying out followed the material act of drawing and that followed the inner conception and design of the drawings.

I assume that language was not involved in this at all, at least not overtly, audibly. Language as *speech* appeared only when I asked Michael what he was doing and he needed to formulate a response. Over the intervening weeks, *semiosis* in relation to this topic had obviously continued, though where before there had been the teacher's *prompt* to link 'like' entities/images by a line, demanding a material, a visual as well as a conceptual/semiotic act, now the conceptual work of drawing entities which were 'like' at some remove in abstraction and ordering them in a layout that *showed* their conceptual order, was done without *speech* or *writing*.

Before, the 'like' entities had been on the page of the exercise book; the task was the linking of entities present and that was done manually/graphically. Now the entities that were (going to be) 'like' had to be imagined, then drawn; at that point the linking had been done conceptually; the linking was then done in the process of laying the cards out in their matched order to show the classificatory schema. *Layout* was the mode used. These processes all involved *transduction*, as well as a 'move' between 'inner' and 'outer' representation. My verbal prompt 'What are you doing there?' then produced a further *transduction*, from *layout* on the floor to a *spoken* account of the principles of layout and classification.

This example has been enormously insightful for me: it exemplifies the 'trade' between inner and outer representation; the evidence and persistence of semiosis once prompted: the *prompt* in school and the action five or so weeks later; the *trans-formative* and *transductive* character of semiosis – whether from the relatively simple task of *classification*, prompted in the classroom, to the later, unbidden, much more abstract version; or the *transduction* of imagined entities → to drawn images → to the ordering in *layout* on the hallway floor → to the *transduction*, finally (as far as this example is concerned) into *speech*.

Given my present professional environment, my interest focuses on *learning*; and therefore on means of getting insightful evidence of learning; on means for the *recognition* of learning; and of course, real questions about *assessment* of learning. Any *principles of assessment* need to include the realization that wherever semiotic work has been done, meaning has been made, whatever the modes in which that hap-pened. It is the meaning made, not the meaning expected, which should be the focus of interest in assessment, at the first step. From there one can elucidate the principles, in this case, of the child's semiotic work. From that position one can attempt to construct a path to the learning that is expected, based now on an understanding of the principles that this learner brings to the task.

My interest is also theoretical. If we were to assess only the child's linguistic account of his images, his spoken commentary, we would have hugely reduced evidence available for assessment: nothing like the richness of the images themselves. The images and the words are not just different, the images are much 'fuller', more precise, more specific as indications of just what the child considered as 'like'. The child's spoken account is hugely general compared to the specificity of the images. The verbal account is a reduction of what was available to be understood and assessed in the visual representation.

Whether from the point of pedagogy or that of semiotics, the central issue is that of *recognition*: first, the *recognition* of learning in the semiotic and conceptual work done as such; and, second, the *recognition* of the work done in all modes. That needs a detailed description of the respective affordances of *speech* and *drawing*.

Transformation

Transformation is a less far-reaching process than that of *transduction*. It describes processes of meaning change through re-ordering of the elements in a text or other semiotic object, within the same culture and in the same mode; or across cultures in the same mode. In other words, the 'translation' of a novel from German to English would fall under the heading of transformation. The process is significant but as it involves the same entities and there is no ontological change, it is much less far-reaching.

The two images shown in Colour plates 9 and 10 stand in a sequence of 'earlier' and 'later' in the children's story in which they occur. They have the same elements; however, the order of the elements has been altered: there has been a transformation; and the viewer's perspective has also altered. That is, there has been a *transformation* in the sequence of elements in the two images; and there has been a consequent *transformation* in the inscribed viewing/reading position. Each can be described; each is meaningful, though differently.

Transformations apply to all syntagms, texts, and semiotic objects: a change from one genre to another – for instance from my tape-recorded account of a meeting to my telling about that meeting later; my writing of a report and then preparing an executive version of it. Similarly, a change of discourse would be seen as a transformation: the mode(s) stay, though different terms and relations appear in the transformed text.

Transformations are processes in which the elements remain while their ordering in an arrangement is changed. Hence a simple statement about *transformations* might be: same mode, same entities, in different order = new semiotic entity (= different meaning). *Transformations*, like *transductions*, can apply to any semiotic object.

The two processes, of *transformation* (re-ordering of elements – within the same mode, leading to change of semiotic object) and of *transduction* (moving meaning from one mode to another, by re-articulating meaning in the entities of the 'new' mode, leading to change of semiotic object) encompass the central aspects of semiotic change. Frequently both processes occur in the one text or semiotic object. Semiotic change always entails change in meaning; the changes in meaning entailed by these two 'operations' are each significant and profoundly different in kind. *Transformation* does not change the ontological constitution of the text/entity, the ontological 'location' of the semiotic object; *transduction* does.

In the rhetorical and design tasks so utterly characteristic of the contemporary social and communicational world, *transduction* and *transformation* are essential processes. As a matter of course many websites now address multiple audiences: in a social world deeply marked by profound difference and diversity it could not be different. This multiplicity might be to do with generation; profession; differences in cultural capital – to use Bourdieu's term – due to education and social class; pleasure; not to mention more specific and equally significant differences: religion, cultural differences of various kinds; gender; and so on. This means that there is a constant need for *translation* in the sense here indicated: each group may need to be addressed taking account of its interests and willingness or not to engage. As one such – entirely innocuous – example, take the website www.poetryarchive.org. It has a homepage, a set of pages for teachers, pages for students; and pages for children. Each of these is designed with clearly distinct styles and aesthetics in mind. Information is transducted, transformed: translated, with distinct modal ensembles.

This leaves a major problem of naming the process usually called 'translation' – a transport of meaning from one 'language' to another. It remains, of course, an instance of *translation* in the sense used here; its specific form is *transformation*. The mode remains: from writing to writing; or from speech to speech. It is a change within a mode, but across cultures. As modes are shaped by the histories of their making in specific societies, modes differ from culture to culture and from society to society. This kind of 'transformation' takes on some aspects of a more profound change. This is especially so if the script systems as well as the cultures differ: the affordances of an alphabetic script, for instance, differ profoundly from those of a character-based script.

Yet these '*transformations* across *mode* and *culture'* are not, in principle, different to those within one culture – though with the addition of cultural difference, that is, the effects of social history in the shaping of mode. It might be necessary therefore to speak of intra-cultural and cross-cultural *transformations* and *transductions*.

Characteristics of states and processes

Meanings of the kind described here often have a characteristic *manner of occurrence* or *appearance*. A social process, action, state, may be permanently as it is; it may be in the process of becoming so; or it may be so intermittently. A social relation (a *connection* let's say) may be *constant* or it may be *intermittent*. The *connection* may be unstable in some other way. Social relations may change their characteristics – they may undergo a change of state. To use an analogy: at some point, the gravy that I stir begins to *thicken*; or the sky outside *darkens* before an approaching storm. The meanings of *characteristics* of states, relations and processes are meanings to which we need to be attentive; and they require signifiers for their realization. Following linguistic usage (it seems unproblematic here), I use the term *aspect* for these meanings: that is, a particular *aspect* of a state, relation, process is brought into focus. These meanings are highly culture-specific.

In human (inter)action and relations, social and affective *proximity* and *distance* – are constant, crucial meanings. What is signalled are relations of *power* and relations of *solidarity*. The perspective from which *power* is viewed, as well as the direction of *power*, need to be specified. Is the point of view one from *lesser power* or one from *greater power*? The more powerful participant may or may not want to insist on the overt (semiotic) recognition of their greater *power*; the ability to make that choice is itself a sign of power. The participant with lesser power has no such choice – unless she or he is prepared to risk giving offence.

Distance – whether spatial or temporal – is a ready signifier of *power*; the more *power* at issue, the greater the *distance* that is felt to exist; the less the power involved, the less the distance that is felt. Following traditional usage here (Brown and Gilman, 1966) I refer to the two poles involved as those of *power* and *solidarity*.

With *power*, as with other social factors, there are meanings – and therefore apt signifiers – around *magnitude* and *intensity, significance* and *importance*. These are often signified by *height, amplitude, length, weight, size, extension* of various kinds. In a given *arrangement* or *syntagm, salience* can be an indicator of social significance – the soloists in a choral performance who stand at the front of the choir; the local dignitary who stands in front of a group of officials for whom she or he speaks. This dignitary may have other indicators of importance at her or his disposal, such as the salience bestowed by a large gold chain as the sign of office.

7 *Design* and *arrangements*: making meaning material

Design in contemporary conditions of text-making

Chapters 2 and 3 sketch a frame in which to think about communication, representation and, importantly, semiotic *production* in contemporary environments. The sketch characterizes the social environment as marked by instability and provisionality; it stresses the role of the market in shaping a habitus of *agency-as-choice* – even though it needs to be said immediately that for many members of society the realities of agency and choice are relatively spurious. These conditions make it possible and demand that individuals assume agency in the production of semiotic entities of all kinds – texts, 'arrangements', practices, objects. They do so not least in relation to the making of *knowledge,* of transforming *information* which they have selected in accord with their interests and needs, into the tools they need in their everyday social and communicational lives.

In this sketch, the environment of meaning-making is radically different to one still active in common-sense imaginations of communication. Yet shifts in authority have made individual *interest* central. These same changes have made formerly stable resources unreliable: *genres* are present, 'there'; yet they are fluid and insecure; representation, understood now as multimodal, is no longer dependably canonical. There *is* choice. What *genre* to use; how to reshape it; what *modes* to use for what purpose and for which audience; all are questions which – in principle at least – need to be dealt with newly in any act of communication.

That is, the environment in which processes of 'realization of meaning' – 'making meaning material' – take place, has to be understood. The frame for action is a rhetorical one; the *rhetor's interest* and assessment of the environment of communication shapes the *ground* of communication; that and the *interest* of *interpreters* of that *ground*, remade as a *prompt,* are decisive in shaping meaning. *Design* is the process of translating the rhetor's politically oriented assessment of the environment of communication into semiotically shaped material. In realizing the interests of rhetor and interpreter, *design* has moved to centre stage.

Design is prospective. It responds to demands which, in some way, are constantly new. Rather than being a competent implementation of conventionally given practices, *design* is transformative, hence inevitably innovative. In contemporary *semiotic production* and *communication* – the two now always linked – *agency* in the *interested* processes of *design* meets with the *affordances* – socially and semiotically – of the resources available for production. *Interest* and *agency* now extend to the choice and the uses of the facilities of *sites of appearance* and the *media* of dissemination.

Design: an essential (re)focusing

The term *design* has quite recently come into widespread use – fashionability even – in areas of the Humanities and the Social Sciences. As with any term that erupts into high visibility, one needs to ask about the reasons. Is there more than just fashion? Is it an indicator of corresponding changes in the larger social environment?

The earlier chapters give one answer. In thinking about 'semiotic production' – whether in relation to language or much more widely – it is possible to delineate a path, over the last seventy to eighty years, which begins with (adherence to) *convention*; solidly, unchallengeably established – other than in fenced-off areas such as the creative arts, grudgingly too in advertising and more recently in popular culture. In that environment, production was seen as *composition* in accordance with well-understood and accepted rules.

The mid-1950s witnessed a turning in that path. Serious challenges began to be made to its direction, above all in popular music. From the 1960s on and moving into the mid-1980s, the path of adherence to *convention* gave way, so much so that *critique* – being a 'critical reader', for instance – has now in turn become a comfortably mainstream road, as semiotic motherhood and apple pie. Now *design* is challenging to become the central term in semiotic work.

To take two concepts – *text* and *knowledge* – as examples. Texts, as *essay*, as *report* or 'story', were *composed*, guided by relatively well-understood and settled generic conventions. From the late 1960s, these conventions began to weaken, the rules began to fray. It became an urgent academic enterprise to subject *generic conventions* to *critique*, to challenge the power that seemed entrenched in and supported by conventions, seen to work to the benefit of some and to the detriment of others. When *critique* replaced *convention*, *composition* became problematic. The 'linguistic turn' (Rorty, 1967) marks that point, with its challenge of the 'innocence' of language and of processes of 'composition'. Yet critique can work only in relation to stable structures and environments; its task is to bring these into crisis. Environments marked by instability, provisionality, fluidity do not lend themselves to critique; the political needs of such environments demand the shaping force of *design*.

In contemporary conditions, knowledge is *made* in many sites: in wikis, in blogs, but also – without fuss or notice – in everyday conversation, in instances of unremarkable, banal interaction; in the compilation, for instance, of personally downloaded music libraries. When knowledge is *made* anywhere, by anyone, 'knowledge' ceases to be 'canonical': witness the increasingly bitter disputes around accounts of evolution. Canonical *representations* of knowledge become unstable, whether as *mode* (Should I use *writing* or *image*?) or as *genre* (Which is apt, the *essay* or the *narrative* or the *cartoon*?). *Writing*, previously the canonical mode par excellence, is giving way to *image*.

The 'school', as society's designated purveyor of hitherto canonical (forms of representation of) knowledge, has an impossible task. When knowledge is made by anyone anywhere, what is, what can and should be the place of the school? The school has the task of upholding canonical forms of knowledge and of representation without the support of clear direction from state or society. In popular culture, the very same practices of production which are censored in the school have acceptance and high status: 'sampling' in music, or 'mashing'. It is an extremely serious matter that contemporary forms of semiotic production – forms of composition – are poorly understood or not at all, as witness the moral panics around 'plagiarism', 'cutting and pasting', and so on (see Aspetsberger, 2008).

The state faces a cacophony of voices of a profoundly diverse society. The school is bound to be at a loss: ontologically, epistemologically, socially, aesthetically, ethically, ideologically. Nor are universities immune from these conditions and effects. Wikipedia appears as a source of reference in student work, including at Ph.D. level; internet sites jostle alongside the canonical media of book and journal in reference lists.

The debate of the 1990s, around *information* versus *knowledge*, has abated somewhat and settled into a new sense that 'knowledge' is always newly made rather than being communicated. What is communicated is 'information'. Knowledge is produced by individuals according to their *interest* and their need in their life worlds at the moment of making (Boeck, 2004). *Knowledge* and *meaning*, as much as the *texts* and *objects* which are their material realizations, are seen as the outcomes of processes of *design* motivated by individual interest.

Chapter 2 sets out some of the *social* and *economic* reasons for the emergence of *design* as the central term in semiotic production: *instability of social environments* (that is, the fragmentation, disappearance of stable, reliable, 'accepted' conventions); the strong insistence on and assumption of *agency* by individuals – including children at ever younger ages: a result of the dominance of the market rather than the state as the major social/political force and, increasingly, the emergence of children as a segment of the 'market' with purchasing power and hence a social force; and this in turn supporting a change from notions of social responsibility to individual choice. What is the case in the world of commodities is no less the case in the world of semiotic actions, with the *multiplicity of semiotic resources* available for the shaping/ realizations of meaning, including meanings of identity.

At the same time, the instability of social environments has destroyed clear and acceptable models for action and behaviour. In the neo-liberal capitalist market, individuals are assumed to take and have responsibility for their actions. The resumption of *agency* by individuals – urged by the state and forced by the market – means that the shaping of meaning and of identity, becomes a matter of individual *design*. A multiplicity of resources provides the means – for those who can act in the market – for their 'individual' shaping of identity, even though the means are those made available to all by the market.

Even those with lesser means or few, are subject to the requirement to assume responsibility for the shaping of meaning in their social environments. The convergence of social conditions, changing semiotic means and affordances in production and dissemination come together to make *design* the usual, normal, taken-for-granted, the necessary and essential semiotic disposition and practice.

What is *design*? A homely example

In my kitchen cutlery drawer there are two potato peelers, shown in Figure 7.1. The one on the right I regard as traditional; that is, as a child I was asked to peel potatoes with a peeler quite like that; and I do so still. The other remains, for me, 'new'. The 'traditional' peeler assumes a particular relation between my right hand and the implement; it also assumes a particular relation between my left hand and the potato. It assumes that the potato fits — snugly, comfortably — into my hand curved around it, leaving about a third of the potato free to be peeled. When I do, my hands touch, the thumb of my right hand partly resting on the thumb of my left hand, acting as a kind of hinge; the fingers of my right hand, curved around the peeler partly rest on/touch the rim of the hand holding the potato. I hold the potato firmly: I feel that I have control in this process, which is comfortably integrated with my body, with the shape of my hands. The action is unforced; it seems natural.

When the potato is too large, this ensemble becomes awkward, the more so the bigger the potato. Now the 'traditional' peeler is less suited for my hand, which can no longer touch and rest on my left thumb; the ensemble is less prepared for the large object to be peeled. Hands, potato, peeler still form an ensemble, but not harmoniously. Now I do notice that I have to hold the peeler at a certain angle to get it to work; I have to give thought to the fact that if the angle is too steep and the pressure of hand and peeler too heavy, the peeler will take too much of the 'meat' of the potato (or apple or carrot) with it; something for which my mother and more so my grandmother would have severely reproached me.

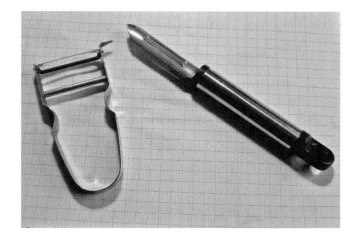

Figure 7.1
Potato peelers:
new and traditional

Usually, the design of this peeler seems to fit naturally into my world. In part, that has to do with the fact that my sense of myself with the peeler makes me choose – without thinking about it – potatoes that fit the ensemble. I don't notice that the peeler configures an ensemble of body, object and process in a specific fashion. In fact, the design of the peeler configures a precise *arrangement* of the world. That *arrangement* is subject to social regulation – how thick the peel can or should be, itself a signifier, among other things, of social conditions surrounding the ensemble and the process – the need to be frugal, for instance.

When I change to my 'modern' peeler I do notice a difference: my relation with both tool and potato has changed. I have to hold the potato differently, not according to the 'natural' 'comfortable' shape of my hand but a shape dictated by the form of the blade, its action of cutting, the shape of this peeler. In fact, the action is much more one of 'slicing' than 'peeling'. I hold this peeler/slicer with thumb and fingers; my hands do not touch. In the process I experience a different relation between myself and the tool, between the tool and the potato. I am doing something *to* it, where before I felt that I was doing something *with* it: I feel distanced. The slicer/peeler is much more effective with large potatoes than the traditional peeler, especially potatoes which do not fit comfortably or at all into my hand.

Of course, the action of slicing may be more congenial to some people than that of peeling; not everyone will feel the need for a more intimate relation with a potato. The peels tend to be thicker with the slicer; reason enough for my grandmother to have ruled it out of her kitchen.

I did do some 'market research', asking two people their views. Both are a generation younger than I am. Both of them feel more comfortable with the 'new' peeler; both feel that it gives them more control. They do agree that the peels are much thicker – but this does not bother them. Where tools are involved, socialization plays its role, making the cultural and technological 'natural'.

At the beginning of *design* stands a task; the parameters of the task and the assessment of the task come from some other source. *Design* starts with the designer's imagining of the task; a knowledge of the resources available to make the tool that will be used to perform the task; an understanding of the characteristics of the object to be worked on or with – carrot, potato or apple; an understanding of the wider social conditions; and a knowledge of the worker/agent and her or his capacities – the fact, for instance, that the hands of a five-year-old differ from those of an adult.

Design projects and organizes the *arrangement* of an entire *ensemble*: of the worker; the object to be worked on or with; of a tool for action with or on the object; integrated in specific ways into the capacities and affordances of the human body; a body with a history of experience of other, prior physical/social processes; an ensemble which is subject more or less, and in different ways, to social needs and regulation of the process. The *design* configures relations of body and tool; of tool and object. It also configures and projects *affect*. The design of the potato peeler is always more than the design of one object or tool: it is the design of a complex ensemble, of an environment of social relations, of social practices and configurations, of purposes, goals, aims, tasks; and of *affect*. A *design* is the imagined projection of a complex, closely interrelated social array in which the designed entity, object, process is used, has social effects, meanings; and produces affect. Identity is shaped in such complex arrays by aspects of *design*, even if in small and seemingly insignificant ways (Latour, 1988; Elias, 1994).

Design in social-semiotic environments

In the semiotic domain, that is, in the domain of meaning, all these features of *design* are present and active. Society, founded on meaning and, in that, on the shaping of identity, rests on *design*, its requirements and principles, whether overtly acknow-ledged or implicitly practised. That is the case in the design of all social environments, whether seen as environments of communication broadly or as environments of learning and teaching specifically. *Design* is at issue in the shaping of all environments of communication and through that in the shaping of social relations everywhere.

An approach to communication and to the production of semiotic entities through *design* – whether as texts or as semiotic objects of any kind – presupposes familiarity with the affordances of all materials involved, of the characteristics of the social environments in which the designed ensembles will be active and of the facilities and affordances of the media involved.

It may seem a large step from the potato peeler – traditional or new – to a website. Still, the point is to develop a frame for thinking about *design* and to test the use-fulness of the example once it is generalized to all instances and domains of *design*; and in particular in semiotic domains, where meaning is the issue. Here I apply the outline of this account to a comparison of two pages of one website, that of the Mayor of London (www.london.gov.uk).

If we start with the homepage of this site, 'Mayor of London' then on the day I visited there were seven 'blocks' or 'modules', neatly arranged in a rectangular pattern. Six of the seven modules have the structure of an image taking up the top half of the module and writing taking up the bottom half. The seventh module, called 'Highlights' consists of a 'menu', a vertically arranged list of ten items.

This 'screen' clearly has a specific social/communicational function, namely to show a range of interesting and significant issues that encapsulate the day-to-day life of London. As a semiotic object it demands not that much semiotic work from its visitor; though it is the visitor who has to order the screen for her or himself. No order is (pre-) given to indicate a sequence for engaging with the screen/page: it is the visitor's interest which decides. At this point I do not wish to engage in an analysis and description of the screen nor of the modules; though of course each module raises questions of a semiotic/discursive/ideological kind.

The other screen, 'Mayor of London: About Us' consists of a vertically arranged list of topics, either briefly described or as a *url* – offering to lead the visitor further. This screen has no images, nor is it arranged from blocks/modules. It is equally clear that visitors come here with different and specific purposes: not casually wondering what

London might have to offer but with a clear notion of seeking something specific. We might ask about the vertically organized layout, rather than a more traditional horizontal one – and especially as there is only writing (except for the framing of the footer).

The task (to be) performed by the *site* is multiple: to provide information; to act as a vehicle for public relations; to communicate, as political work; and no doubt a range of others.

The parameters of the task are, presumably, set from some central (policy-)unit. I don't know if there is such a unit, but let's call it 'The Mayor's Policy Unit'. Here the parameters are elaborated, spelled out, by a 'Working Party': what the tool is to achieve; how it is to be used to do its job. The design-team imagines the task: Who is the audience? What are the purposes? What aesthetic is required? The team needs to understand the resources which are available to make the tool. They need to imagine the object to be worked on or with: the imagined audience.

The rhetor/designer needs an understanding of the wider social and political conditions; in this case for instance, a relatively recent Lord Mayoral election, with political echoes persisting. And there is the need to understand the capabilities of those who will or might want to use the website or whom the party in power might wish to be users of the site.

The *text* constituted by the website overall, as well as its individual pages, should answer these issues. The design task is to move from general specifications to a text which will exemplify the features of the specification. A comparison of two of the pages can make this more concretely visible.

In organization the two pages differ significantly: the *genre* of the Homepage projects a social relation of relative equality: informative; a quasi 'democratic' affect of citizens chattily told about activities of their elected leader, undertaken on their behalf. The page is 'open'; the choice about points of *entry* is left to the interest of the visitor; the items are small, quickly taken in; they offer choices of information packaged as small sub-textual units – modules – consisting of image (top) and writing (bottom); the distribution of word and image, together with the use of colour produces a 'bright' affect. Images are salient, colour is used as a design-feature.

The page 'About us' contrasts markedly; its *genre* is strictly 'informational'; a different social relation to that of the homepage is projected, more formally efficient. In keeping with a social affect of efficiency, the page is sparing in the use modes: 'no wastefulness here; let's keep to the business' seems to be the motto. The layout of the page differs: the items to choose from are presented as a *list* of links with brief glosses, organized as a column of 'lines' with 'headings' for different topic areas: no modular units for this page; the aesthetic is less 'inviting' than that of the homepage. There is much more 'stuff' on the page; it demands effort and attention in engagement. *Writing* is the dominant mode; there is sparse use of *layout* and of (one) *colour*. The visitor needs to do most of the semiotic work.

Genres are projections and realizations of social relations; a different social relation is projected by each 'page'. Each social relation and each genre assumes, implicitly usually, what *semiotic work* is to be done and by whom. In each case we can ask what *semiotic work* has been done *for* the visitor and how much; and what *semiotic work* and how much the visitor is expected to do. What resources are offered and required to make use of the two pages?

Other pages differ yet again; each is generically specific, distinct. *Design* realizes social relations; in that realization in *text* it also projects and constructs social relations. Each instance of the design of a text is the result of *choices*; each feature chosen becomes a *sign* of (aspects of) the social relation. Each *choice* made realizes an aspect of the imagined (and to be projected) social relation. *Choice,* in this as in all environments, is shaped by power: the power to ascribe a social position to those who will engage with the *text*. Each *choice* is a political act. The totality of choices realizes a *style*. *Style* is the politics of choice.

Style is always subject to the effects of the use of social power in assigning value. *Aesthetics* is the result of the application of power in the evaluation of style: *aesthetics* is the politics of style. The two pages display a very different aesthetic; they project different social relations, which embody differing conceptions and relations of power.

Seen in this way, *style* and *aesthetics* are means to connect the social quite precisely to the semiotic. Figures 7.2, 7.3 and 7.4 show three screenshots from the Poetry Archive website (www.poetryarchive.org). Here, some of the telling social differences are *profession* – e.g. *teachers* as against *lay members* of the public; *generation* (as the social construction of age). The choice of modes realizes social difference as semiotic difference – a foregrounded use of writing compared to a mix of image and writing.

In the case of the screen for children, meanings of *generation* are realized by layout, by the shape of the modules and above all by the colour palette: *pastels,* desaturated colours, a range of colours in the lower energy end of the spectrum: all to realize/signify childlike fun, joy and *sensitivity.*

Multimodal design refers to the use of different modes – *image, writing, colour, layout* – to present, to realize, at times to (re-)contextualize social positions and relations, as well as *knowledge* in specific *arrangements* for a specific audience. At all points, *design* realizes and projects social organization and is affected by social and technological change.

To say that a lot has changed in *design* over a given period is to say – and to document it in semiotic/aesthetic form – that a lot has happened socially over that time. This can be tracked and described in specific media and genres. In school textbooks, for instance, there are now many more images than there were, say, sixty or seventy years ago; and their function has expanded and changed. Social change is realized in changes in *design*. *Diversity* is one factor with effects on design. While social changes over time – 'history' – lead to changes in what may be perceived as tradition, convention, or to judgements of 'being too modern', *diversity* may lead to divergence, to exclusion, to inequity in access, to fragmentation. *Design* projects aspects of the social which may not be visible by other means and hence be beyond common-sense awareness. Technological change, such as the introduction of the computer screen or the internet – itself driven by and producing social change – opens up new possibilities for multimodal design.

Figure 7.2
Poetry Archive
website: General
homepage

Figure 7.3
Poetry Archive
website:
Teachers'
homepage

Figure 7.4
Poetry Archive
website:
Children's
homepage

Changes in design: a brief look at recent history

Textbooks, as one such medium, have undergone deep changes over the last century. Society has changed, curriculum and pedagogy have changed in line with social changes; consequently textbooks have changed, both in 'look' and in 'content'. If we compare a textbook for the subject 'English' in secondary schools published in 1930 with one published more recently, we can see – from the point of view of content – that the subject now includes material on 'popular' culture and media. Pedagogically – and for epistemological reasons – where before individuals engaged with the book individually, now there are requirements to engage with materials working in groups. The tasks for engaging are set out, relatively explicitly.

Books have changed; the role of the book has changed; the social relations of book, reader and institution of school have changed. We can see changes in the *semiotic work* of *design* that has been done by design teams and that which is now expected to be done by 'readers'. Now there are full colour images on almost every page, both photographs and drawings; the overall *text*, consisting now of *writing* and *image*, is organized in *layout* of a page which is configured as a *site of display*, a *site of appearance*, a semiotic/layout unit that did not exist and could not have been imagined in the 1930s.

A page, then, was a *page*; a means of presenting parts of what was then the relevant unit of the *chapter*, a unit organized by content. *Content* determined organization; each *chapter* was as long as *content* (mediated of course by author and publisher)

Multimodality

dictated that it should be. The page had no function other than to 'carry' what had been written and was now going to be printed. In contemporary textbooks, the *page* – more usually, the *double-page spread* – determines what is to be represented, how it is to be presented and communicated. Now *content* is shaped by the contingencies of the *site of appearance*. The *page* has become a semiotic unit, that is, a unit of meaning.

What has changed, in other words, it not just subject content; not just the tasks which are set up for learners so as to engage with subject knowledge; what has changed is how these pedagogic interests are graphically realized on paper. Or rather, the 'look', the *layout*, the *arrangement* of the *site of appearance* is a graphic/visual realization of new social relations of the participants in educational environments. *Design*, had of course always been invisibly present; now it has become a major factor in the shaping of social relations and in their semiotic realization. The ordering, the arrangement of materials using the space of a *page* or *screen* is done from the perspective of an educator/*rhetor*, who has an eye equally on 'own interest' (as pedagogue), on students as 'audience', on the 'phenomenon to be communicated', on the 'broader social environment' and on the 'effect of the arrangement'. The *arrangement*, in other words, instantiates the social/educational purposes underlying the design of the materials.

Designers use the resources for making meaning which are available and apt to serve the educational purposes. The category of 'textbook designer' includes writers as well as illustrators, editors, typesetters and other professionals. Each professional group has specific resources and uses their potentials. Different resources – *modes*, *genres*, *discourses* – do specific kinds of ontological, epistemological or pedagogic/ social work. Professionals now tend to operate as teams, as 'an ensemble'; they bring their distinct contributions to the overall design. Increasingly now teachers act as rhetors/designers of digitally mediated materials, bringing their interests and agency into this semiotic work (Jewitt, 2008).

Two examples from Science textbooks (Figures 3.3 and 3.4, pages 48 and 49) can serve to illustrate briefly some aspects of the range of changes in design that have taken place over the last seventy years or so. One is a Science textbook from 1935, the other from 2002. In both books images are used to depict parts of the human body, with writing directly attached to 'anchor' (Barthes, 1977) the meaning of the images. But the placement of the images on the page differs. In the 1935 textbook, placement seems to have followed the then active principle of 'insert Figure X about here'. That principle implies that *writing* is the central means of conveying meaning; that it is functionally dominant in carrying major 'informational load' of the text overall; that *image* is functionally subordinate; and that the sequential logic of *writing* supplies the principle which organizes the ordering of content material on the page and in the chapter.

In the 2002 textbook, *writing* and *image* are placed in *parallel columns*. This principle suggests that *writing* and *image* are on an equal footing. Now it is neither the logic of *image* nor that of *writing* which dominates, but the logic of *layout* – itself of course founded on and exhibiting logics of space. The status relation between *image* and *writing* has shifted from an unequal to an equal position. Their functional tasks have altered: from *illustration* to fully carrying information. Ontologically this implies a shift in the valuation of modes and knowledge: from an ontology in which knowledge constructed in *writing* dominates over knowledge constructed in *image*, to an ontology in which the two bases for knowledge have equal standing.

In the 1935 example, *image* was – spatially – embedded in the sequenced ordering of writing. In the example from 2002, *image* and *writing* are placed – spatially – in parallel. Most immediately, this has *directional* implications: in the 1935 example, there is reference to the *image* at the beginning of the section on 'The Alimentary Canal' and a further reference later in the section. In between, the reader had to turn the page to view the image. Less immediately it has effects on how readers engage with the text, encouraging specific forms of reading, of 'engagement'. One suggests 'attend to *this* first and *that* after'. In other words, the 1935 *layout* does not facilitate a 'parallel reading' of *word* and *image* in the way it does in the example from 2002. Here, *layout* steers the reader into a 'back-and-forth' movement between word and image. It is a mode of engagement which suggests 'attend to these as equally significant; read them in mutual interaction'. In the 1935 example, *layout* steers the reader into a 'first–then' manner of reading. In the 2002 example, the page on which these 'chunks' are laid out is itself part of a larger structure, that of the *double-page spread*. This contrasts with the 1930s textbook, where text-as-writing was 'put' on to pages without much attention to how this played out spatially. What mattered was not where on the space of the *page* an *image* appeared, but where it was positioned in a *sequence of writing*. The *designed page* or more frequently now, the *double-page spread* (here it is both) is organized as a spatial/semiotic unit, linked to the temporal/semiotic unit of 'lesson'; the chapter in the old textbook was organized as a unit of 'content'.

As a multiplicity of modes – *image, writing, speech* and *moving image* – becomes available through the facilities of the contemporary media, the potentials for design alter radically. Resources with particular affordances become available for specific use; here for instance, *lexis* or *depiction* bring implications for generality or specificity; syntactic resources have implications for variable *arrangements* of entities, as well as bringing the means for the expression of the social relations of the maker of a message and its 'reader' – the relation of 'command' for instance. For the designer of the learning materials the question becomes one not just of the '*aptness*' of the representational resources for the specific occasion but also and maybe more so, the question of the design of social relations.

This change means that *participation in semiotic production* within a general – theoretical and practical – frame of *design* now best describes the characteristics of communication in most sites; though least so, still, in schools. That has profound effects on knowledge production. *Social* change has led to an emphasis on the agentive action of all participants in communication, even if differentially, and that in turn has led to the potential agency of individuals in the making of knowledge.

These social and representational changes are everywhere evident in contemporary media. The *participatory affordances* of current media technologies blur former distinctions of *production* and *consumption*, of *writing* and *reading*. The simultaneously global and local *'reach'* of media challenges the boundaries of communities global and local, with severe effects on *genres*; it mixes *contents* both global and local; *ubiquity* of access to information, *convergence* of media and *connectivity* in the sphere of individual lives entails that occasions of and resources for knowledge production and creativity are not tied to particular sites and times. *Multimodality*, representations in many modes, allows and demands the choice of apt communicational resources in all situations.

 The newer dispositions towards agency have deep effects on design processes. All aspects of the domain of meaning are drawn into the new social givens, with far-reaching effects. In relation to the making of texts, for instance, questions of authenticity and authorship have changed profoundly. In *downloading*, *'mixing'*, *cutting and pasting*, *'sampling'*, *recontextualization*, questions such as 'Where did this come from?', 'Who is the original/originating author?' seem not an issue. Much like the use, in former times, of a ruined castle or a monastic building as a quarry, a source of building materials – a large stone here to use as a lintel, another there as part of a wall – existing texts are taken as 'resources' to be 'mined' for the making of new texts. There is a need to understand the practices, epistemologies, aesthetics and ethics of contemporary forms of text *design* and *compositional principles*.

This would need to start with a clear sense of what are now to be regarded as 'compositional elements'. It may well be that the *principles of composition* have not changed very much; the entities that enter into composition have changed. Of course, in the high era of writing, the basic compositional elements were not letters but words and phrases. That is, composition did not start with the production of words, letter by letter. What letter-by-letter practice did do was to re-record, in their remaking, instances of words; had there been another means of producing words 'at one go', so to speak, the letter-by-letter route would not have been taken. Now, the contemporary means of recording, documenting, referring, provided by digital media make quite different compositional elements available (see Chapter 9). Instead of describing a historic building, a landscape, a scene in a market, word by word, my mobile convergent device allows me both to *take* a photograph and to *send* it. I can download segments of written text – longer or shorter – from the internet directly and integrate it into 'my' text which I send on, as 'my' composition.

At the moment these practices and units are discussed in terms of nineteenth-century models; terms such as 'plagiarism' or 'mere copying' are readily – and usually inappropriately – to hand: that is, the invocation of models from an era where conceptions of authorship were clear and legally buttressed in an era entirely differently constituted socially, culturally and technologically – though not yet legally.

In this situation, the notion of *design* and detailed descriptions, analyses and elaborations of *principles of design* can give, instead, relevant means of describing and analysing current *practices of text-making* and the *principles* underlying these practices by certain, usually generationally defined, groups.

What might be termed a 'social common sense' – in reality itself an ensemble of generational layers, gendered differences, distinctive educational background and hence cultural capital – is caught between traditional and contemporary conceptions of authority and agency in relation to the production of knowledge, to the authoring of texts, the authority/canonicity of knowledge and of semiotic forms much more generally. Political authority is contradictory: a demand for 'the new', for innovation and creativity is countered by anxieties around loss of control. Learning has long since left the confines of institutions such as school, university, college; and forms of pedagogy have to accommodate to 'life-long', 'life-wide' learning, that is, learning at *all times*, by those who demand that *their* interests be taken with utmost seriousness, in *all sites*, in *all phases* of professional and personal life. In school, many young people see themselves as authors of the knowledge they want and need, authors of the kinds of texts that meet their social, personal and affective needs – even though authored by processes which bring them into conflict with authority which remains focused traditionally. In that, they come into conflict with the sharply differing, contradictory conceptions and practices of the school. Conceptions of pedagogy held *by* the school as institution are at loggerheads with those held – however implicitly – by those *in* school. To resolve that stand-off productively, conceptions of pedagogy will need to be developed which accommodate the conflicting interests of generation, of power, of politics and of a market-dominated economy – not to mention ethics. Clearly, the agency of learners now has to be taken seriously and placed at the centre of pedagogic attention. Equally clearly, the insights, understandings, values, knowledges which are the result of centuries and millennia of social and cultural work, cannot and should not suddenly be ditched.

Arrangements: making meanings material

Occasionally, in the ceaseless, ongoing meaning-making – whether in social interactions or in the flux of 'inner' semiosis – meanings firm up into visible, tangible, audible, material entities, as signs, complexes of signs, texts, semiotic objects of various kinds: the *fixing* and *framing* discussed in Chapter 5.

That is the issue: 'making meaning material', in some way, making meanings real, in 'realizations'. Meanings-as-resource become material 'arrangements' as *texts* and other semiotic *objects*. These become evident in *sites of appearance* with specific means of *dissemination*. *Fixing* and *framing* entails a momentary interruption of the ceaseless flow of semiosis, provoked by some event, action, process, brought about by a message taken as a *prompt* for a response or by some inner equivalent of that externally produced prompt. The flow of semiosis is 'punctuated' in some way; and 'inner', unmaterialized meaning is given 'outer' material form. It is *fixed* modally, as *speech*, as *image*, as *gesture*, as *gaze*; most usually in *ensembles* of modes, depending on the assessment of the rhetor/designer who shapes the response.

Arrangements of various kinds are in focus here; as are the resources available for producing them. If 'what is to be arranged' was the focus of Chapter 6, now the focus is on the 'means for making *arrangements*'. The *arrangements* – *ensembles* of the kinds of meanings outlined in the previous chapter – are social in their origin and effects; in *ensembles* every aspect of these meanings is given shape in *arrangements*.

Arrangements

Arrangements are the semiotic 'face' of social organization. That means that the social *environments* in which the *arrangements* are produced and which they in turn 'make material' are profoundly significant. That was the point of my brief excursion into the 'emergence'/realization of discourses in architecture. Meaning cannot be discussed without a sense of the shape – the *organization* – of the social environment in which it is produced, whether as *hierarchy* or *network*; as more *web-like* in structure; whether the metaphor invoked is that of the *rhizome* (Deleuze and Guattari, 1973) or that of a *matrix*. These are all possible forms of social organization for which the semiotic theory needs means of expression, realization, materializing. Here too belong social/cultural, ontological (*meaning-*) *orientations* to the world and its production as an ontological-semiotic space: for instance, the social and semiotic significance of *centre* and *margin*, of *vertical* or *horizontal* ordering, of *top* versus *bottom*, of *left* versus *right*; or the variety of possibilities of representation in the realm of actions, events, processes.

The realizing features of the *arrangements* at issue are of many kinds, all at all times related to the *ideological* and *ontological* organizations which shape cultures in a particular society. Formal features – signifiers – such as *lines* and *linearity* versus *squares* and *centrality*, *circular* versus *rectilinear* shapes, *direction(ality)* and spatial and temporal *orientations* (Kress and van Leeuwen, 2006). *Arrangements* are *syntagms,* that is, *orderings* of *signs* or – to put it paradoxically – at times a designed seeming absence of order. All *syntagms*, at whatever level, of whatever kind, express meanings of *affect*, of indications of *factuality/facticity/fictionality*, of kinds of *realism*.

The question is: 'What are the means for making these meanings as *signs*, as *syntagms,* as *texts,* as *arrangements?'* and 'How are these means (to be) used in making apt *arrangements?'*. By and large I will focus on three of these means for making meanings material: on *mode* as the material stuff, the socially shaped material means; on *text* – or equivalent semiotic entity – as the largest level unit in communication; and on *syntagms* as *arrangements* of many kinds. There are many unresolved issues in relation to each of these. In some cases I suggest directions for possible answers – for instance, 'What is a mode?' – but unresolved questions abound: about the types, the functions, the names of 'sub-textual' units in the various modes: units, for instance, that might correspond to the 'movement' in a sonata; the 'panel' in a carved and painted triptych of an altar; to the 'pages' in a website; the 'stanza' in a poem; the 'phrase' or the 'riff' in a musical performance; and questions about the units of which these in their turn are composed, maybe equivalent to the relation of paragraph and sentence in *writing*.

Texts

Texts and their *sub-textual entities* are realized through various resources; many devices are necessary and available to give shape to *text* and *sub-textual units* as well as to the relations between them. My assumption in the theoretical sketch put forward here is that while each *mode* needs to meet the requirements of the three functions – the *ideational, interpersonal* and *textual* – different *modes* do not (need to) have the same *types* of units and entities; nor should we expect that to be the case. As long as we do not take *speech* or *writing* as models, demanding that all modes conform to these – for instance, in having the same entities – we need to learn to feel comfortable with the sense that different *modes* have different kinds of unit. *Image*, as I have said, does not have *words*; nor does *writing* have *vectors*; and layout does not have *tense*. It is that very difference which, among other things, gives modes their distinctive affordances.

Given the range of modes which need to be encompassed in the naming, and given contemporary modes of composition, I will use the term *module* as a catch-all term to name the units which serve to make up *texts* and other semiotic entities. In this I lean on suggestions made by Sean McGovern in his research about a fundamental feature of the semiotics of Japanese composition. *Modular composition* characterizes computer games; in *cutting and pasting* it is a major principle both of the selection and the *composition* of *texts* and other semiotic entities; as it is in *sampling* and *downloading*; in *recording* and *documenting* of various kinds. It is the notion of the (*bric-)collage* as one of the now dominant forms of composition, in which the *module* is central as the element of semiotic production of all kinds. The contemporary notion of the *module*, of *modular composition*, even if not necessarily composition as (*bric-)collage*, can be readily applied as a compositional principle retrospectively, and of course it had been, in 'traditional' forms of composition: in the *text* and the *paragraph*, in the composition of pages in *layout*, in photographs, but also in the 'composition' of buildings: of doors and doorways, of fireplaces, and so on. What is to be 'glued' and how – and what not – is subject to different forms and degrees of regulation at different times in different places.

The *text* (or the semiotic entity), the largest level entity, is recognized – from the maker's as much as from the viewer's/hearer's/reader's perspective – by a sense of its 'completeness' in meaning, in the social and communicational environment in which it is made, in which it occurs and in which it is active: the sense that this unit is complete by itself – in some way – that it 'makes sense' by itself, in its appropriate social environment. The sense of its completeness derives from the 'completeness' of the social event/activity and the environment in which the text is produced and where it 'belongs'; that is, from the fact that the *text* is produced in and shaped by a social activity which has regularity and recognizability for members of a social group. Hence the recognition of completeness is a factor of, arises out of and assumes 'membership' of the group in which the social event has its place and where its meaning is understood.

A part of that sense of completeness, both of the social event and of the semiotic object/*text* rests on features of *cohesion* – a formal attribute – and of *coherence* – an attribute of meaning – internally within the text and of the text with the environment in which it has been produced and is used.

A sense of 'completeness' is essential to the recognition of a *semiotic entity* of any kind, at every level. Within the *text*, the smaller, sub-textual units require their – distinct – sense of completeness: each has to be experienced, both from the maker's and from the viewer's/hearer's/reader's perspective, as a unit, as meaningful, at the level which it occupies within the *text*. If it is not, it will not be recognized and cannot function as a constitutive/constituent part of a *text*. In other words, 'completeness' is relative to the level at which a unit functions. The *text* is special in that it functions in the social environment, it is a part of social practices directly. In that sense, the text's environment is social rather than semiotic. The sense of completeness does not need to be identical for maker and viewer/reader. Indeed, given the definition of communication as resting on interpretation, it could not be the same for the two positions.

To restate: a *text* is a multimodal semiotic entity, seen as 'having completeness', by those who engage with it. Its sense of completeness derives from a (shared) understanding of the social occasions in which it was produced, in which it functions or to which it alludes. The text has features of internal and external cohesion and, as an integrated meaning-entity, of coherence.

The form and the characteristics of *sub-textual units*, the *modules*, are derived from their functions and uses within the text. Putting it this way means that the direction of analysis and of description, of definition and constitution of both the *text* and the *sub-textual units*, is 'top-down'. This is inevitable if the starting point, the point of origin of meaning, is the priority of the social. This contrasts with a 'bottom-up', a 'building-block' approach, in which small units make bigger units and bigger units make very big units. In a top-down approach, *text* and *modules* are seen as shaped by the contingent circumstances of those who make the *text* in its social setting. An account of making the text might be something like: 'I have to write a report; I have these four issues I want to set out, so I better have four paragraphs, one for each of these. I need a paragraph to introduce it; I had best put a sentence at the beginning that says what each paragraph is about; and then I suppose I had better put a summary paragraph at the end.' In this approach, the *modules* of a text – of writing, of image, or multimodally constituted – or of other semiotic entities, are shaped by the interests of the maker of the text, designed by the purposes they meet in the text and in the contingencies of a specific environment – whether that is a website, a pop song, a computer game, a blog.

Signs are the minimal units of semiosis and as such the (minimal) units of *modules*. *Signs* are units of meaning in which 'something to be meant' – a *signified* – is combined with 'something that can mean it' – a *signifier*. *Modules* consist of *signs*; most commonly they consist of several *signs* or *sign-complexes*. *Signs* are units of meaning, which exist as *sign-complexes* in/as *modules*. An example might be the use of a colour (as one sign) with full saturation (as another sign); or a syllable (as one sign) said with a rising intonation (as another sign). This means that a *sign* functions as part of a *sign-complex* in a *module*; a *sign* which does not function in a *module* cannot 'stand on its own'.

A *text* is semiotically and communicationally complete. That makes it distinct from other semiotic entities in its environment. A *text* is *framed*. The framed *text* creates, provides and occupies a discrete 'semiotic space'.

Frames

Frames and *means of framing* are essential to meaning-making in all modes. The frame marks spatial and/or temporal extension and limits of a text or other semiotic entity. My slogan '*Without frame no meaning*' entails that we need to focus on *frame*, on *forms of framing* and on *that which is framed*, at all times, equally.

When painters or film directors want to shape what they wish to represent, they form a rectangle with thumb and fingers of both hands and look at the world through that makeshift *frame*. What is in the *frame* now appears separated from what is outside the *frame*; what is inside the *frame* now forms (or should form) a unity in some way. At a general semiotic level the word 'frame' names the formal semiotic resources which separate one semiotic entity from its environment 'pre-frame' or from other semiotic entities. In this, the *frame* provides *unity*, *relation* and *coherence* to what is *framed*, for all elements inside the *frame*. Without a *frame* we cannot know what to put together with what, what to read in relation to what. If we do not know what entities there are, we cannot establish relations between them. We cannot know therefore where the boundaries to interpretation are: we cannot make meaning. *Frames* and *means of framing* are essential for all meaning-making, in all modes (Goffmann, 1986; Bateson, 2000).

A *frame* defines the world to be engaged with; it excludes and it includes; and in doing that it shapes, presents the world according to the interest and the principles of those who *frame*. Dramatists and stage designers, painters and filmmakers, architects and urban planners, interior decorators, photographers – amateur and professional – have long exploited the potentials of frames. In Photographic Journalism it is a well-understood major device for ideological shaping (Hall, 1982). In Colour plate 14 there is a double frame: that of the photograph; and the frame within the photograph. The first of these gives us a clear sense of being in a space from which we can see through a strongly defined frame into another space, framed by a doorway. The first frame gives us no real sense of the space in which we are located; though it does seem much darker than the space into which we look – and of which we can see only a part. The room into which we might be invited to move has a person in it, and a row of lights hanging from the ceiling takes our eye straight to another frame.

In Colour plate 15 we are in the lighter room. The frame of the photograph again keeps us from seeing everything that we might want to see. A piano is in the far left corner, some easy chairs are lined up along the right hand (largely glassed and curtained) wall; two people seem to be sitting on one of the settees. The emptiness of the room is the overwhelming expression; it seems that what is being framed is emptiness; the pieces of furniture and the people placed in that vast empty space merely reinforce the feeling of being 'lost' in that space.

Modes which have a long history of social use have highly elaborated means for framing. *Sentences* are *frames* in the *mode* of *writing*; *punctuation* is a resource for framing in that mode. When children learn to write (Kress, 1982; 1994), one of the difficulties they encounter – among many others – is that they are familiar with the *framing devices* of *speech*, but not with those of *writing*. In their early experimenting with *punctuation* as *framing*, the questions they pose for themselves are both readily apparent and highly instructive. These tend to circle around two issues: 'How do the framing devices of speech relate to those of writing?' and 'What are the potentials for framing in writing?'. The changes – or 'corrections' – they make to the shape of their sentences give an insight into the questions they pose.

The power of sentences as *frames* to shape meaning can be readily demonstrated in the use of banal examples. Here are three such:

> George came into the room. Mary left.
> George came into the room; Mary left.
> George came into the room and Mary left.

Placement of an element in the frame – here that of the sentence – has effects; so if I invert the order of the clauses in the examples, the meanings alter:

> Mary left. George came into the room.
> Mary left; George came into the room.
> Mary left and George came in to the room.

In *writing*, there are *frames* for units such as *texts*; for *paragraphs* within *texts*; for *sentences* within *paragraphs*; and for *clauses* and *phrases* within *sentences*. The term for the (graphic) means for framing in *writing* is *punctuation*. *Commas, full stops, semicolons, colons, dashes* are 'punctuation marks': each a resource for *connecting* and *separating* entities, so that each can be brought, newly, into a relation with others: *clauses* with *clauses*, *sentences* with *sentences*, etc. All punctuation marks *frame* and in doing so contribute meaning. Some punctuation marks/frames also convey social/attitudinal/affective meanings, such as the question mark '?' and the exclamation mark '!' as *questioning, seeking confirmation, ordering, commanding*. These act as frames for social relations. In *writing*, in English, questions can start with so-called 'Wh- forms': What . . . ?, Who . . . ?, Where . . . ?, or How . . . ? Here, *frames* have been made into words, lexicalized, both to *frame* and *project* a social relation.

Decisions about punctuation as framing are decisions about making meaning. Other frames in writing, the *paragraph* as one such, have equally significant effects. In Guenter Grass's autobiography, *Vom häuten der Zwiebel* (*Peeling the Onion*, 2007) he describes, in a longish paragraph, how, as a thirteen-year-old, he loved reading, lying on his tummy. His mother would come and, using one of her hairclips, pin back the hairs that had fallen across his eyes. Grass concludes the paragraph with the sentence 'Ich duldete das' – difficult to translate, but (in that context) something like: 'I was prepared to allow her to do that to me.' (In the official English translation it is 'I put up with it' – somewhat flat and anticlimactic.)

Grass could have placed this sentence on a separate line, making it into its own sentence-paragraph. The effect of realizing his meaning via the *signifier* of *paragraph* rather than of that condensed concluding *sentence*, would have been to make the comment – with its feeling of an enveloping affection lovingly given and gladly received though, almost, as his due – into the *sign* of a momentous issue, given much different weight as the expression of a young man's relation with his mother.

The material means for *framing* differ from mode to mode. In the theatre there is the framing of the stage, itself a historically shaped and changing form. Attempts to do without the frame of the stage show the power of this frame. The play to be performed itself has framings of *acts* and *scenes*. Amateur photographers carefully frame the scenes they shoot: the doorway, the overhanging branch; in cinemas there are frames – in some, still, a curtain is raised and lowered.

As each mode has its specific means for framing, a social-semiotic theory of multi-modality is required to elaborate these means. In Figure 3.4 (page 49), the image of the digestive system uses colour as a resource for framing. A desaturated pinkish background is used to indicate the whole of the body, which is not the focus of the 'unit of work'; and the saturated blues are used for the organs, which are the focus. *Colour* is a quite different resource for framing to that of a spatial or a temporal gap, an empty *space* or a *pause*; or of a graphic mark such as a *comma*, a *dash*; or the frame made with sound, of an intonation contour, which 'clamps together' the elements within it. *Colour*, as a background 'wash', frames by establishing the 'ground' on which things 'are', 'belong', 'happen', 'take place'. This is other than the framing which marks a boundary. On a road, a single unbroken line is a stronger framing than a broken line; often there is an unbroken line on one side and a broken line on the other: indicating that frames mark boundaries and 'territory' differently for (temporarily) different social groups.

Inevitably, *framing devices* are more elaborated – more conventionalized, more subject to regulation – for modes which have received social and semiotic attention over long periods. With modes which are not so elaborated – and hence not subject to high degrees of control – there is more room for individual innovation. I recall a (then regional) BBC news-'reader' who, having read the evening news, invariably concluded the presentation with the tiniest of nods, eyes firmly pressed together and lips tightly pursed: a full full stop indeed. Some years later, when I saw him presenting the news on national TV, gone were the nod, shut eyes and tightly pursed lips, replaced by an open smile and cheerful 'Good night': a makeover of modal resources; and of identity.

Semiotic entities, *texts* included, have several kinds of *framing*. The 'That's all folks' of old cartoon shows, the 'FIN' or 'The End' of early movies, are one kind. These are the *material framings* of text as text, the fading of the picture at the end, for instance, in early movies; the rising and falling of the curtain in the theatre (still a feature of some cinemas in various parts of the world). Here too belong the various resources of *layout*; and of *colour* which indicate boundaries; white space around print on the page; fences and hedges in suburbia; open spaces in front of buildings.

Then there is the framing of social relations, of *genre*: *generic framing*. Text openings and closings, such as 'Once upon a time, there lived . . .' and '. . . and they lived happily ever after' belong here, as markers of textual beginning and ending: qua 'entry into fairy tale'. We know how to navigate an *interview*, because we understand the generic framing; and we know when a conversation has begun to turn into cross-examination. Texts are framed discursively, as are all semiotic entities; and these framings allow us to navigate the world of institutionally produced knowledge.

The rolling of the credits at the end of a movie is an ambivalent framing; some (aesthetically or fan-oriented) moviegoers regard it as part of the filmic text, while others are already on their way out of the cinema. Ambiguity in framing points to and is a means of realizing social ambiguities of various kinds. Not having a fence between the neighbour's garden and yours in the suburban US (my experience relates to some New England states) seems to mean, I take it, that 'we don't need such things – we're pretty good neighbours here in this community'. Yet the lawn mown with geometric precision exactly up to the border of my/their land contradicts and negates the absence of the fence and constitutes a framing which has to be constantly, newly, reaffirmed. By comparison, the English saying that 'Good fences make good neighbours', takes a pretty pragmatic and for English conventions fairly direct route.

In the case of spatially organized texts, frames can be lines, solid or broken; strong or faint; straight or squiggly; a wash of colour 'behind' the elements superimposed on and framed by that wash; or, in the case of the more traditional page, a clear framing of white space of varying extent around the text overall and around its parts. In *speech*, one function of *framing* – via the means of pitch(-contours) – is to mark information units and the distribution of information (via a perceptibly major pitch movement) – as assumed to be shared and as not shared – and to 'chain together' information units into integrated, internally coherent, larger level units of information (Brazil *et al.*, 1997). In the case of temporally organized texts, various *visual* (the newsreader's closed eyes, his tightly pursed lips, the slight nod) and/or *aural* cues (silence, a fall of intonation to the usual resting point of the voice for a particular speaker; a beat on a drum) exist to signal endings or separations of intra-textual elements from each other.

Elements within the framed entity are treated – in reading, listening, viewing, in the joint reading and viewing of any multimodal text – as belonging to something that has 'unity', coherence. For instance, whatever definition of 'sentence' we might use, its *framing* implies that what is 'in' the frame of the *sentence* belongs there and what is not 'in' that frame does not. Similarly, whatever entity follows on from a *semicolon*, a *colon*, and so on.

Framing devices are *signifiers*, resources for making signs and as such they have meaning-potentials of quite specific kinds. The entities framed by a *colon* are different to those framed by a *semicolon* or those framed by a *full stop*. The meaning of punctuation marks is a semiotic issue; it defines what kinds of intra-textual entities there can be. *Punctuation marks* are entirely conventional, yet the signs made in their use are specific, individually made with this culturally given resource. If I chose to frame a segment of my writing with a comma I have made a sign different to that had I framed it with a semicolon or full stop. In other words, punctuation marks have a meaning potential and allow me to make *my* meaning – as do all framing devices.

Frames *hold together* and they *separate/segment*. The elements within the *frame* are held together and the viewer/reader/hearer is asked to engage with the entities in the *frame* as connected, as coherent, as having some kind of unity. A *bricolage* works because of its frame; take the frame away and it has become an unordered heap of things. At the same time *frames* separate what is in the frame from what is outside; the viewer/listener/reader is asked to regard what is outside the frame as different from what is inside and if connected, as differently connected.

What else is framed?

Frames are specific to modes; they are also – and that is close to a tautology – specific to culture. In Chapter 5, I mentioned some of the cultural/ontological implications of script systems. When children learn to write *characters*, they do so on squared paper; each character is produced as perfectly balanced in a square. The letters of the alphabet are placed on a line. Square and line are frames, in an only mildly extended sense – that is, they indicate, mark out, delineate the space, the site and the manner of appearance.

In a research project with a colleague (Kenner and Kress, 2003), we attempted to understand what sense young learners of different script systems made of the differences in the scripts they were learning. One means whereby we tried to 'get at' their sense of this was to ask them to teach their peers (in the English school, during the week) the script system of their home culture.

On one such occasion, when one of the young Chinese learners was 'teaching' one of his (English) peers how to construct a character, the young 'teacher' several times rubbed off the attempt made by his peer on the black-board. Finally, with unconcealed frustration, he said 'he's doing it wrong'. When my colleague asked what he was doing wrong he said: 'he's not putting it in the square'. My colleague, unable to see the square he was referring to, asked him which square he was talking about. With increasing frustration he pointed at the board. Looking intently, my colleague could see that the blackboard had once been 'squared', though to 'normal' ways of looking, the squares had been all but entirely scraped off by countless cleanings of the board. Neither she nor the non-Chinese young peer had seen the exceedingly faint traces of formerly present squares. For this young 'teacher' on the other hand, they were clearly there; more 'present' than the 'lines' on the blank inside of greetings cards on which I write my message, with the base of each letter placed precisely on the imagined line.

The question: 'Where do *frames* exist?' applies to the framing of all semiotic entities and forms: In the 'world'? In the 'semiotic world'? In the semiotic world that we have, each of us, created in our own heads? In the image of the frames provided by our cultures? It is there that frames exist, firmly lodged, with profound ontological effects. Seeing the world as 'framed' by a line or by a square leads to profound differences in conceptions about the world. The kinds of phenomena relevant here are *direction(ality)* – *arrangements* of elements from *left to right* or from *right to left*; *centre–margin arrangements*; *vertical–horizontal arrangements*; *linear arrangements*, to contrast with *circular, spiral arrangements* or arrangements in *helix* form; or combinations of these. All point to potential use as signifiers of *social forms, structures, processes*, as well as being involved in and emergent in organizing *semiotic arrangements* such as *layout*. They might appear jointly, for instance, in the combination of *linearity* and (left–right) *directionality*. These form a resource of powerfully plausible signifiers for social and/or epistemological dynamics with a wide range of potentials.

Frame, text, communication are inextricably interwoven. Without *frame* no *text*; without *framed entities* no *communication*. Without *syntagms* no order; without *syntagms-as-arrangements* not sufficient stability for *communication*. Without *communication* no renewal of *text* or *frames* or *meanings*. To be in a world of meaning is to be in a world of *frames*, of *framing*, of *syntagms*, of *arrangements* and of the constant remaking of all these in transformative representation. This is so with the seating arrangement of guests at a wedding service in the church: two parties, left and right of the aisle; then the seating arrangements at the reception; and the intensely scrutinized – and felt – meanings of these arrangements: at a wedding; in the church; in a procession.

Other *arrangements* of 'the larger level *social organizations* (and their metaphoric articulations)' are *temporally* and *sequentially* (and usually also *spatially*) organized: *rituals* such as *parades, church services, installations of the new ministers* of a government, *state visits, openings of Parliament, graduation ceremonies* are instances; but so are *family breakfasts* and *mealtimes*. How do these realize social arrangements such as *hierarchy, web, network, rhizome*? Are *parades, church services, state openings of Parliament*, and so on, apt *semiotic arrangements* of such social meanings?

Modes

Modes offer specific orientations to the world, and as such need to be mentioned here, in the section on framing: temporally oriented, spatially oriented or a combination of both. These orientations produce distinct *cultural arrangements* and *orientations,* which differ from the more specific *social arrangements* just discussed in being more general and abstract; that is, they are relatively though not entirely independent of social arrangements; they are not immediately articulated in or applicable to all *social arrangements*. *Mode* brings the 'deep' ontological orientations of a society and its cultures with it. In its guise as *the* means for realizing/materializing meaning – as the answer to the 'With what means?' question – it belongs here. It is as though each mode provides its specific lens on the world and with that lens the world seems organized as specific *arrangements* in space, in time, or both. These 'lenses' produce a complex picture in which ontological and epistemological effects are rolled in with more broadly cultural ones. *Mode*, as the material stuff of *signs*, is central in giving material form to meaning. Given the assumption that 'form is meaning' and that the relation of form and meaning is motivated, choice of *mode* is foundational to meaning-making. *Mode* brings its *logics*, its entities, its *syntagms* and (social and) semiotic *arrangements* more generally. Of course, in other ways, that is the case with the choice of all form, though differently and at different levels.

Relations, processes and connections

Relations, processes and *connections* among entities tend to have relatively stable conventionalized forms in modes which have had a long period of use in a society. Best known, of course are linguistic names; for instance of clause types such as *transitive* or *intransitive*, each of which implies larger level *arrangements* such as – looking at the syntagm syntactically – *subject–verb–object (or complement);* or looking at the syntagm in terms of meaning: *actor–action–affected/involved. Arrangements* of entities can suggest *classification; movement; action* and/or *interaction; state/being;* various spatial or temporal arrangements – whether spatial in *image* or temporal in *music*. Spatial or temporal ordering of entities and elements adds meaning to the *syntagm*.

The social meanings of an *aspectual* kind, as I have called them in Chapter 6, need formal semiotic resources – signifiers – for their expression. A social relation (as a *connection*, let's say) may be *constant* or *intermittent*. Using a *line* to represent that relation in the mode of *image*, might lead to the use of a continuous, unbroken line; or it might be a broken, interrupted, dotted line. To indicate the *strength* of the connection, we might use a *thick* line or conversely a *thin(ner)* line for an *attenuated relation*. For example:

Their relationship was 'pretty steady': as — — — — — — —

Their relationship was 'off and on': as — — – —- – -

Their relationship was 'really fragile': as … … … ….. or as _ _ _ _ _ __ _ _

Their relationship was 'pretty up and down': as _ ….. _ – - — – _ _ —- _

Their relationship was 'solid': as ============

The social connection may not be 'straightforward', that is, it might be unstable in some way and the line representing that relation might therefore be *curvy, meandering*. As with gravy, which at some point begins to change state, so social relations can also undergo *changes of state*: these are culture-specific meanings to which the theory needs to be attentive and to recognize through the provision of signifiers and names.

An action may be ongo*ing* – continuous – *is* walk*ing*; it may be seen as completed – *has* walk*ed*. Here as elsewhere, modes have their specific means for representing such meanings – in the mode of *speech* as in *writing* in English, such meanings can be expressed by specific morphemes, and the several meanings can be brought together to form more complex entities – *inceptive, inchoative, continuous, completed*: the sky dark*ens* (*inceptive + inchoative*) – the sky *is* darken*ing* (*continuous + inchoative*) – the sky *has* darken*ed* (completed + inchoative); or, the gravy thick*ens* (*inceptive + inchoative*) – the gravy *is* thicken*ing* (*continuous + inchoative*) – the gravy *has* thicken*ed* (*completed + inchoative*); and so on.

I am using linguistic examples to make the point relatively accessibly; these meanings – or meanings such as these though different – will occur in many modes. In *gesture*, pace and change of pace may be used; in *image*, *colour* and *saturation* could be used as a *signifier* for such meanings: it might be less saturated on the left of the framed space and gradually change to greater *saturation* towards the right; or it might change in *hue*. In speech the speaker might speak increasingly more *loudly* or *faster*. These resources are specific, socially and culturally: depending on what a society needs or wishes to mean and to express. In speech or in writing, in anglophone cultures, meanings such as *continuous, iterative, simultaneous, inceptive* are relatively common in *speech* and *writing*. That means these meanings are 'there' in the culture; and that makes it likely that these signifier resources exist in other modes in this culture. For instance, parallel lines; walking in step; rhythmic patterns in speech or in poetry; in movement or in gesture; may all serve as *signifiers* of *simultaneity* of *states* or *actions* or of *congruence* and *coherence* of views, actions, values. Visually, the increasingly thicker shaft of an arrow can signal the (social) meaning of the *inceptive* character of a process, and so on.

Depending on the *mode* and its *affordances*, *relations* and *connections* may have any number of forms. I may stand close to someone at a party as a means of making meaning; or turn away from someone. I may glance at someone or avert my glance, an action performed with the mode of *gaze*.

Metaphor

Metaphor as *frame* is one of the major categories of a social-semiotic theory. Multimodality and the notion of transduction add complexity and intensity to that fact. *Aptness* and *likeness* are not the same: *likeness* is what it says: 'X is like Y'; that is, *likeness* focuses on what seems to be the *criterial* feature of what is to be *represented* and says that something else is like it. *Aptness* focuses on 'fitness for purpose': 'this is the best fit (the most apt) for this purpose here'.

Likeness points to the relation of *analogy* and *frame*; in principle it provides a frame for two elements in an *iconic* relation. *Analogy* is the foundation of *metaphor*. Hence every *sign*, being formed on the basis of *likeness* and on the *principle of analogy*, is (formed as) a *metaphor*. *Aptness* speaks about the *resources which are available* in the making of signs: 'these resources are the nearest best fit'. The questions that need to be asked in relation to *aptness* is 'Apt for whom?', 'Apt to what?', 'Apt to whom?'. *Analogy* is shaped in a dual response: to features of the *entity* or phenomenon to be signified and to the demands of *power* with its effects in skewing the sign – the relation of signifier and signified – away from transparency and in its direction. *Power* acts to ensure, where possible, that *metaphor* stays within boundaries set in certain ways in specific environments. *Power* acts as a *frame* on the extent of *transformations* – for instance by setting limits on *what is taken as 'X-like'*.

Signs, and hence *signifiers*, come from specific social places and cultural sites. The red-and-white check tablecloth in a restaurant – in England as in other places in Europe – is a signifier of 'Mediterranean-ness'. The oversize peppermill waved by the waiter over my plate is a *signifier* of 'Italian-ness'. Many signs/signifiers bring, with the *frame* of their *provenance*, additional meanings into a specific mode – whether an instrument in music – the ukulele, the mandolin; or a French accent in speech, pronouncing *maison* with a nasal vowel; or a beret as part of my dress.

What is signified in *frames* can be traced back to the *interest* of the maker of the sign. For the three-year-old, wheels proved *criterial* for representing cars; just as some years later flames drawn shooting out from the wheels of a different car signify power and speed, flames and guns mounted on the car are by then both *criterial* as *signifiers* of 'car'. *Signs*, in this theory are at all times the result of a motivated connection of a *signified* – a *meaning* – and a *signifier* – a *form* which is already *apt* to mean that *meaning* in a *frame* that provides the space for the link of analogy.

Foremost among the terms integral to this theory is that of *affordance*, a term which points to the potentials and limitations of specific *modes* for the purposes of making *signs* in *representations*. *Affordance* rests, on the one hand, on the *materiality* of the *stuff*, which *work* in *social environments* has fashioned into a *cultural* and *semiotic resource* on the other hand. The *materiality* of the *stuff* of which modes are fashioned means that they have distinct *meaning-orientations* to the world, which I have called *logics*.

Discourse: ontological and epistemological framing

Texts are always multimodal, so the *rhetorical* and *design decisions* lead to the making of *ensembles of modes*; these are themselves assembled as *orchestrations of modes*, in which purposes and needs of the maker of sign-frames are brought together with *affordances* in the best possible manner, from the *rhetor's* and the *designer's* perspective. *Ensemble*, in this context, names an emphasis on the *modal multiplicity* of the text, while *orchestration* names an emphasis on the *aptness* of the selection, the mutual interdependence and the 'semiotic harmony' of such ensembles. Within such *orchestrations* there are: *elements* and *processes* which *link* and *reach across* modes – *transmodal elements* or *processes*; *elements* which *link between modes* – *intermodal elements* and *processes*; and those which *link within modes* – *intramodal elements* and *processes.* Such *framing* and *linking devices* are essential in overall multimodal *textual organization.* I pointed to *intramodal elements* when I mentioned the function and meaning of punctuation marks earlier: question marks, dashes, colons, etc. These all have meaning-potentials, whether *trans-, inter- or intra-modal.*

8 Multimodal *orchestrations* and *ensembles* of meaning

The world arranged *by me*; the world arranged *for me*

The meanings we make and encounter in all aspects of our daily lives are complex. Texts – spoken, gestured, written, drawn, mimed and any combination of these – are the means of making some of these complex meanings material. By means of texts we can communicate if not all then at least those meanings for which the modal resources of our cultures provide means of representation.

Texts are made by me as 'messages' for others; and others make texts as 'messages' for me, so to speak. Most of the texts I make – as coherent complexes of signs – actually go entirely unnoticed by me and by others: they are meaningful all the same and still function as means of making my way in the world. Here I look at *texts* as complexes of signs from two perspectives, that of *arrangements* and that of *movement*. *Arrangements* are made by me – as a modal *ensemble* made for myself or for others – or else someone has made an *arrangement* as a modal *ensemble* for me. *Arrangements* are made as *ensembles* in a world of *movement*: I, as maker of meaning *move* in the world, literally, in different ways; and the world around me is in *motion*, in constant *movement*; and more often than not, I *move* in a world *in motion*.

Much – probably most – meaning made by me and by others goes unnoticed or at least, is noticed but below the (conscious) semiotic radar, so to speak. When I cross a street I need as much information as I can get about my immediate environment: the speed of an approaching car; its positioning on the road; maybe the blinking of an indicator. I assess what else is happening on the road and what the implications are, for me and for others. I know that the Number 91 bus will not turn left here; I try to see where drivers are looking and what that might suggest; I try to make eye contact with the driver of the car nearest; she or he might give me a fleeting signal – a nod, a finger gesturing that it's fine to cross the road: all this in fractions of a second.

I interpret all this stuff and so for me this is communication, even though most of it is not intended as such by anyone. The blinking indicator is, yes; the positioning of the car on the road most likely is not. No court of law would accept my interpretation of 'what was communicated' – but law and reality go their own ways. All of that stuff has regularity: if it did not, I could not use it as a basis for my decisions. Most of it is not recognized as *mode*: not overtly seen as a regular, never mind as a 'codified' means of making meaning. Nevertheless, from all of this I make what become for me useful meanings, of different kinds. My judgement about the speed of the car tells me, accurately enough for me to act on, whether it is likely to stop; its position and orientation on the road gives me information whether it is intending to turn before it gets to me or to overtake a cyclist; or whatever. I take these as different kinds of information – and interpret them as *signs* on the basis of quite different kinds of evidence: eye contact; the finger suggesting 'OK, go on'; speed; the indicator; all come to me as information through different material and via different senses. The stuff I am 'taking in' is a diverse, complex set of materials, which I turn into the *signs* of a multimodal ensemble of my own making. The ensemble and all the action that precedes and goes with it is based on my interest. My interest directs my attention, guides my framing of this moment and that shapes the selections I make from this segment of this world here and now.

I don't spend all of my day crossing roads – or sitting down for that matter. And of course, I also *hear* what goes on around me; at times I even *listen*. Most mornings, conditions permitting, I go for a walk. I humour myself that I am walking 'against the clock'; and so I don't like stopping or slowing down when I cross a side street, to turn round and see if a car is coming. I *listen* instead. If I can hear a car, I try to judge from the sound whether it is slowing down. If not, I cross the road without looking. My attention and my framing of informational *stuff*, my consequent selection from that stuff and my *making of my ensemble* of information is shaped by the contingencies of the immediate situation.

If I was sight-impaired my disposition and orientation to the world and the informational stuff it provides for me to make meaning with would be profoundly different and so would, as a consequence, my attention, framing, selection. Now my major resource would be the 'soundscape' of the street; the sounds in the spaces of the underground station; the sounds of a park in a city. I would *hear* 'perspective': that motorbike sound seems further off than this bus sound; that car has passed me, this other one behind me is not slowing down; that one is approaching. I have at times watched people who are sight-impaired negotiating what are complex environments for sighted people: I am thinking of an underground station in London which I use regularly. What for me, relying mainly on *sight*, is a cacophony of *noise*, is, I assume, for a sight-impaired person a rich environment of *sound*, as orderly perhaps and as regular as the flood of *sight*-impressions are for me. My more general point is that at any moment we occupy distinct positions and that (difference in) position entails differences in attention, framing, selection. This applies to all of us, at each and every moment in each and every environment; always in specific ways.

At times my attention is solicited; and the request is supported by varying degrees of power. The captain of the flight I am on tells me over the intercom that I should, for my own sake, attend to the safety demonstration that the cabin staff are about to give. Now the framing is not mine; or at least, it is not, if, unlike most of my fellow passengers, I choose to attend to the demonstration. There are spoken instructions; gestures pointing out the location of the emergency exits. There is the actional performance: this is how the buckle is done up; this is how you fasten the lifejacket;

the oxygen mask is put on like this. However, the spoken 'Place the mask over your nose and mouth and pass the strap over your head' is much clearer for me as a *demonstration* than it is as a spoken message alone. *Demonstrating* the use of the oxygen mask, or of the lifejacket, works better for me than the spoken instructions, which do not tell me which or where 'the buckle *here*' actually is. In the demonstration I can *see* it; I cannot *hear* it from the *speech*. Some airlines encourage passengers to 'study' the card with its written and visual instructions at the same time as the demonstration is going on.

This too is a *multimodal ensemble*; though this time it is clear that the material has been carefully arranged *for me*. Different meanings have been allocated to specific modes, in a particular sequencing. This *ensemble* has been *orchestrated*, much as the *orchestration* of an otherwise simple tune. It has been 'scored' with care and precision. The modes involved have been chosen with rhetorical intent for their affordances and the orchestration has been designed with the characteristics of the specific environment – the difficulty of hearing the intercom announcements; the noise in the cabin; the somewhat stressful atmosphere; and the generally uninterested audience – all in mind.

We might reflect whether the *demonstration* also serves as a quasi 'auxiliary channel' for communication. On a plane where Portuguese is the first language used, the *demonstration* provides enough information for me to be sufficient by itself. We might conclude from that that the *actional mode* of the *demonstration* is the *foregrounded* mode for me and that for me it carries *equal* or even *major communicational load*. For a speaker of Portuguese, on that same plane, the spoken mode may well be the foregrounded mode. My 'position' affects how I engage with a multimodal ensemble; it is essential to be aware that that is more likely than not to be the condition in most cases of communication; though our attention is rarely drawn to that.

Of course, when I am crossing the road, I make my *multimodal ensemble* out of the many resources available. Yet here too, in the plane just before take-off, this carefully *orchestrated ensemble* meets up with *my interest* (or lack of it) and it is still *my interest* which shapes my *attention* and guides my *framing* of this moment – even though the ensemble had been carefully *framed* for me. In other words, presenting an *orchestrated ensemble* does not of itself guarantee or determine my *attention*, nor my *framing* and not therefore my *interpretation*. It does however provide the 'ground' on which my *selection* and *interpretation* take place. The ensemble makes certain resources available in a specific order; that is the material, the ground, from which I shape the prompt which is the basis of my interpretation.

That is a fundamental point in communication: the difference between the outwardly directed making of the *sign* → text → message by someone *for me* and *my* inwardly directed *making* of a new *sign* in my *engagement* with that *signifier* → text → message. It is easy to lose sight of that crucial difference, lodged between the necessary emphasis on the double process of sign-making: that of the 'initial' maker of the sign as a *ground* for me and that of my engagement with that sign/ *prompt*. The initial maker of the sign – the sign that becomes the *prompt* for my *response* – 'sets the ground' on which my *attention* focuses (or not), and *framing selection* and my making of a sign/meaning for myself takes place. To repeat: that is a fundamental point about communication and about theories of communication alike. The recognition of multimodality makes theorizing what is a complex process just that much more complex.

The issues of *orchestration* and *ensembles* are entirely related and yet distinct; the former names the process of *assembling/organizing/designing* a plurality of signs in different modes into a particular configuration to form a coherent arrangement; the latter names the results of these processes of design and orchestration. *Orchestration* describes the processes of *selecting/assembling/designing* the semiotic 'materials' which seem essential to meet the rhetor's *interests* and which will be given shape as the semiotic entity of *text* as an *ensemble*, through the processes of *design*. *Orchestrations* and the resultant *ensembles* can be organized in *space* and they can be organized in *time*, in *sequence*, in *process*, in *motion*. The basic principles of design apply to both kinds of ensembles, *spatial* and *temporal*; some principles apply separately and differently to each of the two types of *arrangement*.

The world arranged by me, the world arranged for me: orchestrating ensembles, staging of *movement, motion, 'pace'*

The *ensemble* (the *genre*) of the safety demonstration on the plane is carefully orchestrated and it 'unfolds' in time. Different modes are foregrounded at different moments in the sequence and different modes carry specific information. By and large, modes are used aptly: *gesture* to 'point to' specific aspects; *speech* to *explain* and *recount*; *action* to *demonstrate*; and were we to look at the safety card there would be *images* to *show* specific situations and *writing* to provide *complementary information* for the *images* in specific ways. The temporal unfolding is intended to reveal information in a staged sequence for me.

The next example shows a specific instance of an entirely usual example, as complex as my account from the plane. It is meant to push the exploration of *multimodal orchestration* and of *multimodal ensembles* a step further. The example comes from a series of science lessons on 'blood circulation' in a class for thirteen-year-olds in an inner London school (Kress *et al.*, 2001). The class has had three lessons on blood circulation and this is the fourth and last lesson on this topic. Before the students had come into the classroom, the teacher had drawn a large circle (with two lines, to make a 'tube' with an inner and an outer ring) on the whiteboard (Figure 8.1). At the top of the circle he had drawn a symbol to indicate the heart. As the students enter the classroom – after a mid-morning break – this image is there on the board. During the lesson the teacher modifies the diagram several times; by drawing arrows on it as he suggests the direction in which the blood is moving and which organs the blood is 'visiting'; by adding a second loop on the top (Figure 8.2) to indicate that the structure of the circulatory system is in fact more complex than the first drawing had indicated. His drawing on the diagram during the lesson allows him

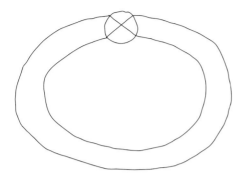

Figure 8.1
Blood circulation: circle

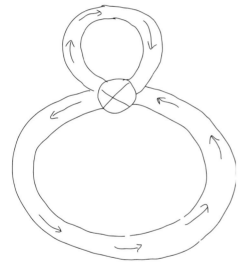

Figure 8.2
Blood circulation: arrows and loop

to develop a more complex model from this simple one. However, he also 'modified' the diagram in other ways, which were no longer visible afterwards. He did this by 'overlaying' gestures on the diagram with his hand: moving his hand over the circle in the direction of the blood's circulation; placing his hand lightly on the diagram at various points to indicate the organs visited: 'It goes to the lungs . . . to the small intestine . . . to the cells . . . to the heart.'

In this sequentially unfolding ensemble, at times *speech* is foregrounded, with the *image* as the focus of what is said. At first he uses *gestures* alone in relation to the diagram, to indicate the location of organs. He then picks up a marker pen and *draws* arrows inside the circle, at points which he had previously indicated in *gesture*. The *image* is now permanently modified. A bit later in the lesson, the teacher bends down and from below the desk he gets a *3D model* of the upper part of a human torso; he places this in front of him on the desk. This model is a three-dimensional *classification* of the relevant curricular entities. These are three-dimensional parts of the model: detachable object-entities in many cases – the front of the chest, the heart, the front of the heart, arteries – all of these are also curricular knowledge-entities. *Gesturally* he relates part of the *model* to parts of his own *body*, to establish an empirically founded equivalence between real body and model and, through that, to establish the *realism* of the *ensemble* and of the theoretical construct of *blood circulation*.

The *multimodal ensemble* is transformed successively throughout this sequence. At various points it consists of (different) *orchestrations* of *image* (the successively modified diagram), *speech, gesture, 3D model,* and his own *body* as well. The *configuration/ orchestration* of the *ensemble* is constantly adjusted by the rhetor/teacher, in relation to his sense of pedagogic need. The *ensemble* and its parts – the diagram as well as the 3D model – are constantly transformed: through the *gestural overlay*; through other *actions* by the teacher and by his *gestures* linking the *3D model* with *his body* as the empirical grounding and guarantor of the scientific 'security' of the ensemble. Having taken the front off the model, exposing its insides and pointing to the heart he says, with his elbows tucked closely into his body: 'It needs something to start pumping.' He accompanies that by bellows-like movements with his elbows and arms, moving his tucked-in arms away from the body slightly, then pressing them into the body again. Interspersed with this he makes several contracting gestures with his hands – made into fists and then opened again – to indicate the contracting action of the heart muscles, a gesture made several times in quick succession.

The teacher's talk (where // marks off intonation-information units):
'We can think about it // as a circle of blood like this // going round // and at various points // say // the lungs are here // the small intestines here // and the cells are here // and the kidneys up here // okay // so it's going all the way around // and what it needs // is something to start pumping it again // to give it a bit more motion // to go around // okay //.'

The teacher's actions:
Points at head; traces finger around circle; returns hand to heart; draws on arrows; places opened hand at left of diagram; places opened hand at bottom left of diagram; places opened hand at bottom right of diagram; places opened hand at top right of diagram; draws arrows on circle; points at heart; bends elbow; arms at side, makes bellows action; makes bellows action three times; puts lid on pen.

Here, in a rough transcription, we have an ensemble of *speech, image* as diagram, *gesture*. There is also the *teacher's positioning* while he is conducting this demonstration: the *orchestration* of an *ensemble* in a multimodal fashion by the teacher.

It is relatively straightforward to understand the *functional specialization* of the modes here; the mimetic clenching and unclenching of the teacher's hands to suggest the contraction and expansion of the heart muscle; the bellows-like pressing in of his arms into his upper body. What is less clear is their modal *interrelation*, in two ways. In terms of their *functional load*, *gesture, action* and *speech* seem to share the load – *gesture* and *action* alone would not be sufficiently explicit; *speech* alone would be neither explicit enough nor would it be as persuasive. So while *speech* 'names'; *gesture* mimes; *action* 'enacts' in a manner that is easy to re-enact for the students in an 'inner' mimetic action: to 'feel', to 'experience' in 'inner' mimetic remaking. Nor is the direction in meaning of the modal interrelation quite clear: do the gestures/actions *illustrate* or *demonstrate* the meaning of 'pump'? – that is, is there an implied 'If you want to know what is meant by the word "pump", look at this'; or do the words supply a name for the persuasive action? – that is, an implied 'If you need a lexical hook, a metaphor to make sense of this action, then what about the metaphor "pump"?'.

In ensembles of this kind the contingent status of modes becomes clear: is word made explicit by action? Or is action 'given meaning shape' by a word and drawn into lexical classification? The *ensemble* offers a *ground* which, in its multimodal orchestration is *multiply meaningful*; and so the effects for the students of the interrelation and interaction of the modes in the teacher's *orchestration* are difficult to predict. The ensemble offers a choice of routes of meaning-making in interpretation, which the students can take up according to their interests. And that may well be what the teacher 'intends': offering several distinct means of access, all of which are in their potentials differently plausible for all students at different moments. No doubt this has worked before; for the teacher and for the students.

So what more general strategies of meaning-making can be draw out of this example? The hugely abstracted diagrammatic representation of 'blood circulation' remains on the board throughout the whole lesson. That is, the most abstracted representation *persists* throughout, on the board. It provides a stable backdrop against which the constantly changing orchestration can be developed. Much later, when the teacher has placed the 3D model on the bench in front of him, or later still, towards the end of the lesson, when he refers to a textbook to show how all this is represented in canonical form in a book, the abstract representation still remains. In its most general form, as a large abstraction of the topic it remains a constant, stable presence and a constant backdrop to the teacher's gradual building up of the detail of a dynamically varying ensemble. Constantly there, providing rocklike stability – 'This is what we are talking about' – and yet constantly modified, from moment to moment. Neither speech nor writing could fulfil that task. The gestural overlay over the image serves the function of adding necessary specific detail, gradually. Yet once the gestures have been made, they are also 'gone' – vanished, no longer visible. No permanent, recorded trace of them remains. This has great advantages for the teacher: the lungs are not actually 'there' where the gesture had placed them; nor is the small intestine 'there', next to the lungs on that circle. Nor for that matter are the cells an organ in the way the lungs are, nor are they 'there' between small intestine and kidneys, where both speech and gesture had placed them. But the gestural placing – accompanied by speech – has given them sufficient ontological status, enough *realism* for the effect to have been achieved. More than that, as they are not recorded, the specific effects or details of the gestural overlay cannot be challenged. There is no accountability for what can no longer be seen. It is not possible for a student to say 'But Sir, you *said* the cells were *there* and your *gesture pointed it out*.' 'There' has done its function doubly: by suggesting a real presence and location and by making that real presence and location impossible to challenge.

This shows (just one of) the different functions of speech and of gesture: *speech*, to *name*, to *lexicalize* – the *cells*, present everywhere in the body, are given a *name*, and as a noun, like nouns that name the other organs, they are explicitly classified as being like other organs; and *gesture* to *locate* an entity in the relevant space, to *localize* it in a specific site. In this part of the lesson sequence, *speech* follows *gesture*: gesture *indicates, points out, localizes, makes real*; while *speech names*, gives a *name* – after the (gestural) event – to *actions, processes, entities* which have already been established through *image* or *gesture* or other *action*.

In doing so, speech acts as a means of 'ratification': something that has been done by another mode is 'ratified' through its naming in *speech*. Had the teacher actually drawn the organs in the 'correct' place on the circle, it would have been a problem in two ways: the *epistemological commitment* given by that action – 'The lungs are there' – could not have been supported, for plainly they are not; nor could the *classification* of cells as an organ just like other organs be supported. Both naming and placement 'there', when plainly they too are not, could easily have been challenged by the students, thereby undercutting the whole pedagogic and theoretical edifice. The transience of *gesture* serves ideally in that respect: it makes the points that need to be made clearly and strongly; and, having made them, gesture is gone.

A *gesture* may precede the *name* and its *naming*; or the *name* may precede the *gesture*. Each possibility gives the other a different, a specific function. It may be simultaneous with the mention of a name. Each of these possibilities shifts the relative mutual relation of the modes to each other. Speech may 'fill' the more open, maybe still vague meaning of the gesture; it makes it explicit. Where the gesture *illustrates* the name, it gives a concreteness, substance, a 'reality' to a verbal entity – 'If you wish to know what pumping is, then watch this.'

The classificatory act of naming serves its purposes differently: it draws a gestural entity into what is in most domains the most developed cultural classificatory means in Western – and maybe in other – cultures; but gives it no visible form. As a 'word' the name is not a problem in the teacher's orchestration here; as an *image* it would be. Any problems with the word can be dealt with later; whereas as *image* – say, of the cells as an 'organ' – it would be visibly and ontologically and in plain common sense – unsustainable. As I suggested, the use of an image would undermine the credibility of the whole 'performance'.

Frequently, in temporally organized multimodal ensembles, the orderings within ensembles change, quite as the choice of musical instruments in the orchestrations of a melody in a musical text changes in the course of its performance. Such re-orderings have implications for genre, for discourse and epistemology. Often, in sequentially organized ensembles, one mode is prominent for rhetorical (as well as at times for 'real' reasons); then another, then another.

The example of the 'persistent circle', that is, a sign which remains present to an audience for an extended duration, is not in any way an isolated instance in multi-modal ensembles. In a research project on the school subject 'English' (Kress *et al.*, 2005) we saw how teachers had designed the walls of 'their' classrooms as spaces for the display of those aspects of 'English' which were for them representative of the subject as they saw it and/or as they wanted the students to see it. Many teachers displayed writing done by the students, framed in different ways. Others used the walls to display their 'own' materials – images, bits of writing from different places, posters. All of this happened in the context of tight policy regulation around the subject, so these 'designs' were one available means for teachers to position them-selves in relation to policy, to the students and to their sense of the subject. It offered the possibility for the realization of their sense of what they thought English 'was', what it 'was for' and importantly, 'who it was for'. Two examples are shown here.

In Figure 8.3, the walls are covered in images and posters drawn from (the teacher's sense of) the culture of the students in their lives outside of school. A student coming into this classroom might get the sense that 'English is the subject which relates to my everyday life outside school, and gives me means of making sense of it.'

In a different school (all the schools were within the 'inner London' area), the walls (Figure 8.4) are decorated with carefully mounted, framed, and displayed curricular concepts from the National Curriculum for English. A student coming into this room might think that 'knowing English means knowing the concepts of the National Curriculum for English so that I can pass the exam with a reasonable hope of success'. Students coming in to this room might get the sense that English – just like the subject Science – is defined by the concepts set out in the National Curriculum.

Figure 8.3 What English is for: English as popular culture

Figure 8.4 What English is for: English as National Curriculum

The significant effect in each case, communicationally speaking – ignoring the quite profoundly different suggestions about what English is and *is for* – is the persistence of one element of the ensemble that makes the complex sign of 'English': the display on the walls. It is a constant, silent, unavoidable and insistent visual message of what English is. Being unspoken and unwritten, it is a message beyond challenge. It would be difficult for a student (or parent or maybe even head teacher) to challenge either conception of English by saying 'I really don't agree with what you're saying English is (*for*).' That statement can be met with 'What do you mean, what exactly have I been saying about English?'.

In a multimodal social-semiotic approach, what applies to these classrooms applies to all environments in which we lead our lives – large or small, brief or persistent, permanent or transient. Cities and their streetscapes have such constant, insistent and irresistible effects. Streetscapes constitute both curricula and pedagogies; more effective for being unspoken and impossible to challenge – other than by avoiding and leaving them. I often try to imagine the kinds of affect, the kinds of life which are projected, and the lives which could or *could not* be led in the 'scapes' of the different places I encounter.

In sequenced, temporally 'unfolding', 'staged' ensembles, modes occur in a temporally ordered fashion. I mentioned the precedence of *gesture* over *speech* in the example from the Science classroom. This is a common communicational phenomenon in 'English' in England, especially where a topic is 'difficult' for whatever reason – a word that is socially awkward or conceptually difficult, not remembered or not quite right for some reason. Here gestures often precede; and maybe they do so always, if we count the hesitations, the so-called *umms* and *errs* in speech.

Usually of course we are so immersed in the flow of ongoing communication that we are unaware of this sequencing. It is easy however (and need not be noticeably impolite) to 'step back' for a moment or two and observe. Gestures are invariably, and contrary to popular view, specific in form, that is, they can be readily related to the spoken utterance which eventually follows. Often, when speech follows as ratification, the gesture is some dynamic forward movement made with the hands, a kind of forward rolling of both hands, or a gestural outlining of the 'shape' of what that thing not yet spoken might be or might look like.

These things are social and therefore learned; hence they differ from culture to culture. I became aware of this relation of gesture to speech quite some time ago, when I was involved in looking at someone else's data over some period of time. I had seen written transcripts of bits of the data many times. On this occasion, it was the first time I was invited to view the actual videos. Three six-year-olds in a primary classroom were playing at being teacher and students. The 'teacher' would 'prefigure' her spoken address to one of the two 'students' with a slight turning of her head towards the 'student', then a turning of her body, prior to her 'nominating' him verbally to speak. In watching the video it became absolutely clear to me that speech *ratified* (the word I thought of at that time) what had already been established in *gaze, posture, movement* and *action*.

In the research project of 'visitor studies' mentioned in Chapter 3, we noticed that two people will be in conversation in some part of the exhibition when one of them begins to 'move' – actionally and gesturally: first a shift in gaze, then a slight bodily (re-)positioning, and a complex staged ensemble of 'shifts' is enacted prior to a spoken 'I think I'll just have a look at . . .' We know these things from our own experience; they point to much 'inner movement', 'thinking', which is 'prefigured' by an orchestration of several modes and communicated by means other than speech before being *ratified* in speech. Usually the other member of the 'pair' is aware of this communication and makes complementary modal adjustments: the spoken ratification comes as no surprise.

Ratification is a process whereby meanings sketched or introduced in one mode are subsequently re-articulated in a mode which is relatively more explicit in relation to the topic at issue. This raises methodological points about the *sequencing, ordering,* '*staging*' of modes in multimodal ensembles, questions about which mode is prior, about what semiotic work is being done with the prior mode and about the functions of the subsequent modes in an ensemble; as well as about the purposes and effects of this staging of communication. For the Science teacher the modal staging has several advantages: sequential clarification is a kind of repetition which, not being in the same mode, is not experienced as a repetition; and it enables a form of repetition which is also an ontologically and epistemologically different (re)statement. As a restatement it allows different students to engage with 'the same' issue via routes which may be affectively, sensorially or culturally more congenial to them. At the same time it affords a fuller exploration of the topic at issue.

The conditions of power which obtain in a given environment have effects on what kinds of modal 'stagings', ordering and sequencing of information are possible.

Aesthetics, style and ethics in multimodal ensembles

All communication is movement. Interacting in dialogue is movement: my interest directs my attention; it frames a part of the semiotic world. I select from the *prompt* that I receive and construct a complex sign/text/ensemble as my response in return; which I pass on to my interlocutors. Turning the pages of a book is movement, preceded by the movement of my eyes over the lines of print and the simultaneous 'inner' movement of my interpretation of the written, ordered material. Entering into the syntax of the linguistic, written 'stuff' that I am engaging with, is movement of a quite different kind. This is not to speak of the 'movement' of connecting the ensemble which I am interpreting with other text-ensembles that seem to me to connect, more or less distantly; nor to speak of the movement of what I have been taught to call 'my imagination'.

There are movements of different kinds, in different environments, with different prompts and with different effects. Reducing the turning of the pages of a book to the same activity as the movement I engage in when I range across texts of a similar kind in my recollection to form connections with a text I am engaged with at the moment, is to empty the idea of movement of any real significance. What kind of activity am I engaged in when I am 'flicking' from channel to channel; how does it differ from my prior movement across a printed TV programme? When I am engaged in the 'navigation' of a website on the internet via the screen of my laptop it is a specific kind of movement; as is the movement of the 'mouse' in my hand. Do different media invite or demand specific kinds of movement across the different kinds of textual arrangements; and do these lead to different forms of imagination? And if so, what are these?

Movement and meaning are intertwined, so there might seem to be no need to draw attention to movement and the *pace* of movement – if attention to meaning already takes care of all of these. Yet the integration of multimodality with the facilities of the screen as site of display and of dissemination has unsettled what had long been a 'naturalized' kind of semiotic movement, that of the *reading* of pages. In the era of the joint dominance of the page and writing, the movement of the eye across written text; the reader's engagement with the syntax of the writing; the turning of the page and the move from chapter to chapter were habituated, unnoticed, invisible, *naturalized*.

The screen, as an inherently *spatially organized site of display*, coupled with the affordances of the digital technologies, has shifted the centre of semiotic gravity to the new arrangement of the *facilities* of the *screen* and *image-dominated representation*. In that new arrangement, *writing* is not disappearing by any means, though it is being remade. *Writing* is newly organized by the demands of the spatial logic of the visual mode which dominates the 'screen'; and remade too by the new functional relations of image and writing.

Engaging with screens and their representations requires new forms of movement. The notion of the *reading path* in its traditional form (Kress and van Leeuwen, 1996/2006) becomes problematic, maybe redundant. Or rather, it needs to be re-theorized in the light of the theory which asserts that 'communication happens when there is interpretation' and that 'interpretation is a response to a prompt', then the *reading path* is made by the reader's interest in response to the *arrangement* of the *prompt*; it becomes the documentation of the 'semiotic movements' of the person who has engaged with a specific *ensemble*.

In Chapter 3 I considered a BBC website for children (Figure 8.5). Here I want to comment briefly on the homepage for adults from that same date in 2005. The colour is light blue, black print/fonts, with other colours used – 'realistically' – where it seems apt: for two small portrait photos, and a small image of Turner's *The Fighting Temeraire* in the top right corner. Where the children's website invited its 'visitors' to move across the site according to their interest, the site for adults – still more traditional – is displayed in three columns which are organized by topics/themes: 'Sport', 'Browse', 'Television', etc., with a 'menu-bar on the left, with topics such as 'Health', 'News', 'Lifestyle', 'Society and Culture'. In other words, there is more order(ing), more direction, more sense of predicted movement, both conceptually, in terms of topics and spatially in terms of left to right ordering of the columns and top-down ordering within each column. The movement imagined and suggested for the two

Figure 8.5
CBBC homepage
2005

sets of readers differs, even in colour – 'staying' with the single dominant blue of the site for adults compared to moving across, over, around, the multiple colours in the site for children.

My interest is in the *uses* of modes, more than in the *forms* of multimodal texts, though the two are intricately related. My questions are: What modes are used, in what arrangements; and how do modes and arrangement project, signify and appeal to the kinds of audiences imagined as 'viewers'/'visitors' of these two sites? I am interested in the kind of movement that is imagined in the engagement with the two screens by the designer of each of these two homepages.

The layout of the two 'pages' is deeply different; and my assumption is that difference of 'generation' of audience is projected here. I will not engage in description here, other than to point to notions of 'orderliness' and to the aesthetics of the two 'screens'.

Both forms of layout/textual arrangement are the result of the constant trans-formative work of a decade and a half of homepage design; the equivalent screens now, in 2009, are already very different, with a discernible 'direction of travel' toward an aesthetic of movement, colour, 'fuller' multimodality in the case of the CBBC site; and a 'catching up' in the direction of modular organization for the BBC site. The instability of the genre – profound by contrast with previous periods – points to the instability of the social world of the audience which the designers of the websites are dealing with and attempting to project and capture.

The two kinds of layout offer different forms of engagement with the screens. The more orderly arrangement of the BBC homepage is meant to appeal to a generation which might still be used to more traditional pages and their layout, and which still had – in potential – a reading path. *Choice* is not the issue – both homepages offer the possibility of choosing; rather the issue is how the possibility of choice is mediated via the arrangement of the page. The BBC site is arranged in terms of *columns*, each with internally orderly choices, which can however be selected in any order. In the case of the CBBC page, there is a clearly modular organization: a 'collection' of self-contained textual blocks, larger than those on the BBC page (where only a few modules exist – the units here are still more paragraph like).

The other immediately striking difference lies in the aesthetics of colour. In the original, the BBC colour range is narrower: four shades of a light blue, three of these desaturated. Small inset images – two photographs of people, one photograph of a painting and a reproduction of a diagram – use colours other than the blue. The CBBC site uses a much wider range of colours: yellow, red, green, mauve, purple, pink; all of them are saturated colours. This use of 'childlike' colours is matched by the use of fonts and images which suggest the subjectivity of a very young child – somewhere between 10 months to 4 years maybe (I am assuming here a congruence with the colour of toys for children).

In terms of *genre* there is an absolute difference: of projected habitus of 'reading' or of 'engagement' with the site; in forms of 'realism' of the two sites: a fantasy 'surrealism' for the CBBC site and a near 'everyday realism' for the BBC site; and of course in terms of the projection of *social domains*: pleasure/fun/play as against the calmer, more serious domain of the person who enjoys being 'informed' as much as she or he enjoys being entertained. On the BBC screen, 'reading' remains connected to traditional forms: the dominant, foregrounded mode is *writing*. However, the reader of the screen is no longer tied to a strict *reading path* as they would have been in older TV programmes, where time of day and day of the week were the organizing principles. Here the principle is 'interest', expressed via the notion of 'topic'. Within that arrangement the reader is free to choose according to their interest.

'Reading' of the CBBC site is first of all based on a notion of 'engagement' with visual, image-like modules. That is clearly also on the basis of interest – and 'reading' is first and foremost engagement with entities conceived as visual not verbal. In terms of the organization of content this is less by 'topics' (e.g. sport, news) than by 'programmes' (e.g. Backstage, Superheroes) and 'activities' (e.g. Games, xchange, shoebox zoo).

Aesthetics is the category which seems essential to make analytic inroads here, about characteristics of the imagined readership, of the relation of web design (standing in for the authority which has commissioned and approved the web design) and viewer/reader. *Aesthetics* as the politics of *style* – with *style* as the politics of choice and *ethics* as the politics of (e)valuation – allows me to ask what kind of viewer/

reader/visitor, is imagined, with what tastes and habitus, what lifestyle, what age/ generation, what gender. It also allows me to speculate whether the reader/viewer/ visitor is likely to be attracted by the proffered forms of *engagement* – with a relation to the reader's imagined subjectivity: 'serious' yet 'light', interested in the public domain yet not stolid, generationally not all that specific but certainly beyond their mid-twenties; or by the proffered *aesthetic,* in image and colour, oriented to fun, to play, to choice among those things which are there to choose from.

If we assume that *genre* is the 'entexting' of the social relations which obtain in a particular social encounter, then both the offered forms of reading/engagement and the offered kinds of modal resources – for instance *writing* versus *image*; one colour scheme rather than another; one kind of *font* rather than the other; this form of *realism* rather than that; movement versus none – are signs of an imagined social relation and are therefore part of the *genre* of a textual form/semiotic entity. In this, both *genre* and *modal choices* are indications of the rhetor's and then the designer's sense of their audience and their relation to that audience. Both speak of specific *aesthetics.* That makes the category of *aesthetics* into a social, political and cultural category of central significance.

It is possible and I think useful to use the notions of *style* and *aesthetics* and to speak of two entirely distinct aesthetics – using that term in the way I have described it as 'the politics of style' and with that 'the politics of taste' – as social judgements based on social valuations supported by varying degrees of power. This definition of *aesthetics* includes, for me, a projection of the characteristics of the audience to whom this aesthetic will be and can be appealing. That of course applies to both websites and its distinct audiences. In using the term 'political' here I am referring to the power involved in the ascription, implicitly, of a 'taste' to each of the two audiences.

9 Applying the theory: learning and evaluation; identity and knowledge

Learning and identity in a communicational frame

The world of meaning has always been multimodal. Now, for a variety of reasons, that realization is once again moving centre-stage. A range of questions arises from this re-recognition. In education, for instance, the question of what theories are needed to deal with *learning* and *assessment* in a multimodally constituted world of meaning is becoming newly and insistently urgent. That question also poses, in a more general form, the issues of *identity* and *knowledge*: *identity* seen as the outcome of constant transformative engagement by someone with 'the world', with a resultant enhancement of their capacities for acting in the world. In that frame, *knowledge* is seen not as the outcome of processes regulated by power and authority but of everyday, entirely banal processes of meaning-making by individuals in their engagement with the world. The augmentation – in the processes of learning – of the individual's capacity is at the same time a change in *identity* of the person.

Teaching and *learning* are *communication*: they are reciprocal aspects of one relation. *Learning* is the obverse of *making meaning*. *Learning* is the result of a semiotic/conceptual/meaning-making engagement with an aspect of the world; as a result the learner's semiotic/conceptual resources for making meaning and, therefore, for acting in the world, are changed – they are augmented. This augmentation of an individual's capacity is at the same time a change in *identity* of the person who now has different capacities for acting – in whatever way – through *knowledge*-as-tool to deal with problems in that individual's life-world.

Given that *teaching* and *learning* are instances of communication, they invoke theories both of *communication* and of *meaning*. In this frame, *assessment* is the evaluation from a specific perspective of the kinds of augmentation there have been. *Assessment* deals with a relation between *that which was (expected) to be learned* – explicitly as a curriculum or implicitly as 'experience' – and *that which has been learned*.

Irrespective of the environment in which learning happens, it is the learner's interest which frames her or his attention to what becomes *that which is to be learned*, and which therefore functions as the curricular prompt.

A major issue for *assessment* is what might constitute data of *that which has been learned*. A common means of getting such 'data' has been to ask someone, in some way or another: *what* they (thought that they) might have learned; or *how* they felt that they had learned. Methodologically and in terms of the semiotic theory proposed here, that seems thoroughly unsatisfactory. Instead I use the notion of *signs of learning* (Jewitt and Kress, 2001). A *sign of learning* shows some *difference* in the *capacities* of the learner in their making as signs as the result of learning.

There is then the issue of *assessment* itself and differences between *(e)valuation* and *assessment*. These have been the substance of a vast academic endeavour, captured in shorthand by the two terms *formative* and *summative assessment*. Given that valuation happens in all environments in respect to all our actions, always, a theory of assessment ideally applies to all environments and all forms of *evaluation*; its focus would be on what *metrics* can or might be used in different instances of *(e)valuation*.

Evaluation has application in relation to *identity*, through its effects on the individual evaluated by whatever means. For instance, *evaluation* matched with power can, will be and usually is meant to have normative effects. Even in non-institutional environments and with small power differences or none, *evaluation* has effect as feedback and what is done with that feedback.

Communicational environments are complex, and learning environments no less so. They are marked by a plethora of phenomena all of which can, potentially, become *prompts*; whether they do or not depends on the *interest* of a participant; her or his *interest* directs their *attention* to the *ground*; this 'interested attention' *frames* an aspect of the communicational environment as a *prompt*; the characteristics and the 'shape' of the *prompt* provide the basis on which the *interpretation* proceeds; the participant *engages* with features of the *prompt;* and he or she forms their interpretation.

The action which follows the *prompt* is based on the *interpretation* that there has been; it is a *sign* of and based on that *interpretation*. If we switch our lens from *communication* to one of *communication-as-learning* then this is a *sign of learning*. If we switch from that to the lens of *identity*, we see a change in the capacity for action of an individual: a change – however slight – in *identity*.

Reading as design

Through the lens of *learning*, the rudimentary theory sketched here focuses on the *learner* rather than on the teacher and on teaching. The lens of communication focuses on much the same phenomena as 'everyday practices' and seeks to understand them as such – and in their effects on the shaping of identity.

Unlike the traditional page, designed with a (pre-) given order of engagement/ reading, the website shown in Colour plate 2 needs the reader's *ordering-as-design*. The reader's interest determines how she or he will engage with the page and establishes the order in which its elements are 'read'. It is the reader's interest which provides the *design* of this page in that respect. In that, the question of modes of representation is in the foreground. On a first scanning of the site it is not at all clear that *writing* provides the first means of engagement. Placement of the elements does not determine the order of 'reading-as-engagement'. 'Reading' is now a matter of the design of the 'page' or the 'screen' by the reader. That suggests – and projects – a different disposition for the reader or learner, a different identity to one which is expected to follow a predetermined path.

If 'reading' follows the route of *interest, attention, engagement, prompt, framing,* it becomes ever more difficult to imagine and to maintain that for such readers *learning* – when it is encountered as such – does not follow the same route as *reading*. Readers who read according to *a design of their interest* – even though on the *ground* of someone else's prompt – are likely to take much the same attitude in relation to their semiotic engagement with other domains in their world. In other words, dispositions developed in one area – reading – are likely to become principles that will be applied elsewhere; or, looking at it the other way, principles from elsewhere – the 'market' let's say – are brought into this semiotic domain.

It might be objected that 'reading' for pleasure is one thing and that *reading/ engagement/learning* in an institutional site of learning is another: there is the issue of power. Here I will focus briefly on that. In Chapter 3 I briefly referred to a research-project on visitor studies in museums in Stockholm and London. Museums do not, usually, exercise power over their visitors in relation either to *communication* or *learning*. As I mentioned earlier, the data was designed to elicit signs of the visitors' engagement as learning through the photos they had taken, the map they had drawn, as well as through the recording of the talk between them and their partner. This was an attempt to minimize the effect – if any – of felt power the visitors might have had of needing to conform to expectations, authoritatively buttressed.

In Chapter 3 I showed two of the maps produced by visitors (page 40); an imme-diate objection might have been that 'these are not maps'. But it is precisely the absence of power which allowed the emergence of profoundly different notions of what a map is, something that does not usually emerge or become visible either in the presence of power or in the fast-paced interactions of everyday life. The (relative) absence of power allows the emergence both of the individuals' interest with which they come to the exhibition and the effect of that interest in the visitors' engagement with an exhibition.

An exhibition is designed; its designer(s) have specific aims: not just to show objects, images, reconstructions, or to tell stories of the prehistory of a nation; they have specific social purposes in mind. These are often not overtly stated; though in interviews with curators or the curatorial team it is clear that much discussion, framed by larger-level policies of the museum around such purposes, had been had.

Increasingly, museums are sites of 'social education': proposing to their visitors conceptions of a social and cultural kind: a curriculum of social education. An exhibition is thus the design of a learning environment. As with other institutional sites of education the question 'Whose interest is to dominate?' then comes to the fore. Is it the interest of the museum, or that of the curator, or the interests of the visitors? In other words, the situation can become quite like that of the school – teacher – student. Depending on how this is seen and implemented, the actions of visitors, their responses will be evaluated.

Semiotically speaking, an exhibition is a message; it is meant as a *prompt* to the visitors who come to engage with it. *Pedagogically* speaking, an exhibition (re)presents a curriculum for the visitor/learner. In that context, the maps are indications of how aspects of the overall design-message have engaged the visitor's interest; they are *signs of interest* and *signs of learning*.

The maps are of real interest, whether from the perspective of *communication* or of *learning*. They are not in any way a full account of the meanings made by either of the two visitors. Yet they do give a clear sense of a difference in interest; of a consequent difference in attention and framing; and of distinctly different *interpretations* of the same *ground*. These differences can be taken to rest on differences in identity; including the sense of identity the visitors felt that they should or could assume in that setting.

These are questions for the curator and they are the motivation for engaging in 'visitor studies'. Looking with the lens of *learning* and *assessment* these are *the* questions. What principles did each of the visitors/learners apply in their engagement with the curriculum of the exhibition? What consequences follow for the pedagogue? Then come considerations of the path which the (curator as) teacher might have wanted the (visitor/) learner to take.

The curator might wish to understand the reasons for the differences in interpretation. One is provided by the notion of *interest*. As it happened, one of the visitors was an 11-year-old boy, whose school had its mid-term break; so his mother took him out for a day to the museum. His interest was caught by a display that showed that Heathrow airport covered a Neolithic site, a reconstruction of which was shown. His interest is expressed in the map: but that is the case equally clearly in all the maps. The prehistoric camp map was drawn by one of two German 18-year-old students, who were very engaged with the exhibition – and the task they had been given. A *teacher* needs to be equally interested in such differences and in their origins; though that is not the usual path taken in forms of assessment.

The matter of *modes* arises here via the question of *rhetoric* and *design*: that is, the question of rhetoric goes to the initial conception of the exhibition and from there to the overall 'shaping' of the exhibition: in the selection of its objects, in its layout, in its lighting, in the salience given to particular themes and areas and to the modes chosen in representing specific meanings. Are three-dimensional objects more salient, more 'attractive', more noticeable than written captions or than longer written accounts/explanations? Are painted scenes more engaging than three-dimensional tableaux? What effect does lighting have in creating *affect* and *mood*? Is the distance at which visitors are able to engage with objects – for instance, the question whether they are available to touch an object – a significant matter? The question of *affect* has to be addressed in the case of the exhibition: the wrong affect will 'turn off' potential visitors.

Through the lens of *teaching*, *effectiveness* is likely to be judged in terms of *assessment* of some form or other. *What has been learned* is now the centre of attention. The question appears in two ways as: 'How can we assess learning expressed in *modes* other than those which are dominant in formal educational settings – what theoretical and practical means do we have to assess learning in different modes; how do we assess multimodally?' and as 'What knowledge about modal representation and therefore about multimodal assessment do we actually have?'.

While the first question is about 'means', the second question is about 'recognition': 'How do we or *can* we *recognize* learning when it is expressed in the non-dominant mode(s)?', 'How was the curriculum expressed in terms of modes and how is *what has been learned* now represented modally?', 'What is actually recognized as *means of representation* of learning, as means of knowing?'. It is a question of 'visibility': What is *visible* to the 'eye of assessment'? What is it possible, actually, to see?

Semiosis, meaning and learning

Learning is not a term that belongs in semiotics. So can there be a (*social*)-*semiotic* theory of learning? And what might we mean by *learning*? Notions of *learning* are products of the theories in which they are developed. Theories are historical, social and hence ideological products of the manifold social and political forces of the time of their making and use; theories of *learning* are no exception. *Learning* in institutional settings is a political matter and as such highly subject to power and ideology. Beyond that, there is the question of disciplinary difference; a psychological, linguistic, social or anthropological, never mind a pedagogical theory of learning, will each produce distinctly different understandings of *learning*.

And, can one ever talk about *learning-as-such,* or can we only ever talk of learning in specific contexts? Contemporary theorizing in parts of the Humanities and the Social Science favours that latter view. Here there are confident claims that the brains of younger generations are now differently wired, due to the effects of contemporary technologies.

Such questions point in two directions. One is: 'Is learning always shaped in essential respects by the structures, resources, participants and environments of the occasions of learning?'. The other is: 'Is there *learning as such* irrespective of the circumstances in which it takes place?'. Both of these are central to *multimodal social semiotics,* in that they focus on the role of the social and the material resources in and through which meaning is made and by which learning therefore takes place.

Questions of meaning and of learning are in essence the same questions, though posed from distinct disciplinary perspectives – one semiotic and one pedagogic – and posed therefore with different purposes. One cannot have a theory of learning without a theory of meaning, however implicit that may be; a theory of learning always entails a theory of meaning. Meaning is the stuff of semiotics, hence semiotics is inevitably and centrally implicated in any theory of learning. Semiotically speaking, *sign-making is meaning-making* and *learning* is the result of these processes.

The term *learning* tends to be used when these processes happen in institutions with particular purposes and forms of power, with institutionally organized sets of entities as a *curriculum*, with which learners are required to engage. In these sites, that is, in the environment of a *pedagogy, learning* usually has associated with it metrics for assessment. These have the aim of making *social subjects* according to the purposes of the social group 'standing behind' the educational institution. The question 'What is *learning*?' implicitly raises the question 'What is *not learning*?'. My answer is that '*not learning*' refers to the same processes and phenomena as *learning* does, though outside of institutional framings and their metrics. Outside those framings, these are called *experience, development, meaning-making*, and so on.

The conception of the motivated sign, with the interest and agency of the sign-maker evident in the shape of the sign, has direct implications for assessment. The sign – say, either one of the two maps – is the result of its maker's interest and is an apt reflection of that interest. The maker of the sign has made the form of the sign as an apt expression of the meaning she or he wanted to be represented. For the recipient of the sign therefore, the *shape*, the *form* of the sign, is a means of forming a hypothesis about the maker's interest and about the principles that he or she brought to their engagement with the *prompt* which led to the making of the sign – whether the experience of the visit to the museum-exhibition – or the experience of a series of lessons in the classroom.

The makers of the maps have *made* signs; they could not have *used* an existing sign: there was no such a sign to be used. In the making of these map-signs, criterial features of the exhibition are selected. The signs were *made*, for reasons which were entirely *motivated* by the interest of the maker in the circumstances obtaining at the time of their making.

If we took the museum examples as instances of *learning*, then the question of how to assess *what was learned* can only be done by recourse to multimodal means: modally, *what was to be learned* is distinct from the *representations* which document *what was learned. Three-dimensional objects* have been transducted into *two-dimensional images*; '*spaces*' have become *images*; the transformational process of *selection* has led to the *deletion* in the maps of most of what was there in the 'curriculum' of the exhibition.

'Recognition'

I want to re-emphasize two notions: that of *interest* and that of the *principles* used in the engagement with an aspect of the world shaped by interest. The examples on page 180 are examples from two primary schools in North London. The children are six years old, and the topic of their (Biology) lessons was 'Frogspawn'. Here are two *signs of learning*, each from a child in one of the two classes.

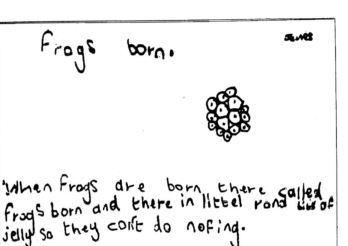

Figure 9.1a
Frogspawn 1

Frogs born.
When frogs are born there called frogs born and there in
littel rond bits of jelly so they con't do nofing.

Figure 9.1b
Frogspawn 2

Tadpole + frog
I already knew that frog's have Baby's. I have learnt tath
tadpole come out of frog's sporn. I also learnt that thay Brev
uder water. hawever the most interesting thing was that the
tadpoal are the blak spots.

The examples illustrate *sign-making* as *learning*. The *interests* of the sign-makers lead him (Figure 9.1a) and her (Figure 9.1b) to select what was criterial for them about an entity at the moment of its representation. What the sign-maker takes as *criterial*, determines what she or he will represent about that entity; only what is *criterial* is represented. Representation is always partial.

The maker of the text of Figure 9.1a decided to 'spread' the meaning he wished to represent across two modes, *image* and *writing*. Where the maker of Figure 9.1b uses *writing* to represent '*the most interesting thing*' namely '*that the tadpoal are the blak spots*', the maker of Figure 9.1a uses *image* to *show* the black spots in his carefully drawn image of frog spawn. The issue of *recognition* presents itself yet again: is the teacher likely to see this as a very nice picture or as a carefully made *visual account* of a scientific fact?

Both sign-makers saw the black spots as criterial, though they chose to represent them in different modes. In Figure 9.1a, the drawing precedes the writing and in this way it frames the writing in significant ways. In Figure 9.1b, the 'same' fact is embedded to the written judgement '*the most interesting thing . . .*'. Again the question posed for the two teachers is whether to accord to *embedding of fact to written judgement* higher status than to the embedding/*framing* by the *drawing*; or the other way around – that is, accord to the child's visual presentation of *empirical reality as prior* a higher status; or to treat each as legitimate alternative accounts. Both of these possibilities are worth exploring with the class.

I am not, here, so much interested in a detailed analysis of the two texts – for instance that the maker of Figure 9.1a foregrounds the explanation of the (for him new) concept '*when frogs are born there called frogs born*', while the maker of Figure 9.3b foregrounds her knowledge '*I already knew that frogs have Baby's*'. I am interested in the principle of *recognition* as a heuristic device for the teacher. From the perspective of identity I am interested in the clear and precise indications of 'serious-ness' on the makers' parts; a seriousness that finds different routes of expression. That includes the recognition of both makers' interest in *precision,* which appears among other things in their transcription of their own speech: 'so they *cont* do *nofing*' where the transcription of the North London vowel in *cont* as –o- and of the 'standard language' consonant –th- in *nofing* as –f- are signs of acute hearing and accuracy in transcription; as are the –ay- in *thay*, and the (voiced) –v- as a transcription of the 'standard language' voiced -th- in *Brev*; as is the loss through nasalization of the –n- in '*uder* water'.

Not least of course, precision appears in their 'transcription' of the unknown term 'frogspawn' – semantically transcribed as 'frogs born' and syntactically transcribed as 'frogs sporn' – i.e. 'frog's sporn' – a nonsense term lexically, yet syntactically well motivated.

All signs are metaphors which embody the interest of the maker of the sign – whether the sign of a *letter* as transcript of a *sound*; of a concept – such as the black spots in frog spawn – as *image* or as *word*; or of an unknown word/concept – as in 'frogs born' or 'frogs sporn'. Given the principle that *signs* function as *concepts*, we can say that *concepts* are the result of the work of the sign-maker, and represent her/his interest in relation to the world which is in focus. As a consequence, the semiotic as much as the conceptual resources of the individual are the result of their work in their engagement with their (social and cultural) world. *Identity* is the effect of the semiotic/social and conceptual work done by an individual.

This can be translated into a view of learning in two ways. One is to say: what the sign-maker does, settles, if only for this moment, the world of signs and the state of his or her 'inner world'. Here it has settled an understanding of what *frogs born/frogs sporn* is. With that, it has for a moment changed their capacities for making (new) meanings and for future meaningful action in and on the world. It has changed the intellectual/conceptual potential of the meaning-maker, and in this it has changed this individual. *That is a result of learning.* The second would be to say: *interest* and *partiality* operate in quite the same way in *learning* as they do in representation. But in any case I would say that learning and the work of identity formation are not separable, other than as a theoretical convenience.

How should principles and practices of assessment deal with that? What is to be assessed? Is it *learning*; is it *conformity to authority*; or is it *identity*? Multimodality and social semiotics are neutral in this respect in principle, though they do sharply pose the matter of *recognition*: 'What is *recognized* as a sign of learning?'. At this point it might be useful to propose a *definition of learning*.

> Learning is the result of the transformative engagement with an aspect of the world which is the focus of attention by an individual, on the basis of principles brought by her or him to that engagement; leading to a transformation of the individual's semiotic/conceptual resources.

This provides a *social*-semiotic view of *meaning* and *learning*. The (social-semiotic) *multimodal* view adds an insistence that meaning is made in a multiplicity of modes, always in *ensembles of modes*. All present evidence of learning; all in different ways; and all need to be taken care of in forms and practices of assessment.

Recognition, metrics and principles of assessment

From the perspective of a semiotic theory of learning, the following might be said: the *concept/sign* which the child has made gives us an insight into his 'stance' in the world, with respect to a specific entity or phenomenon. As a general principle we can take all *concepts/signs* to be precisely that: an indication of the *interest* of the sign-maker in their relation to the specific bit of the world that is at issue; an indication of their experience of the world. Both *concept* and *sign* are shaped by that, and give us a sense of the criteria, the principles, the *interest* which led the child to the representations he made. It is a point where we need to think about apt *metrics* for assessing/evaluating what learning had gone on.

Is our interest in learning? This is a strange question to put; though other questions suggest themselves, which make it somewhat less strange. For instance: 'Is our interest in producing *conformity to authority* around 'knowledge'? or 'Is our interest actually in *environments and conditions of learning*?'.

In societies dominated by the forces of the market in conditions of intense diversity, we cannot attempt to construct a plausible approach to assessment without the consideration of the different aesthetics which govern contemporary social life. Signs made 'outwardly' are the best evidence that we can get for understanding the 'inner' processes of learning. The *visitors' maps, the frogspawn examples,* the *classification examples,* are all *signs of learning.*

I have attempted to draw out two strands in an approach to assessment: the need to be clear about a theory of learning as the underpinning of forms of assessment; and related to that the need for *principles of recognition of learning.* Here I briefly restate them:

1. Work produces change; change is meaningful; semiotic work is work and produces meaning.
2. Meaning is made in all modes; learning takes place in all modes.
3. Signs are made in response to *prompts* on the basis of the sign-maker's *interest,* in transformative engagement with characteristics of the prompt.
4. The sign made in response to a *prompt* points to the *principles* at work in the sign-maker's engagement with the prompt.
5. Learning is best seen in the frame of a learner's principled transformative engagement with the characteristics of a prior prompt in terms of the learner's interest.
6. Signs of learning constitute apt data for any form of assessment.
7. The question of assessment is a question *either* of attention to metrics of conformity *or* to principles of semiotic engagement. As a slogan we can speak of an opposition between *metrics of learning* and *signs of (principles of) learning.*
8. In contemporary environments of communication as of learning it is implausible to restrict notions of effective communication to the mode of language alone. Assessment is no exception.

10 The social semiotics of convergent mobile devices: new forms of composition and the transformation of *habitus*

(Elizabetta Adami and Gunther Kress)

The social frame for the semiotic analysis

One of the recurring concerns in the book so far has been that of principles and forms of contemporary composition/text-making. The constant emphasis on social conditions represents the view that the social is prior: the facilities/affordances of the new technologies can only be used along the lines that the social conditions make possible. The assumption of agency by individuals in conditions of the dominance of the (neo-liberal) market over the state is one effect of that. The waning of stability and canonicity in terms of knowledge, genres, discourses is another effect. An ideology of choice pervades the semiotic domain as much as it does others. So the interest in the communicational and social effects of contemporary technologies – here in the shape of a mobile device – is a concern in this book; it is a widely shared interest and concern. In particular this is so in relation to contemporary or likely future practices and forms of text-making.

Chapter 2 presented a sketch of some aspects of the contemporary world which need to frame any consideration of communication. This chapter returns to that interest specifically by focusing on contemporary communicational technology in the shape of a convergent mobile device. It is a means of drawing together many of the issues discussed so far and a response – however vaguely articulated – to a number of convergent factors in contemporary 'Western', 'developed' societies mentioned in that earlier chapter. From an economic and cultural perspective 'globalization'; from a social and cultural perspective 'diversity', more or less intense; from a social perspective 'fragmentation', 'mobility', 'instability'; from a representational and cultural perspective 'instability' and 'provisionality'. The effects of these social conditions on communication are profound; and especially so when matched up with the affordances of digital technologies.

A major effect of the shift from state to market – in anglophone societies at least – is the move from a responsibility to values of the social to values of individual satisfaction. Where identity was formerly constructed through the achievement of social position and of position in work or profession, solidly localized and firmly fixed, identity is now constructed through the exercise of choice in consumption in the market.

Choice assumes agency in relation to a range of options; the ensuing disposition (however spurious) of agency in selection is carried by the young from the market into the school, where their assumptions meet the former structures of authority in relation to values, knowledge, and semiotic action in representation and communication.

The third unsettling force comes from developments in contemporary media, which, in their facilities run in parallel to these social conditions. Current technologies of communication unsettle former patterns of communication, which had developed along with former social givens.

The formerly settled patterns of communication – (at least relative) stability of genres, of discourses, of knowledge – can no longer be assumed. The return to the questions of rhetoric over the last two or three decades is one consequence: when social conditions are unstable and provisional, each occasion of communication requires, in principle at least, an assessment each time of the communicational environment in terms of power, characteristics of participants, of their expectations, their tastes and style preferences. Equally, in the design of messages, the suitability of available cultural/semiotic resources has to be assessed newly and on each occasion. Hence a move to realize rhetorical purposes in messages which will be apt to the requirements of specific situations and instances of communication.

This is the frame within which we analyse one convergent media device, both to understand its specific affordances as well as its likely 'uptake' in communication; and, more significantly still, its likely effects in terms of the production of a habitus of communication.

The affordances of Smartphones: a social-semiotic account

The analysis focuses on the 'affordances' (Kress and van Leeuwen, 1996, 2006) of Smartphones. Every medium, every technology that we use to represent and to communicate – to make and to disseminate meaning – has affordances, both of material and social possibilities and constraints. If the formation of identity and subjectivity is a process of meaning-making by and about ourselves and of our 'life-world' (Kress and Pachler, 2007), as in our view it is, then the media we use and the affordances they offer – what they facilitate, what they hinder and inhibit – influences how we make meaning and hence how we come to shape our identity in this respect.

Smartphones are portable 'media convergence' devices which bring together the functionalities of several (formerly) separate digital devices. They have been introduced into the media landscape relatively recently; nevertheless they are increasingly the devices being used in everyday life. Understanding their affordances casts light on to the processes and skills that they foster, as well as on those which they do not; they illuminate how we learn to make meaning of the world through their use. In using such devices we shape *habitus* and the way we approach and conceive of our life-world. This promises – among other things – a more principled basis for their adoption or rejection in school than when adoption had been argued on the less clear sense of technology as a (positive or negative) phenomenon in itself. More generally, it promises an understanding of the interaction of life-world and this specific technology and the longer-term likely social effects.

Various types of Smartphone are available; the one analysed here is the Nokia N95, as an instance. Without wishing to deny the specificity of the affordances that each model entails, the observations are meant, broadly, as indicative of general trends underpinning the affordances of the whole category of Smartphones; and of trends in communication we can discern.

The analysis focuses mainly on the design of the device and its affordances and to a lesser extent on the software and the main functionalities. Some general observations are drawn in terms of skills and *habitus* that these affordances might foster or hinder and these are considered in terms of the implications which might follow from the use of mobile devices in communicational/social contexts.

Affordances of the hardware

When the device is closed (Figure 10.1a), its shape and the options differ significantly from traditional mobile phones. It has a relatively large, coloured screen with thumbnails, which occupies three-quarters of the device; a relatively small section is devoted to buttons. The touch input section has a central five-way navigator, with other buttons of various dimensions arranged symmetrically around it.

The section devoted to the visual output is bigger than the one devoted to the kinaesthetic input, which is for navigation rather than for textual input, so that the device resembles an advanced version of a *Game Boy* rather than of a mobile phone. Only when the device is 'open' (by sliding the front part vertically over the back, Figure 10.1b) does one see it as a mobile phone: a keyboard appears and the size of the screen becomes proportionally less significant, at about a half of the size of the device.

Figure 10.1a
Smartphone closed

Figure 10.1b
Smartphone open

Although different models vary in shape, most share the priority given to visual output and navigational input over written input. The radical change in the shape of these devices is a significant clue to the designers' intentions about the kinds of representations fostered and the semiotic modes thereby foregrounded or backgrounded; not to mention the manual skills needed to use the device.

'Shape': designers' intentions and social implications

New communicational potentials and priorities have brought design features other than shape to the fore: the larger the screen, the better the output for the functionalities which rely on the visual mode, such as imaging, Web browsing and GPS positioning (but also selection of audio files). The still relatively small dimensions do keep the device portable; though easy portability is now counterbalanced by the need for maximum usability of the different media functionalities, which, in output rely more and more on the visual. The traditional phone functionalities are less prominent. You cannot 'txt' (one of the main functions presently associated with mobile phones) nor compose a phone number, without sliding the device open. Shape is a clue to the designers' interest in functionalities of the device; those devoted to phoning are backgrounded.

The design of these devices emphasizes their 'convergence' characteristics – the fact that they merge several traditional digital devices such as camera, video camera, laptop, GPS navigator, gaming mobile device, portable music player. The mobile phone function may be becoming a bit less relevant. Shape effects how the device is handled. Because of their relatively large size, the devices are frequently not held to the ear when they are used as a phone; instead, they might be kept in a bag or pocket and used with earphones (wireless or not), and carried in the way an MP3 player is. In several of its functionalities, it is held with both hands outstretched, horizontally – when taking pictures or videos – or held horizontally or vertically in the lap, using the fingers of both hands to manipulate them (like handling a *Game Boy*).

The representational affordances

Visual output has clearly become the priority. Its prioritizing is at the expense of access to the alphanumeric keyboard of touch input in the textual mode; the touch input section still remains available for navigation, with the five-way navigator below the screen. The alphanumeric keyboard is covered to keep the device reasonably small. That is, in order to facilitate immediate access to certain modes, others are backgrounded. Written production in particular is given lesser priority in favour of navigation and (internet) access to image and written text and the *capture of images*. As a result, 'content generation' and 'text creation' is now more likely to be done by means of representation-as-selection, 'framing' and copying of semiotic material available via, e.g. the internet.

This changes the way we conceive of representational means and meaning-making in the world, favouring selection, 'capture' and transformation rather than 'production from scratch' – as a traditional view might still describe it – transformation or 'transduction' (Bezemer and Kress, 2008; Kress and van Leeuwen, 2006). In other words, now we can directly forward a 'link' or a 'file' where before *production* might have been 'transduction' of ensembles of modes as texts from the written to the visual or from the visual to the verbal. In this way action on or in the world is more likely (the kinaesthetic input) to happen through selection from among options and forwarding these as (existing) 'links' rather than to use the affordances of writing to describe what we wanted to represent and communicate.

The software affordances

The options on the visual output are arranged as menus whose logics we already understand, generally speaking, since a semiotics of interfaces based on menus is now widespread in the (Western) digital environment. This leads to a conception of semiotic (inter-)activity as a matter of 'navigation' and 'selection' among options. Semiotic action – whether as representation, production or communication – is coming to be seen as selection-driven. This in turn might lead to notions of 'semiotic agency' more and more becoming a matter of selection from among predetermined templates; and an ensuing sense of (multimodal) text as *bricolage*.

The thumbnail 'carousel' and the issue of 'aesthetics of interactivity'

The addition of moving visual entities is becoming more and more widespread in the design of digital devices, in MP3 devices for instance; in operating systems for computers; in webpage design; and so on. The feature adds an aesthetics of motion-as-(inter-)activity, since the idea of action is generally associated with movement. The movement of visual entities on the screen as an effect of a touch suggests control through action and more specifically is suggestive of physical handling and acting on the objects.

One can trace a development in software design. With traditional mobile phones there is neither *logical* nor *spatial proximity/continuity* of *action* and *effect*: a touch on the keyboard results in an effect on an element on the screen – a rectangle framing the thumbnail. With touch-screen devices like the *iPhone*, for example there is both *logical and spatial* proximity/continuity of action and effect – a touch *on* the object moves it – so that the perceived gap between virtual and real handling of objects is narrowed. By means of software which simulates the laws of physics, interactivity with icons mirrors the aesthetics of interactivity with 'physical' objects; and so the perceptual boundaries between virtual and real are blurred (Roschelle and Pea, 2002).

Figure 10.2 Aesthetics of interactivity

The functionalities

Imaging

The device has two camera lenses, one on its back (so that you can see on the screen what happens in front of you and photograph it) and one on its front (so that you can see yourself on the screen while handling the device and photograph yourself). The screen shows what is in focus and taking a picture is just one click away. This material of the imaging functionality makes it highly usable, so the user of the device is easily 'seduced' into the photographic 'capturing' of reality and as a consequence becomes motivated to understand this function, and begins to see the world around as reality to be selected and 'captured'. As a result, many more images of everyday life are taken with this device than with a digital camera. Representing reality by selecting and 'capturing' becomes a 'naturalized' activity. In this way, present reality is conceived in terms of possible future needs of representations of past event, in terms of usability as representation and artefact, rather than of living experience. On the one hand, every representation can achieve further significance and, as representation has little cost, many more events and objects may seem worth being represented. Once represented, they are framed (Bateson, 1972) and achieve a new meaning. On the other hand, the environment may be being lived so as to represent it; and the life-world may be turned into an artefact to be (re)used. That can be done on the spot, by uploading the artefact on the Web or sending it to friends, for example. As a consequence, life lived offline is directly connected to online life, for instance to one's YouTube or MySpace profiles which now are 'literally' lived and enacted by means of representations. Life lived offline may become subordinated to life lived online or lived *for* life online.

Mobile Web access and usability: changes in social habitus

Mobile Web browsing reduces the need for planning ahead for activities which happen away from non-mobile sources of information; and it reduces the need for organizing the information needed to carry out activities ahead of time. In effect this makes strategic (global) planning redundant. The mobile phone had already made social networks more 'mobile' and meetings more contingent. For certain generations it already seems like a remote past when one had to arrange times and place of meetings well ahead of time: a time when things became really complex and difficult if any changes to previously made plans were contemplated. With mobile Web browsing, interpersonal mobility and connectivity afforded by the mobile phone joins the mobility of ubiquitous information access, so that planning of either is becoming less necessary. This may make the everyday seem or be more densely packed and at the same time make planning for future events seem an unnecessary imposition. Planning may come to be felt as a constraint on the freedom to follow the desires of the moment in real time. Where timetables and activities are predetermined, in the context of institutions – such as the school for instance, as in many forms of work, this may produce tensions and have consequences in terms of affect.

It is inevitable that different kinds of human social dispositions, subjectivities, identities will come to evolve with the use of these facilities. Already it seems evident that a generation fully used to immediacy and ubiquity of access finds it increasingly difficult to cope with social institutions and regulations of the former kind. In this respect the 'school' is the most 'exposed' institution and it is 'the school' which is most in the firing-line.

If ubiquitous access to the Web obviates much planning (Fisher and Konomi, 2007), it also eliminates the need of moving semiotic materials from one medium to another or of transducting meanings from one mode to another. Taking notes on Post-its – in their time themselves signs of a then new fragmentation and mobility of information – printing ticket confirmations or receipts become virtually unnecessary and pointless when they are accessible via these devices. This radically changes the media and semiotic 'landscapes' of everyday life-worlds (Kress, 2003). More and more, representations are selected and re-used in different contexts rather than transducted or produced for each new context; *recontextualization* of signifiers (form) becomes more usual than the production of new content and form in each context. It is a foregrounding of the function of framing as production over more traditional production of content – as in writing, for instance.

Accessibility of information reduces risks of certain kinds. This produces a changed attitude to life, time, relations and world: being informed to optimize time and experiences avoids 'time-wasting', when time is felt as a highly valued commodity. Discovery, rather than an exploration of the unknown, becomes an information-driven experiencing. Experiencing life becomes an activity shaped and framed by accessible information; and 'learning' may come to get confused with grabbing information – reliable or not – about the environment.

Furthermore, if the environment is supplemented with detailed online information, the 'reality' of the environment is produced offline and online at the same time and in the same place. This blurs the boundaries of virtual and real even more because the so-called virtual no longer has a pre-assigned place and time – for instance, at home or in the office on the PC or laptop. The 'virtual' can now be accessed on the spot to check on the 'real'. The online is an extension of the offline and vice versa.

Mobile Web browsing becomes easy, at least potentially. However, using the facility is not necessarily easy. Web browsing on a mobile device is very different from Web browsing on the PC or laptop, both in touch input and in visual output as the screen of the mobile device shows a limited portion of the webpage only. Due to its small size the complete page is unreadable. Keying in information about searches is cumbersome given the reduced affordances of the mobile keyboard.

Emailing

Mobile email can become a form of mobile Web browsing in as much as sites and times of interaction are merged with activities and environments online and offline. An email can be read online while the sender is talking face-to-face to the addressee about the contents of that email. The textual input affordances of the device make reading *incoming* emails (and forwarding them) easier than writing emails. This is another instance of the affordance of representation-as-selection: it is more likely that selected artefacts are emailed – by forwarding incoming emails or by sending photos or weblinks – rather than writing texts.

There are some textual features which allow one to tell whether an email is from a mobile device – briefer texts, very little or no introductory or closing elements, implicit reference, (lack of) punctuation and capitalization, spelling and spacing; sometimes just pictures or weblinks are sent with no – or small – written captions with them. The widespread use of these devices might come to foster a new genre, the 'mobile email', characterized by *representation-as-selection* more than by *representation-as-new-production*, compared to emails from PCs or laptops. This fits with the trend we have mentioned already.

'Positioning'

The GPS positioning function enables users to situate themselves via a representation of geography. Here a typed input, say an address, results in a visual topological output, say a geographical representation. A paper road map, framed and selective, shows an area and its locations as both context and content; its user can focus on location and route from any given point of view. The GPS dynamically visualizes a given position and the desired route on the screen in relation to the user's actual position. The reference point as the point of view – focus versus context – is automatically framed on the screen; as the former changes, the context is reframed as well. This amounts to a – presently – paradoxical situation, where the individual is both the constant centre and constantly de-located. By doing this with the mobile device, geographical representations of one's actual situation are recorded while being experienced. Here too, life-world becomes representation/artefact, and movement becomes visual output.

Moreover, the *self* is positioned in the representation on the screen. This displacement of the self, geographically represented in real time, adds to the capturing/representing of experiences of the imaging function and to the blurring of boundaries between online and offline reality.

Phoning and messaging

Many options of the phoning/messaging functionality of the device are new, compared to traditional mobile phones; these mainly deal with combining phoning and messaging with the other functionalities so that one can show the artefacts being documented/recorded to the person called, for example. The addressee's device needs to be suited for real-time sharing of the 'semiotic entities' afforded by the sender's device. Hence the spread of such devices is likely to be fostered by social networks. This is likely to give rise to new uses of these devices, in which representations are collectively transformed in multi-'authored' chains of semiosis.

Lifeblog

The *lifeblog* is a chronological multimodal representation of the user's activity with the device. It is a multimodal diary, automatically recorded and assembled while using the device. All of life turns into a visual artefact, which is (re-)usable, since each artefact from a lifeblog can be edited and transferred to other devices (cf. the notion of 'act as artefact' in Roschelle and Pea, 2002 and the admitted risks of 'Big Brother' overtones of continuous surveillance).

In a lifeblog, the ephemera of existence are captured and recorded automatically, with all the related consequences of fulfilled existential needs of 'leaving a trace' of your existence in the world (LeJeune, 1975; and the literature dealing with 'life-writing'). As the device automatically records/documents, there is, on the one hand a new question about what 'selection' might mean, while on the other hand there is no need for the effort of transducing one's experiences: that is, to select them according to the interest of a specific moment and purpose, hence to frame them subjectively, and to transduct them in writing in a specific genre, as happens in writing a journal. A *trace* is automatically left; self-reflection can be left out or be left to later.

The affordances of the multifunctionality feature

At its best, 'mobility' is foregrounded in the use of each functionality; the 'live' aspect – as 'immediacy' – is preferred over a concern with 'quality' of the artefact, which can always be edited later or once it is uploaded on to another device.

This advances, by a further step, a *habitus* fostered by the introduction of the digital, in which editing and post-production has little cost. In a multifunctional device, customizing each functionality option is an activity which has greater semiotic cost. The digital camera, for example, has an image-capturing functionality and has options to maximize the 'capture' of reality in every context. The device discussed here has *several* mobile functionalities, among these an imaging functionality, and it in turn has the option to maximize the 'capture' of reality in every context.

The result of the availability of multiple functions is that real-time mobility, connectivity and synergetic use of all the potentialities are prioritized over a fine-grained use of each of them. This affordance of media-convergence devices is homologous with social trends of contemporary life to change *habitus* in terms of favouring immediacy, quantity and 'multitasking' instead of accuracy, focus and depth. Since each functionality is more likely to be used in its default settings rather than by being 'personalized' through using its advanced options, it mirrors contemporary social trends, by facilitating a *habitus* where agency is first of all a matter of selection among template-based options, from software tools to commodities and services. In each case, 'personalization' entails greater semiotic costs and becomes, therefore the realm of the expert, that is, highly competent users. Choosing from among (pre-)given templates the one which (most) aptly fulfils immediate needs becomes normal. In turn this means that users adapt their 'needs' to fit the range of pre-set templates.

Here too, selection and text-making as *bricolage* becomes the signifier of a contemporary notion of creativity, in which personalization as choice of the immediately available is most favoured and the semiotic work of more elaborated design is less favoured.

The multifunctionality of the device brings other material constraints, which require skills of estimating and balancing their use for optimizing resources in line with personal needs. Since the extent of the use of one functionality leads to a possible compromising of other uses – a compromise between my interest in that use and my interest in having the device available for other functionalities – it is the user's interest which establishes a priority among uses. So real-time and just-in-time use of its affordances might be the greater priority, though it might not. Maximization of use is a signifier of what the user sees as optimization of resources.

Implications

The semiotic analysis here is framed with several questions in mind. From a social and economic perspective: 'What kinds of skills are likely to be needed and in what environments?' or, from an educational one: 'What kinds of skills are foregrounded by the affordances of media-convergence devices and how can they be used for educational purposes?'. We might ask the question which has been posed several times already: 'What forms of habitus are most facilitated by this device and what forms are less or least facilitated?'. And we might ask questions about gains and losses, socially, culturally, economically and communicationally: 'What cultural capital is least facilitated and most likely to be lost, what cultural goods are most facilitated?'.

We have answered some of these questions, implicitly and explicitly. It is difficult to sort these into positive and negative features: depending on social environments, on life-worlds and their demands, on uses and social valuations, they will be evaluated as either or both. Here are some features of the device that may be seen positively – always depending on wider social circumstances:

- It offers flexibility of sensory engagement with the environment.
- It allows adaptation of previous knowledge drawn from heterogeneous phenomena.
- It facilitates real-time mobility, multitasking and synergetic use over fine-grained focus and accuracy.
- It favours learning '*how to* processes', rather than the *what* of '*content accumulation*'.
- It favours real-time selection of apt options according to micro – individualized – interests; with more semiotic work needed for considering meso- or macro-design.
- It permits individual optimization of certain resources.
- It fosters tactical (local and operational) planning more than strategic (global) planning.

We can say that mobile (learning) environments are now (more) constituted through: *how to access, select, capture, use* and *transform* global/collective information and events for local/individual aims, relations and activities in real time. It remains to think about how learning, identity formation, social subjectivity may be affected in this.

The affordances of these convergent devices run in parallel with contemporary social trends in fostering a *habitus* which conceives of action – and agency – as matters of navigating and selecting among options and which sees content generation in the form of representation-as-selection. Through the facilities they offer, the devices contribute to a continuing and increasing blurring of the boundaries between virtual and real, offline and online; between times and sites of leisure and work; where information about activities and relations about the self, life and life-world and the environment – social and cultural more widely – can be documented/recorded/ 'captured' – as representation and artefact; to be selected, edited and (re-)used later and as needed as contemporary means of recording, storing, recollecting and shaping experience.

As a result, *production* is taking the form of *documentation, recording* and *trans-formation*; and (newly shaped) *consumption* takes the form of *transformation* of the ephemeral into tangible representations for (re)use.

When a life-world becomes mobile in this sense, there is a tendency to lose tolerance of any 'fixing', of planning of life; these are now perceived as limitations of freedom of agency and choice: trivial yet telling examples are 'pre-booking' or 'time and content scheduling' such as school timetables and the curricula of formal and informal learning.

When the environment is ubiquitously augmented with information, any possibility of exploration of 'the unknown' becomes difficult to recognize: when all of the world is treated as known, knowable and instantly accessible, the horizons of the new, the unknown have receded beyond visibility. Risk taking is avoidable; 'learning' is seen as grabbing all possible kinds of information – reliable or otherwise – about the environment at issue. Experiencing life is conceived of as 'being in motion', fully supplied with on-the-spot information, 'delivered' in real time. Usability, selection (choice within given possibilities), *bricolage* and mobility are values that (have) come to signify a contemporary notion of 'freedom' and 'creation'.

Over time, the introduction of a new technology, with its specific and at times sharp-edged affordances/facilities, into a life-world generates newly shaped needs and new purposes. Initially the device is used according to the purposes brought from the most immediate past; yet using the device brings a change in the habituations of the user. It is a reiterative process: drawing on experiences of devices known and on previous purposes one comes to learn (some of) the potentials of the new device; thinking what it might be made to do, it is used for newly shaped purposes; its functionalities are shaped to the needs of the user whose uses – and identity – is reshaped in that process. With enhanced mobility, connectivity and means for capturing and representing reality, one aim might be to be more mobile, more connected, capturing and representing more of life and reality.

Gains and losses: some open questions

Technologies are cultural resources. They are taken up or not; inserted or not into life-worlds by social agents according to actual or felt social requirements and constraints. In that, they follow and foster contemporary social transformations while being shaped by them.

These mobile devices and their affordances instantiate far-reaching global trends. Large questions arise which cannot be answered straightforwardly; yet it is necessary to try at least to formulate some of the questions. As a first step: it is not helpful either to stigmatize mobile technology or to worship it as a panacea to any problem. We think it is wise to start by describing its affordances and its limitations, in specific environments. We might then evaluate as far as possible what is gained and what is lost in adopting the device, in the far-reaching shifts between foregrounded and backgrounded skills, dispositions and potential social *habitus*. The social effects of the technologies reach across many social domains, yet in trying to estimate gains and losses it will be essential to focus on specific domains, on their requirements and demands. We could, for instance, reflect on the rationale of communicational practices which might be affected by the affordances of the technology and by the habitus engendered in its use, perhaps particularly by young people.

We do think that schools and universities – as well as other institutions – must engage in a serious, searching investigation of the communicational (and pedagogic) affordances of such devices and make decisions about potential action in the light of calm assessments of the perceived needs of specific social aims for education. This chapter and this book are meant as one resource in such an aim.

It will be essential to ask about the desirability of skills such as those in the list below for young people and appeal to the schools' responsibility to engage with these in a seriously reflective manner:

1. The ability and skill to act flexibly in representation, communication, text-making and knowledge creation with a disposition to adaptability.
2. To understand principles of learning as the effect of sustained engagement by a learner with aspects of a learning environment, for instance through selection as framing and as transformation.
3. To have the skills and required disposition towards *production* with contemporary media in the creation of semiotic artefacts.
4. To be at ease with real-time decision making.
5. To be at ease with multitasking.

Schools will need to provide 'navigational aids' which enable individuals to be reflective in their use of skills of:

1. 'Awareness' in selection.
2. Full understanding and creative and transformative use of templates.
3. A willingness to challenge boundaries of what is provided; for instance in the 'personalization' of templates provided in convergent (and other) technologies.

Schools will need to be aware of and prepared to take the initiative to fill gaps of what is not afforded, or of what is backgrounded; especially in relation to:

1. Reflection on the use of resources in relation to aims, purposes and designs.
2. The ability to engage in self-reflection.
3. Fostering a disposition towards agency which values representation-as-content creation.
4. Making full and confident use of the creative potentials of representation-as-transduction.
5. Fostering positive dispositions toward reflective risk-taking and exploration of the unknown.

6. Encouraging fully 'involved' attitudes to the students' life-world, as 'experiencing'.
7. Encouraging the foregrounding of strategic dispositions; of *design* as prospective; and of participation in the design and shaping of the social world: a disposition towards 'architecture' and 'building' rather than one of mere navigation and selection among given options.
8. A settled ethical view of communication as the question about benefit or dis-benefit to members of the designer's community.

References

Aers, D.R., R.I.V. Hodge and G.R. Kress (1982) *Literature Language and Society in England 1580–1680,* Dublin, Gill & Macmillan.

Andrews, R. and C. Haythornthwaite (eds) (2007) *The SAGE Handbook of e-learning Research,* London, Sage.

Aspetsberger, F. (ed.) (2008) *Beim Fremdgehen erwischt! Zu Plagiat und 'Abkupfern' in Kuensten und Wissenschaft,* Innsbruck, Studien Verlag.

Bachmair, B. (1996) Fernsehkultur: Subjektivität in einer Welt bewegter Bilder, Opladen, Westdeutscher Verlag.

Bakhtin, M. (1986) *Speech Genres and Other Essays,* Cambridge, MA, MIT Press.

Barnett, R. (2003) *Beyond All Reason: Living with Ideology in the University,* Buckingham, Open University Press.

Barthes, R. (1968/1977) 'The death of the author' in *Image Music Text,* London, Fontana.

—— (1977) *Image Music Text,* London, Fontana.

—— (1978) *Image Music Text* (trans. Stephen Heath), New York, Hill & Wang.

Bateson, G. (1972) *Steps to an Ecology of Mind,* Chicago, University of Chicago Press.

—— (2000) *Steps to an Ecology of Mind: Collected Essays in Anthropology, Psychiatry, Evolution, and Epistemology,* Chicago, University of Chicago Press.

Bernstein, B. (1996) *Pedagogy Symbolic Control and Identity: Theory, Research, Critique,* London, Taylor & Francis.

Bezemer, J. and G.R. Kress (2008) 'Writing in multimodal texts: a social semiotic account of designs for learning', *Written Communication* 25: 166–95.

Blumler, J.G. and E. Katz, (1974) *The Uses of Mass Communications. Current Perspectives on Gratifications Research,* Beverly Hills, CA, Sage.

Boeck, M. (2004) 'Family snaps: life worlds and information habitus', *Journal of Visual Communication* 3(3): 281–93.

—— (2002) 'Information, Wissen und medialer Wandel', *Medien Journal* 27(1): 51–65.

Brazil, D., M. Hewings and R. Cauldwell (1997) *The Communicative Value of Intonation in English,* Cambridge, Cambridge University Press.

Brice-Heath, S. and B. Street (2008) *On Ethnography: Approaches to Language and Literacy Research,* New York, Teachers College Press.

British Deaf Association (1992) *A Dictionary of British Sign Language,* London, Faber and Faber.

Brown, R. and A. Gilman (1966) 'The pronouns of power and solidarity' in Giglioli, P.P., *Language and Social Context*, Harmondsworth, Penguin.

Chomsky, N.A. (1965) *Aspects of the Theory of Syntax*, Cambridge, MA, MIT Press.

Colapietro, V.M., T.M. Olshewsky and C.S. Peirce (1996) *Peirce's Doctrin of Signs: Theory, Applications, and Connections*, Berlin, Mouton de Gruyter.

Cope, B. and M. Kalantzis, (1997) *Productive Diversity,* Sydney, Pluto Press.

—— (eds) (2000) *Multiliteracies*, London, RoutledgeFalmer.

—— (2008) *New Learning. Elements of a Science of Education,* Melbourne, Cambridge University Press.

Deleuze, G. and F. Guattari (1973) *A Thousand Plateaus: Capitalism and Schizophrenia* (trans. Brian Massumi), Minneapolis, University of Minnesota Press.

Dervin, B., L. Foreman-Wernet and E. Lauterbach (1986) *Sense-Making Methodology Reader: Selected Writings of Brenda Dervin*, Cresskill, NJ, Hampton Press.

Diamontopoulou, S. and G.R. Kress (forthcoming) 'The museum, the exhibition and the visitor: A social semiotic account'.

Dixon, R.W. (1976) *The Dyirbal Language of North Queensland,* Cambridge, Cambridge University Press.

Douglas, M. (1966) *Purity and Danger*, London, Routledge & Kegan Paul.

Eco, U. (1979) *A Theory of Semiotics*, Bloomington, Indiana University Press.

Elias, N. (1994) *The Civilizing Process: Sociogenetic and Psychogenetic Investigations,* Oxford, Blackwell.

Fairbrother, F., E. Nightingale and F.J. Wyeth (1935) *General Science, Part III,* London, G. Bell & Sons.

Fairclough, N. (1989) *Language and Power,* Harlow, Longman.

—— (1993) *Discourse and Social Change,* Cambridge, Polity Press.

Fisher, G. and S. Konomi (2007) 'Innovative socio-technical environments in support of distributed intelligence and lifelong learning', *Journal of Computer Assisted Learning* 23(3): 38–50.

Foucault, M. (1982) *The Archaeology of Knowledge and Discourse on Language,* London, Tavistock Press.

Fowler, R.G., R. Hodge, G.R. Kress and T. Trew (1979) *Language and Control,* London, Routledge & Kegan Paul.

Gee, J.P. (2004) *What Video Games Have to Teach Us About Learning and Literacy,* London, Palgrave.

Gee, J.P. (2007) *Social Linguistics and Literacy: Ideology in Discourses*, New York, Routledge.

Gee, J.P., G. Hull and C. Lankshear (1996) *The New Work Order: Behind the language of the New Capitalism,* Boulder, CO, Westview.

Gibson, J.J. (1986) *The Ecological Approach to Visual Perception,* Hilldale, NJ, Lawrence Erlbaum.

Goffmann, E. (1986) *Frame Analysis: An Essay on the Organization of Experience,* Boston, Northeastern University Press.

Göhlich, M., C. Wulf and J. Zirfas (eds) (2007) *Pädagogische Theorien des Lernens,* Weinheim, Germany: Beltz.

Goodwin, C. (2000) 'Action and embodiment within situated human interaction' *Journal of Pragmatics* 32: 1489–522.

Grass, Günter (2007) *Vom Häuten der Zwiebel*.

Hall, S. (1982) 'The determination of news photographs' in S. Cohen and J. Young (eds) *The Manufacture of News*, London, Constable.

Halliday, M.A.K. (1967) *Intonation and Grammar in British English*, The Hague, Mouton.

—— (1967/68) 'Transitivity and theme in English, Parts 1, 2, 3', *Journal of Linguistics* 3(1, 2 and 3).

—— (1978) *Language as a Social Semiotic*, London, Edward Arnold.

—— (1984) *An Introduction to Functional Grammar,* London, Edward Arnold.

Halliday, M.A.K. and R. Hasan (1976) *Cohesion in English*, London, Longman.

Hjelmslev, L. (1961) *Prolegomena to a Theory of Language,* Bloomington, Indiana University Press.

Hodge, R.I.V. and G.R. Kress (1979) *Language as Ideology*, London, Routledge & Kegan Paul.

—— (1988) *Social Semiotics*, Cambridge, Polity Press.

—— (1993) *Language as Ideology* (2nd edn), London, Routledge.

Insulander, E. (2008) 'The museum as a semi-formal site for learning', *Medien Journal,* (Special issue: *Lernen: Ein zentraler Begriff fuer die Kommunikationswissenschaft*) 32, Jahrgang Nr 1/2008.

Jewitt, C. (2003a) 'Computer-mediated learning: the multimodal construction of mathematical entities on screen' in Jewitt and Kress (eds).

—— (2003b) 'Rethinking assessment: Multimodality, literacy and computer-mediated learning', *Assessment in Education: Principles, Policy & Practice* 10(1): 83–102.

—— (2005) *Technology, Literacy, Learning: A Multimodal Approach*, London: Routledge.

—— (ed.) (2009) *Handbook of Multimodal Analysis*, London, RoutledgeFalmer.

Jewitt, C. and G.R. Kress (eds) (2003) *Multimodal Literacy*, New York, Peter Lang.

Jewitt, C., G.R. Kress, J. Ogborn and C. Tsatsarelis (2001) *Multimodal Teaching and Learning. The Rhetorics of the Science Classroom.* London: Continuum.

Kaplan, N. (1995) 'Politexts, hypertexts, and other cultural formations in the late age of print', *Computer-Mediated Communication Magazine* 2: 3.

Kenner, C. and G.R. Kress (2003) 'The multisemiotic resources of biliterate children', *Journal of Early Childhood Literacy* 3(2): 179–202.

Kenny, A. (1994) *The Wittgenstein Reader*, Oxford, Blackwells.

Kress, G.R. (ed.) (1976) *Halliday: System and Function in Language*, Oxford, Oxford University Press.

—— (1978) 'Towards an analysis of the language of European intellectuals', *Journal of European Studies* VIII: 274–91.

—— (1982) *Learning to Write*, London, Routledge & Kegan Paul.

—— (1984/89) *Linguistic Processes in Sociocultural Practices,* Geelong, Deakin University Press and Oxford, Oxford University Press.

—— (1991) 'Critical discourse analysis' in Clyne, M. (ed.) *Linguistics in Australia,* Canberra, Academy of Social Sciences, 163–80.

—— (1993) *Learning to Write* (2nd edn), London, Routledge.

—— (1995) *Writing the Future: English and the Making of a Culture of Innovation,* Sheffield, NATE.

—— (1996) 'Internationalization and globalization: rethinking a curriculum of communication', *Comparative Education* 32(2): 185–96.

—— (1997a) *Before Writing: Rethinking the Paths to Literacy,* London, Routledge.

—— (1997b) 'Visual and verbal modes of representation in electronically mediated communication: the potentials of new forms of text', in Snyder, I. (ed.) *Page to Screen: Taking Literacy into the Electronic Age,* London, Routledge.

—— (1999) 'Genre and the changing contexts for English language arts', *Language Arts* 32(2): 185–96.

—— (2000a) *Early Spelling: Between Convention and Creativity,* London, Routledge.

—— (2000b) 'Design and transformation' in Cope, B. and M. Kalantzis (eds).

—— (2000c) 'A Curriculum for the future', *Cambridge Journal of Education* 30(1): 133–45.

—— (2001) 'The punctuation of semiosis', in Meinhoff, U. and J. Smith (eds) *Intertextuality and the Media: From Genre to Everyday Life,* Manchester, Manchester University Press.

—— (2003) *Literacy in the New Media Age,* London, Routledge.

—— (2005) 'Gains and losses: New forms of texts, knowledge and learning', *Computers and Composition* 22: 5–22.

—— (2008) New Literacies, New Democracies (A challenge paper) unpublished.

—— (2009) 'Assessment in the perspective of a social semiotic theory of multimodal teaching and learning' in Wyatt-Smith, C.M. and J.J. Cumming (eds).

Kress, G.R. and R. Hodge (1979) *Language as Ideology,* London. Routledge & Kegan Paul.

Kress, G.R. and N. Pachler (2007) 'Thinking about the "m" in m-learning' in N. Pachler (ed.).

Kress, G.R. and T. van Leeuwen (1996) *Reading Images: The Grammar of Graphic Design,* London, Routledge.

—— (2001) *Multimodal Discourse: The Modes and Media of Contemporary Communication,* London, Edward Arnold.

—— (1998) 'The (critical) analysis of newspaper layout' in Bell, A. and P. Garrett, (eds) *Approaches to Media Discourse,* Oxford, Blackwell.

—— (2002) 'Colour as a semiotic mode: notes for a grammar of colour', *Visual Communication* 1(3): 343–69.

—— (2006) *Reading Images: The Grammar of Visual Design* (2nd edn), London, RoutledgeFalmer.

Kress, G.R., C. Jewitt, J. Ogborn and C. Tsatsarelis (2001) *Multimodal Teaching and Learning: The Rhetorics of the Science Classroom,* London: Continuum.

Kress, G.R., C. Jewitt, A. Franks, J. Bourne, J. Hardcastle, K. Jones and J. Reid (2005)

English in Urban Classrooms: A Multimodal Perspective on Teaching and Learning. London, RoutledgeFalmer.

Kress, G.R., Ogborn, J., Jewitt, C. and Tsatsarelis, C. (1996) 'A satellite view of English: Some lessons from Science classrooms', *Language Awareness* 7(2, 3): 69–89.

Kuhn, T. (1968) *The Structure of Scientific Revolutions*, Chicago, University of Chicago Press.

Labov, W. (1966) *Language in the Inner City: Studies in Black English Vernacular*, Philadelphia, University of Pennsylvania Press.

—— (1972) *The Social Stratification of Language in New York*, Cambridge, Cambridge University Press.

Lakoff, G. (1987) *Women, Fire and Dangerous Things*, Chicago, University of Chicago Press.

Lakoff, G. and M. Johnson (1982) *Metaphors We Live By*, Chicago, University of Chicago Press.

Lankshear, C., J.P. Gee, M. Knobel and C. Searle (1997) *Changing Literacies*, Buckingham: Open University Press.

Lankshear, C. and M. Knobel (2003) *New Literacies*, Buckingham, Open University Press.

Latour, B. (1988) *Science in Action: How to Follow Scientists and Engineers through Society*, Cambridge, MA, Harvard University Press.

—— (2007) *Reassembling the Social: An Introduction to Actor Network Theory*, Oxford, Oxford University Press.

van Leeuwen, T. (1996) 'Moving English: the visual language of film' in Goodman, S. and D. Graddol (eds) *Redesigning English: New Texts, New Identities* London, Routledge.

—— (2000) *Speech Sound Music*, London, Macmillan.

—— (2005) *Introducing Social Semiotics*, London, RoutledgeFalmer.

van Leeuwen, T. and C. Jewitt (eds) (2001) *Handbook of Visual Analysis*, London, Sage.

LeJeune, P. (1975) *Le pacte autobiographique*. Paris, Seuil.

Lemke, J. (1998) 'Multiplying meaning: visual and verbal semiotics in scientific text' in Martin, J. and R. Veel (eds).

—— (1999) 'Typological and topological meaning in diagnostic discourse', *Discourse Processes* 27: 173–85.

Leu, D.J., Jr. (2000) 'Our children's future: changing the focus of literacy and literacy instruction' *Reading Online*. www.readingonline.org/electronic/RT/focus/index.html

McNeill, D. (1988) *Gesture and Thought*, Chicago, University of Chicago Press.

—— (2000) *Language and Thought*, Cambridge, Cambridge University Press.

Martin, J. (1993) 'A contextual theory of language' in Cope, B. and M. Kalantzis (eds) *Powers of Literacy and Literacies of Power*, Lewes, Falmer.

Martin, J. and R. Veel (eds) (1998) *Reading Science*, London, Routledge.

Maybin, J. and G. Moss (1993) 'Talk about texts: reading as a social event' *Journal of Research in Reading* 16(2): 138–47.

Morris, C.W. (1970) *The Pragmatic Movement in American Philosophy*, New York, Braziller.

Myers, G. (1990) *Writing Biology: Texts in the Social Construction of Science*, Wisconsin, University of Wisconsin Press.

—— (2001) 'Putting the text back into practice: junior age non-fiction as objects of design' in Jewitt and Kress (eds).

New London Group (1996) 'A pedagogy of multiliteracies: designing social futures' *Harvard Educational Review* 66: 60–92.

Nunberg, G. (ed.) (1996) *The Future of the Book,* Brussels, Brepols.

O'Halloran, K. (2005) *Mathematical Discourse: Language, Symbolism and Visual Images*, London, Continuum.

Oliver, M. (2005) 'The problem with affordance', *E-Learning* 2: 402–13.

Pachler, N. (ed.) (2007) *Mobile Learning: Towards a Research Agenda,* London, WLE Centre, Institute of Education.

Pachler, N., Ben Bachmair and John Cook (2010) *Mobile Learning: Structure, Agency, Practices*, New York, Springer.

Palmgreen, P., L.A. Wenner and K.E. Rosengren (1985) 'Uses and gratifications research: the past ten years' in Rosengren, K.E., L.A Wenner and P. Palmgreen (eds) *Media Gratifications Research: Current Perspectives*, Beverly Hills, CA, Sage.

Peirce, C.S. (1991) *Peirce on the Semiotic,* Chapel Hill, University of North Carolina Press.

Postman, N. (1993) *Technopoly: The Surrender of Culture to Technology*, New York, Vintage Books.

Rampton, B. (1995) *Crossings: Language and Ethnicity among Adolescents,* Harlow, Longman.

—— (2006) *Language in Late Modernity,* Cambridge, Cambridge University Press.

Rorty, R. (1967) *The Linguistic Turn: Essays in Philosophical Method,* Chicago, University of Chicago Press.

Roschelle, J. and R. Pea (2002) 'A walk on the WILD side: how wireless handhelds may change computer-supported collaborative learning', *International Journal of Cognition and Technology* 1: 45–68.

de Saussure, F. (1983) *Course in General Linguistics* (trans. R. Harris), London, Duckworth.

Schütz, A. (1981) *Theorie der Lebensformen,* Frankfurt, Suhrkamp.

Schütz, A. and T. Luckmann (1984) *Strukturen der Lebenswelt, Band 2*, Frankfurt am Main, Suhrkamp.

Science Education Group (2002) *Salters GCSE Science Y11*, Oxford, Heinemann.

Scollon, R. and S.W. Scollon (2000) *Intercultural Communication: A Discourse Approach*, Oxford, Blackwell.

Sebba, M. (1993) *London Jamaican: a Case Study in Language Contact*, Harlow, Longman.

Selander, S. (2008) 'Designs for learning: a theoretical perspective' *Designs for Learning* 1(1): 6–9.

Shannon, C.E. and W. Weaver (1998) *The Mathematical Theory of Communciation*, Chicago, University of Illinois.

Sharples, M., J. Taylor and G. Vavoula (2007) 'A theory of learning for the mobile age' in R. Andrews and C. Haythornthwaite (eds).

Snyder, I. (ed.) (1997) *Page to Screen*, London, Routledge.

Street, B. (1995) *Social Literacies*, London, Longman.

—— (1998) 'New literacies in theory and practice: what are the implications for language in education' *Linguistics and Education* 10(1): 1–24.

Tuman, M. (1992) *Word Perfect: Literacy in the Computer Age,* Pittsburgh, Pittsburgh University Press.

Unsworth, L. (2001) *Teaching Multiliteracies across the Curriculum: Changing Contexts of Text.* London, RoutledgeFalmer.

Wallerstein, I. (2001) *Unthinking Social Science,* Philadelphia, Temple University Press.

Whorf, B.L. (1966) (J. Carroll, ed.) *Language and Thought,* Cambridge, MA, MIT Press.

Williams, R. (1985) *Keywords: A Vocabulary of Language and Society,* London, Fontana.

Wittgenstein, L. (1935) *Philosophical Investigations,* New York, Prentice Hall.

Wulf, C. (2005) *Zur Genese des Sozialen: Mimesis Performativität, Ritual,* Bielefeld, Transcript Verlag.

—— (2006) *Anthropologie kultureller Vielfalt. Interkulturelle Bildung in Zeiten der Globalisierung,* Bielefeld, Transcript Verlag.

Index